Memory a

Series in Psychology

Advisory Board

George Mandler
William Kessen
Robert Zajonc
Brendan Maher

Series Advisor for this Volume:

George Mandler

Memory and Attention

An Introduction to Human
Information Processing

SECOND EDITION

Donald A. Norman

University of California, San Diego

John Wiley & Sons, Inc.
NEW YORK · LONDON · SYDNEY · TORONTO

10 9 8 7 6 5 4 3 2

Copyright © 1969, 1976 by John Wiley & Sons, Inc.

All rights reserved. No part of this book may
be reproduced by any means, nor transmitted,
nor translated into a machine language without the written permission of the publisher.

Library of Congress Cataloging in Publication Data

Norman, Donald A
    Memory and attention.

    (Series in psychology)
    Bibliography: p.
    Includes indexes.
    1. Human information processing. 2. Memory.
3. Attention. I. Title.
BF455.N66   1976   153.1'2   76-236
ISBN 0-471-65136-2
ISBN 0-471-65137-0 pbk.

Preface to the First Edition

There are many reasons for writing books. This one could have been written to serve as a textbook, or as a source of reading selections for students, or as a vehicle for my own viewpoint about psychological processes. This book has been written for all of these reasons, and yet for none of them. The primary reason is that it has been fun to write.

The format of this book follows the format of a seminar, for that is how it has come into being. Basically, I have written what I have done (or wished I had done) during a seminar entitled "Memory and Attention." In a course, one hopes to give the student a feeling for the history of a subject, a working knowledge of the modern literature, and some grasp of the nature of the problems faced by the researchers in the field. This is accomplished by expository lectures, reading assignments, and critical evaluations of the literature. Throughout such a seminar, the temptation to add personal thoughts about the problems and their solutions is never resisted. I have tried to do the same things in this book.

This book is biased. It treats the human as a complex system, struggling to impose organization on the information received through the sense organs. This type of bias—always asking about the general structure of processes which the human used to detect, recognize, attend to, and retain incoming information—allows me to organize in a meaningful way a good deal of our knowledge of the structure of human perception, attention, and memory. At the same time it makes it difficult, sometimes impossible, to discuss the more traditional psychological theories and experiments. As a result, the book consists of a very restricted survey of attention, memory, and pattern recognition. The restrictions are deliberate. I have tried to minimize the number of issues discussed in order that important ideas not be lost in a jumble of details.

Briefly, then, I introduce a broad selection of topics through a restricted set of papers and concepts. Most topics are discussed through excerpts from the original papers. Not only does it make little sense for me to paraphrase the words of the original, but much of the flavor of the field can only be experienced by reading the variety of styles and jargon used by the individual researchers. Some papers introduce the history of each area and its relation to other fields. The major effort, however, is concentrated on the examination of recent ideas and issues. Usually the modern work branches out in many directions and, of course, it is too early to tell which way the field will eventually develop. The works selected here are chosen to give the reader an understanding of each topic and some feeling for the problems and theories that can be used in its study. As a result, I have been somewhat arbitrary in my selection of studies, choosing them for their generality and the ease with which they could be inserted into the framework of the text.

Thus, the book does follow the seminar in many ways. Although one cannot provide a comprehensive survey of the literature in a single course, the hope is that the reader will end up with an understanding of the basic issues, an idea of where he can find more detailed information, and the ability to read the journals with understanding and insight. In keeping with the spirit of the seminar, I have reserved the right to comment and censor: eliminating from published writings whatever is irrelevant for the present context and making comments where appropriate.

This book is designed for the sophisticated beginner. No knowledge of psychology is assumed and technical terms are explained as they are introduced. Some of the problems are subtle, however, so that the complete novice to psychology may have difficulty. Many of the fields discussed here are now the subject of elaborate mathematical theories. I have resisted the temptation to elaborate on these models, primarily by promising to put them in a sequel, if ever there should be one.

I wish to thank George Mandler for his advice and encouragement during the construction of this book and, in general, simply for putting up with me. David Rumelhart has read all the chapters with care and his comments have helped to improve the final product. The format of this book, the frequent use of excerpts from the published literature, would not have been possible without the efforts of the authors from whose works I have selected. I wish to thank the publishers and authors of these papers for their permission to use these materials.

Donald A. Norman

La Jolla, California

Preface to the Second Edition

Data driven and conceptually driven, resource limits, depth of processing, the representation of knowledge; these are the ideas that characterize this new edition; these are the ideas that tie the latest results together into a consistent picture of human information processing. One of the most exciting aspects of these ideas is the range of phenomena that they cover. The fields are expanding. Now we can cover topics that would have seemed completely unreachable a few years ago. The study of human information processing is becoming the study of the human. This book covers only a limited range of topics, but it is highly suggestive of the way in which other areas can be studied. Clinical issues, states of consciousness, practical skills and public performance, and interpersonal relations are all touched on briefly; all can be expanded by some serious efforts.

The first edition of this book concluded with a hope that, with sufficient new research, the book would become obsolete. The hope proved to be true. New evidence and new sophistication have come into our life; each year brings a significant increase in our understanding of mental processes. When I wrote the first edition, the concept of mental rehearsal was just barely being discussed. Almost no one studied mnemonic techniques, and the question of studying the representation of knowledge within long-term memory simply did not occur to most people. Today we know enough to fill a book on each topic. Furthermore, the approach described here has grown to encompass most areas of psychology—from the ones explicitly discussed, to education, to clinical settings and, finally, to a variety of applications. These are indeed exciting times.

The present edition seeks to remedy the effects of the passage of time. I have retained the flavor and essential elements of the first edition, but I have brought it up to date. Also, I have retained enough old material to give the history of each area. In addition, I have kept a general level and have introduced the issues of memory and attention through an understanding of the general principles about cognitive systems. Finally, I have added sections (and a chapter) on applications. For these reasons, I hope that the discussions will remain current even as new experiments and new developments occur.

Several areas of development have been deliberately excluded: In particular, I have not discussed work on reading, word recognition, and language. These topics are mentioned, of course, but my focus is mainly on the major problems expressed by the title—memory and attention. To try to do otherwise would enlarge the book beyond reason. The students who read this book will acquire sufficient background material to understand the primary literature, both in the areas covered here and in related areas such as reading and language.

As usual, my work has been enriched by active interaction with my colleagues. I especially thank the people who allowed me to use their ideas in the excerpts that are reprinted here. My ideas have been greatly influenced by my collaborators Danny Bobrow, George Mandler, and Dave Rumelhart and, most especially, by the students who have comprised the LNR Research Group. Ed Smith provided a useful formal review of the deficiencies of the first edition. Julie Lustig put this book together—editing, compiling, and empathizing.

Donald A. Norman

La Jolla, California

Contents

Memory and Attention

1
The Problems

The history of the formal study of human memory and attention is rich and varied. It is easy to trace a written record of speculation about these aspects of the human thought processes to the Greek philosophers, and the dedicated scholar could, no doubt, find earlier records. In fact, as early as 86–82 B.C. the Romans had a textbook of techniques for improving one's natural memory entitled *Rhetorica ad Herennium.* The rules given in *Ad Herennium* for establishing an "artificial" memory are still used today by practitioners of the art of memory, although since the invention of printing, this art is no longer of great value. To the Greeks and the Romans, rhetoric was an important part of life, and to the orator a reliable memory was of great importance. Today, with convenient access to libraries (and our acceptance of orators who speak from written notes), we have little need to memorize whole books, poems, or orations. Hence, the art of memory has fallen into disuse. But the rules established in the Greek and Roman world are still valid and useful today for those who wish to improve their memory. Modern science, with all its power, has added little to our knowledge about the practical art of remembering things.

The early practitioner of the art of memory realized that attention is a prerequisite of memory. In 400 B.C. the written rules of memory contained statements such as, "This is the first thing: if you pay attention, the judgment will better perceive the things going through it."[1] This simple quotation sets the stage for what follows. The orators wanted prac-

[1] My source for the early history of memory and for this quotation is the book *The Art of Memory*, by Frances A. Yates. Chicago: University of Chicago Press, 1966. Copyright © 1966 by Frances A. Yates. We shall return to this topic in Chapter 7.

tical rules for improving their ability to use memory. Today, we want understanding of the psychological principles that underlie the rules.

Basic Issues

Let us start by reconsidering the quotation, "If you pay attention, the judgment will better perceive the things going through it." This is a common idea. We need to alter the words only slightly in order to recognize it in its modern form: "Now Jimmy, if you don't pay attention, you will never learn." The statement, we feel, must be true. What does it mean? What is this process called "attention"? What does it mean to start or stop paying attention? Obviously, the way we apply attention to one task or another is a psychological problem, for there is often no external sign that a person is or is not paying attention (although sometimes we stop paying attention by shutting our eyes).

What about perception? The quotation tells us that attention leads to better perception. Does this mean that if we place only half of our attention on a subject, we will perceive it only half as well? Now, immediately, we get to the heart of the whole problem. Can we consider attention to be a finely divisible process, sometimes putting 20 percent of its capacity to work on a problem and sometimes 70 percent? If so, what are we doing with the other 80 or 30 percent? Is attention something with a limited capacity that must be divided among the jobs at hand? Is perception a continuous process, dependent on the amount of attention bestowed on the objects to be perceived? The whole statement presupposes a particular mechanism of human processing.

This whole statement about the relationship of attention, perception, and learning is quite unsatisfactory to the psychologist. Naming something "attention," something else "perception," and yet something else "learning" adds to our vocabulary, but not to our knowledge. The psychologist will not be satisfied until he can point to a specific process—the sequence of operations that performs transformations and makes decisions on sensory information—and identify this as a mechanism of attention. Then he tries to state the specific properties of each component of the overall process and show how they are related to other aspects of human abilities. The ultimate in specification is a model that describes in detail the operations underlying attention, perception, learning, and memory.

In order to study the mechanics of human thought processes, we must take a great leap in time from the Greek and Roman era to the 19th and 20th centuries. Although the phenomena have long been known, systematic scientific investigation of psychological processes has only recently begun. In the chapters that follow, we shall examine the progress of theories and experiments about the way humans process information by looking at two restricted fields: attention and memory. We do this by following the discussions of experimental psychologists, looking at some of their research, and discussing their theories. In so doing, it will be seen that even these two fields encompass a wide variety of problems, so many in fact that we divide them into many smaller sub-problems. There is often little agreement about the proper breakdown of these problems, or even about the interpretation of the facts about any particular subproblem. It is often unclear how the theories proposed for each subproblem can ever be connected. These issues complicate the study of attention and memory, but they also enrich it. Modern psychology is a fascinating subject, not only because the subject matter is so interesting, but also because the area is so new and unexplored that all of us can take part in its development. So, although the apparent contradictions and gaps in the works that follow can be read with dis-couragement, they should be read with excitement. Ask yourself where the problems are and see if you can provide the extra bit of insight or evidence that would set them straight.

Organization of the Book

Before we get into the subject matter, it may be useful to outline the overall organization of this book. The arrangement may be com-pletely inaccurate as a model of human performance, but it is useful as a guide in understanding the problems that follow.

First, we view the human as a processor of information. In particu-lar, we are concerned primarily with verbal, meaningful information in acoustical and visual form. The aim is to follow what happens to the information as it enters the human and is processed by the nervous system. The sense organs provide us with a picture of the physical world. Our problem is to interpret the sensory information and extract its psychological content. To do this we need to process the incoming signals and interpret them on the basis of our past experiences. Memory plays an active role in this process. It provides the information about the past necessary for proper understanding of the present. There must be temporary storage facilities to maintain the incoming information while it is being interpreted, and it must be possible to add information about presently occurring events into permanent memory. We then make decisions and take actions on the information we have received.

Someplace along the line, the capacity of the human to deal with incoming information is severely limited. It is as if at some stage of the analysis of incoming information, only a small portion of the incoming signal is selected for further processing. The study of the phenomenon of attention is the study of this limitation and selection.

The procedure just described ignores the interconnections among the levels of processing. We would like to peel back the different levels one by one, starting with an understanding of the sensory organs, moving through sensation and perception and, finally, ending at decision making and thinking. Unfortunately, the trail ends soon after it starts. We have not yet finished the analysis of the most elementary level, sensation, and we have just barely started with perception. Beyond that, well, our lack of results is not from a lack of trying. One problem is that no process can be analyzed in isolation. We can, for example, analyze sensations only through the responses made by our experimental subjects, and these responses must be the result of the whole structure of their psychological processes, from sensation through decision making. It is only in recent years that we have learned to disentangle the sensory from the decision process. As a result of the fact that each level of psychological processing can be studied only through the other levels, our research in one field progresses slowly because it requires the simultaneous development of experimental skills and analytical techniques for understanding other fields.

The arrangement of this book follows the organization just described. We start with the problem of attention and the limits on our ability to process information (Chapter 2). Attention cannot be studied in isolation from other processes, and so we are unable to come to a final understanding of attention at this point. As a result, we proceed to a discussion of how information arriving at the sense organs is identified and recognized as meaningful patterns: the problem of pattern recognition (Chapter 3). This chapter introduces some new principles of processing, in particular, the distinctions between bottom-up and top-down analysis (which we call data driven and conceptually driven processes). Chapter 4 returns to the study of attention, first looking at some new phenomena, then using the processing principles introduced in Chapter 3 to put together a new picture of attention.

Both attention and pattern recognition depend heavily on the properties of memory, so starting with Chapter 5 we study memory. First comes the study of sensory memories and short-term or primary memory (Chapter 5), then an analysis of the relation between depth of processing and the retention of information (Chapter 6). Chapter 7 examines some of the strategies of memory storage. Chapter 8 examines some of the recent work on the representation of information within long-term memory, including the study of images and of semantic networks. In Chapter 9, we have some fun, examining the stories told by professional performers about the need for practice of their skills, relating these stories to the principles of attention and memory discussed in the book. Finally, Chapter 10 picks up some pieces, discussing topics that are too interesting or important to leave out, but that do not yet fit neatly into the structure of the rest of the book. These last two chapters mark the areas where I expect new developments and growing interest to occur. These chapters offer a preview of what might come.

One warning before we get down to business. The problem with studying mechanisms readily available to everyone's own inspection through introspection is that we cannot find out anything surprising. We spend years of careful research in the laboratory, meticulously separating the details of a process and experimentally determining the unreasonableness of alternative processes. When we finish, friends and students who are not psychologists say: "You mean it took you 10 years to discover that? I knew it all along, why didn't you ask me?" This can be rather discouraging. The answer to these comments is that there is a difference between the level of our understanding derived from careful experimentation and that derived from careless introspection. One is precise and detailed, often mathematically specified and capable of accurate prediction and explanation. The other is vague and imprecise, lacking in detail and often conflicting with the opinions of others. That the two results do concern the same processes and usually confirm one another should be satisfying, not discomforting. It would be peculiar if our careful study of thought processes led to results that were at odds with all of our intuitions.

Suggested Readings

The readings and discussions contained in this book present a restricted survey of the literature and theoretical points of view in the fields of attention, memory, and pattern recognition. The restrictions are deliberate, both by personal biases and also to minimize the number of issues discussed in order that the important ideas not be lost in a jungle of details.

Although this policy is satisfactory for the purposes of introducing the problems of human information processing, it is not satisfactory for the students who have finished the book and wish to continue reading. Therefore, I have added a selected bibliography of references at the end of each chapter. These references are accompanied by a brief discussion of their importance. The bibliography is, of necessity, incomplete, but by emphasizing review articles, readers will be able to focus rapidly on the literature relevant to their particular interests. In addition, the interested readers should use the journals that are listed in the references for general sources. If an article of interest is found in a particular journal, then it is likely that the same journal will also contain other interesting articles. Thus, it is often useful to sit down with a stack of journals, dating from the most recent issue to issues about five years old, and then simply skim the tables of contents for interesting readings. Another procedure is to use the *Science Citation Index,* published quarterly by the Institute for Scientific Information, Inc., to find those newly published papers which reference the papers discussed in this book.

2
Attention

Every one knows what attention is. It is the taking possession by the mind, in clear and vivid form, of one out of what seem several simultaneously possible objects or trains of thought. Focalization, concentration, of consciousness are of its essence. It implies withdrawal from some things in order to deal effectively with others.[1]

We start with attention and with William James. William James was one of the first modern experimental psychologists (although he himself did few experiments). He believed in studying the mind by using every tool he could find: logic, introspection, and experimentation. His goal was to describe the functions of psychological processes, and he succeeded admirably. His massive textbook *The Principles of Psychology*, first published in 1890, makes good reading today.

As our first quotation from James states, the effects of attention are known by everyone. We cannot fully appreciate all that takes place at any one time. When we concentrate fully on a book, noises in the environment fade from consciousness; when our thoughts wander in a lecture, we find ourselves unable to recall the speaker's message, although we were aware that he was speaking. We can generate examples endlessly. Let us try rather to determine more exactly the nature of attention and the quantitative bounds on its limitations. Then, we may be able to construct the type of logical process that is involved in limiting and controlling attention.

[1] From William James, *The Principles of Psychology,* Vol. 1. New York: Henry Holt and Co., 1890. Pages 403–404. (Republished by Dover, 1950.)

The Phenomena

William James deserves our study because he has carefully set forth his opinions about attention, letting us gain a deeper understanding of the many aspects of the phenomenon before we attempt to explain them. First, we follow James as he examines the problem of simultaneous attention. Granted that we have trouble attending to several simultaneous events, exactly how many items can we attend to at the same time? This problem is basic. We can immediately consider two different types of processes which might be responsible for the limitations of attention: one, a serial process which can do but one thing at a time, and the other, a parallel process which can do a number of things simultaneously, but with some upper limit to the total number of operations it can do at any one time.

A serial device requires some method of switching among the tasks that it is trying to do. If the switching can be performed with sufficient rapidity, there may be little loss in the information obtained from any given task. Parallel processes do not need to be switched from one task to another, but in turn, imply a good deal of complexity and redundancy in the mechanism that analyzes incoming information. The distinction between serial and parallel processes is of much current interest. Unfortunately, although James raises the issue, he gives us little help in resolving it, for he concludes that both possibilities might exist.[2]

*Attention**

WILLIAM JAMES

If, then, by the original question, how many ideas or things can we attend to at once, be meant how many entirely disconnected systems or processes of conception can go on simultaneously, the answer is, *not easily more than one, unless the processes are very habitual; but then two, or even three,* without very much oscillation of the attention. Where, however, the processes are less automatic, as in the story of Julius Caesar dictating four letters whilst he writes a fifth, there must be a rapid oscillation of the mind from one to

---

* *William James.* The Principles of Psychology. *Vol. 1. New York: Henry Holt and Co., 1890. Page 409. (Republished by Dover, 1950.)*

[2] In the readings that follow throughout the book, the original writings have been edited for continuity. Figures and footnotes have been renumbered to correspond to the numbers used here, and occasional sentences referring to sections of the author's paper that are not included in this book have been deleted. The symbol . . . marks a short deletion of material from a quotation, and the symbol — — — marks a lengthy deletion. My comments are printed in this style of type and lengthy quotations appear in this style of type.

the next, and no consequent gain of time. Within any one of the systems the parts may be numberless, but we attend to them collectively when we conceive the whole which they form.

The point seems to be that the number of things we can do depends on the difficulty of each task. A well-learned task, such as walking, takes little effort and does not impede us in our performance of another. A more difficult task such as walking along a high, narrow ledge requires more concentration and may completely impede our efforts to hold a conversation.

Given that the number of things to which we can attend at once is very limited, what is our perception of events to which we are not attending? The act of switching our attention to an event may both blur our perception of that event and cause confusion in our judgments of its temporal properties. These are the critical observations for the experimental investigation of attention, and they suggest a method of study. If attention is the result of a serial device, should there not be difficulty in determining the details and time sequence of events that occur during the absence of our attention? Again, let us return to the descriptions of William James before we go to more modern versions.[3]

When the things to be attended to are small sensations, and when the effort is to be exact in noting them, it is found that attention to one interferes a good deal with the perception of the other. A good deal of fine work has been done in this field, of which I must give some account.

It has long been noticed, when expectant attention is concentrated upon one of two sensations, that the other one is apt to be displaced from consciousness for a moment and to appear subsequently; although in reality the two may have been contemporaneous events. Thus, to use the stock example of the books, the surgeon would sometimes see the blood flow from the arm of the patient whom he was bleeding, *before* he saw the instrument penetrate the skin. Similarly the smith may see the sparks fly *before* he sees the hammer smite the iron, etc. There is thus a certain difficulty in perceiving the exact *data* of two impressions when they do not interest our attention equally, and when they are of a disparate sort.

Professor Exner . . . makes some noteworthy remarks about the way in which the attention must be *set* to catch the interval and the right order of the sensations, when the time is exceeding small. The point was to tell whether two signals were simultaneous or successive; and, if successive, which one of them came first.

The first way of attending which he found himself to fall into, was when the signals did not differ greatly—when, e.g., they were similar sounds heard each by a different ear. Here he lay in wait for the *first* signal, which-

---

[3] William James. *The Principles of Psychology, Op. cit.* Pages 409, 410, and 424–427.

ever it might be, and identified it the next moment in memory. The second, which could then always be known by default, was often not clearly distinguished in itself. When the time was too short, the first could not be isolated from the second at all.

The second way was to accommodate the attention for a certain *sort* of signal, and the next moment to become aware in memory of whether it came before or after its mate.

> *This way brings great uncertainty with it. The impression not prepared for comes to us in the memory more weak than the other, obscure as it were, badly fixed in time. We tend to take the subjectively stronger stimulus, that which we were intent upon, for the first, just as we are apt to take an objectively stronger stimulus to be the first. Still, it may happen otherwise. In the experiments from touch to sight it often seemed to me as if the impression for which the attention was* not *prepared were there already when the other came.*

Exner found himself employing this method oftenest when the impressions differed strongly.

— — —

THE EFFECTS OF ATTENTION

Its remote effects are too incalculable to be recorded. The practical and theoretical life of whole species, as well as of individual beings, results from the selection which the habitual direction of their attention involves.

— — —

Suffice it meanwhile that each of us literally *chooses,* by his ways of attending to things, what sort of a universe he shall appear to himself to inhabit.

The immediate effects of attention are to make us:

    (a) perceive
    (b) conceive
    (c) distinguish
    (d) remember

better than otherwise we could—both more successive things and each thing more clearly. It also

    (e) shortens 'reaction-time.'

a and *b*. Most people would say that a sensation attended to becomes stronger than it otherwise would be. This point is, however, not quite plain, and has occasioned some discussion. From the strength or intensity of a sensation must be distinguished its clearness; and to increase *this* is, for some psychologists, the utmost that attention can do. When the facts are surveyed, however, it must be admitted that to some extent the relative intensity of two sensations may be changed when one of them is attended to and the other not. Every artist knows how he can make a scene before his eyes appear warmer or colder in color, according to the way he sets his attention. If for warm, he soon begins to see the red color start out of everything; if for cold, the blue. Similarly in listening for certain notes in a chord, or overtones in a musical sound, the one we attend to sounds probably a little more loud as well as more emphatic than it did before. When we mentally break a series of monotonous strokes into a rhythm, by accentuating every second or third one, etc., the stroke on which the stress of attention is laid seems to become stronger as well as more emphatic. The increased visibility of optical after-images and of double images, which close attention brings about, can hardly be interpreted otherwise than as a real strengthening of the retinal sensations themselves. And this view is rendered particularly probable by the fact that an imagined visual object may, if attention be concentrated upon it long enough, acquire before the mind's eye almost the brilliancy of reality, and (in the case of certain exceptionally gifted observers) leave a negative after-image of itself when it passes away. Confident expectation of a certain intensity or quality of impression will often make us sensibly see or hear it in an object which really falls far short of it. In face of such facts it is rash to say that attention cannot make a sense-impression more intense.

But, on the other hand, the intensification which may be brought about seems never to lead the judgment astray. As we rightly perceive and name the same color under various lights, the same sound at various distances; so we seem to make an analogous sort of allowance for the varying amounts of attention with which objects are viewed; and whatever changes of feeling the attention may bring we charge, as it were, to the attention's account, and still perceive and conceive the object as the same.

> *A gray paper appears to us no lighter, the pendulum-beat of a clock no louder, no matter how much we increase the strain of our attention upon them. No one, by doing this, can make the gray paper look white, or the stroke of the pendulum sound like the blow of a strong hammer—everyone, on the contrary, feels the increase as that of his own conscious activity turned upon the thing.*

Were it otherwise, we should not be able to note *intensities* by attending to them. Weak impressions would, as Stumpf says, become stronger by the very fact of being observed.

I should not be able to observe faint sounds at all, but

*only such as appeared to me of maximal strength, or at least
of a strength that increased with the amount of my observation. In reality, however, I can, with steadily increasing attention, follow a diminuendo perfectly well.*

The subject is one which would well repay exact experiment, if methods
could be devised. Meanwhile there is no question whatever that attention
augments the *clearness* of all that we perceive or conceive by its aid. But what
is meant by clearness here?

c. Clearness, so far as attention produces it, *means distinction from
other things* and *internal analysis* or *subdivision.* These are essentially products of intellectual *discrimination,* involving comparison, memory, and perception of various relations. The attention *per se* does not distinguish and
analyze and relate. The most we can say is that it is a condition of our doing
so. And as these processes are to be described later, the clearness they produce had better not be farther discussed here. The important point to notice
here is that it is not attention's *immediate* fruit.

d. Whatever future conclusion we may reach as to this, we cannot deny
that *an object once attended to will remain in the memory,* whilst one inattentively allowed to pass will leave no traces behind.

William James leaves us with a very complete description of the
phenomenon of attention. He describes its variety, its nature, and its
effects. Not much can be added to the overall picture, but all of the
details must be filled in. We have just read that attention can alter the
temporal order of our perceptions; why? We have read that attention
affects retention, clarity, and reaction time; why? Even with a good
description of the phenomenon we still know little of the mechanism.

Attention received much study following William James. Eighteen
years later, in 1908, Edward B. Titchener wrote from his experimental
laboratory at Cornell that one of the few things psychology could credit
itself with achieving was the discovery of attention. Titchener credited
the German introspectionist Wundt with the doctrine of attention, dating
its inception as 1860, but, commenting further on the critical importance
of attention, Titchener pointed out that "the discovery of attention did
not result in any immediate triumph of the experimental method. It was
something like the discovery of a hornet's nest: the first touch brought
out a whole swarm of insistent problems." (Titchener, 1908, Chapter 5.)

Titchener tried hard to specify the attributes of attention by such
"laws" as the law of prior entry in which he stated that, "the stimulus
for which we are predisposed requires less time than a like stimulus,
for which we are unprepared, to produce its full conscious effect. Or,
in popular terms, the object of attention comes to consciousness more

quickly than the objects that we are not attending to." But Titchener was forced to conclude that, "although the discovery of a reliable measure of attention would appear to be one of the most important problems that await solution by the experimental psychology of the future" (Titchener quoting Külpe), "the discovery has not yet been made." All these statements apply today, some 70 years later.

The study of attention declined from the early years of the century until the 1950s. Then, in England, a group of researchers started a whole new series of studies, this time with a specific theoretical model of the attention process in mind. Several dramatic changes in scientific technique had occurred in those interim years. Mostly as a result of tremendous impetus to scientific work produced by the second world war, communication engineers had developed powerful electronic systems and analytical techniques, including the digital computer and related topics in automata and network theory.

Selective Attention and the Cocktail Party Problem

One of the first studies to come out of the new era of experimentation exemplifies many of the characteristics of the research. It was conducted by an Englishman, E. Colin Cherry, in an American laboratory at the Massachusetts Institute of Technology. The study was one of experimental psychology, but it was performed in the MIT Research Laboratory of Electronics and was published in a physics journal, the *Journal of the Acoustical Society of America.* Such interdisciplinary research is characteristic of modern psychology.

Cherry addressed himself to the problem of selective attention, or as he put it, "the cocktail party problem." The cocktail party serves as a fine example of selective attention. We stand in a crowded room with sounds and conversations all about us. Often the conversation to which we are trying to listen is not the one in which we are supposedly taking part. There are many different aspects of the cocktail party to interest psychologists. (We ignore the idea that it is a comfortable way in which to conduct research.) First, what is our selective ability? How are we able to select the one voice that interests us out of the many that surround us? Second, how much do we retain of the conversations to which we do not pay attention?

The first problem, selective attention, is not trivial. It implies a very complex analysis of the sounds that arrive at our ears—an analysis so complex that it cannot yet be performed by electronic devices. The second problem, the measure of our knowledge of rejected sources of speech, tells us how well the attention mechanism selects and rejects channels of information. These two problems, we will see, characterize the most recent research, for they are at the core of the phenomenon: we select what is relevant; we reject the rest.

As you read Cherry's paper, note several things. First, humans use all the information that is available in performing their tasks. When we are required to separate two simultaneously spoken messages, we do so by physical cues such as the idiosyncrasies of the speakers' voices, their spatial location, their intensities, and whatever else we can find to distinguish them. If these physical cues fail, we use psychological ones, such as the grammatical or semantic content of the spoken material. If we are asked to specify just what aspect of the situation allows a human to select one voice from others, we cannot give a simple answer. Second, note that Cherry's experiments indicate that his subjects knew little of the characteristics of the rejected channel, but as you read his convincing demonstration of this fact, ask yourself how we are able to switch our attention to new voices or events when the occasion arises, if we are unaware of the content of those other events. The inconsistency between our apparent lack of knowledge of rejected channels and our selective ability governs the conclusions and studies of the rest of this chapter.

Some Experiments on the Recognition of Speech, with One and with Two Ears*

E. COLIN CHERRY

INTRODUCTION

The tests to be described are in two groups. In the first, two different spoken messages are presented to the subject simultaneously, using both ears. In the second, one spoken message is fed to his right ear and a different message to his left ear. The results, the subject's spoken reconstruction, are markedly different in the two cases; so also are the significances of these results. Before examining such possible significance, it will be better to describe some of the experiments.

THE SEPARATION OF TWO SIMULTANEOUSLY SPOKEN MESSAGES

The first set of experiments relates to this general problem of speech recognition: how do we recognize what one person is saying when others are

* E. Colin Cherry. Some experiments on the recognition of speech, with one and with two ears. Journal of the Acoustical Society of America. 1953, 25, 975–979. Copyright © 1953 by the Acoustical Society of America. With permission of author and publisher.

speaking at the same time (the "cocktail party problem")? On what logical basis could one design a machine ("filter") for carrying out such an operation? A few of the factors which give mental facility might be the following:

(a) The voices come from different directions.
(b) Lip-reading, gestures, and the like.
(c) Different speaking voices, mean pitches, mean speeds, male and female, and so forth.
(d) Accents differing.
(e) Transition-probabilities (subject matter, voice dynamics, syntax . . .).

All of these factors, except the last (e), may, however, be eliminated by the device of recording two messages on the same magnetic-tape, spoken by the same speaker. The result is a babel, but nevertheless the messages may be separated.

—   —   —

At the subjective level the subject reported very great difficulty in accomplishing his task. He would shut his eyes to assist concentration. Some phrases were repeatedly played over by him, perhaps 10 to 20 times, but his guess was right in the end. In no cases were any long phrases (more than 2 or 3 words) identified wrongly.

In a variation of the experiment the subject was given a pencil and paper, and permitted to write down the words and phrases as he identified them. Subjectively speaking, his task then became "very much easier." Times were shortened. It appears that the long-term storage provided assists prediction.

Numerous tests have been made, using pairs of messages of varying similarity. Some test samples consisted of adjacent paragraphs out of the same book. The results were consistently similar; the messages were almost entirely separated.

However, it was considered possible to construct messages which could not be separated with such a low frequency of errors. Such a test is described in the next Section.

INSEPARABLE SPOKEN MESSAGES. USE OF CLICHÉS OR "HIGHLY-PROBABLE PHRASES"

As a final test in this series, using the same speaker recorded as speaking two different messages simultaneously, a pair of messages was composed which could not be separated by the listening subject. The messages were composed by selecting, from reported speeches in a newspaper, 150 clichés and stringing them together with simple conjunctions, pronouns, etc., as continuous speeches. For example, a few of the clichés were:

    (1) I am happy to be here today,
    (2) The man in the street,
    (3) Stop beating about the bush,
    (4) We are on the brink of ruin,

and the like. The corresponding sample of one speech was as follows:

"I am happy to be here today to talk to the man in the street. Gentlemen, the time has come to stop beating about the bush—we are on the brink of ruin, and the welfare of the workers and of the great majority of the people is imperiled," and so forth.

It is remarkably easy to write such passages by the page. Now a cliché is, almost by definition, a highly probable chain of words, and on the other hand the transition probability of one cliché following another specific one is far lower. The subject, as he listened to the mixed speeches in an endeavor to separate one of them was observed to read out complete clichés at a time; it appeared that recognition of one or two words would insure his predicting a whole cliché. But he picked them out in roughly equal numbers from both speeches; in such artificially constructed cases, message separation appeared impossible. The speeches were of course read with normal continuity, and with natural articulatory and emotional properties, during their recording.

It is suggested that techniques such as those described in the preceding sections may be extended so that they will shed light on the relative importance of the different types of transition probabilities in recognition. For instance, speeches of correct "syntactical structure" but with no meaning and using few dictionary words may readily be constructed. [Lewis Carroll's "Jabberwocky" is such an instance; similarly, "meaningful" speeches with almost zero (or at least unfamiliar) syntactical or inflexional structure (Pidgin English).] Again continuous speaking of dictionary words, which are relatively disconnected, into "meaningless phrases" is possible; the word-transition probabilities may be assessed *a priori,* with the assistance of suitable probability tables. Further experiments are proceeding.[4]

UNMIXED SPEECHES; ONE IN THE LEFT EAR AND ONE IN THE RIGHT

The objective, and subjective, results of a second series of tests were completely different. In these tests one continuous spoken message was fed into a headphone on the subject's left ear and a different message applied to the right ear. The messages were recorded, using the same speaker.

The subject experiences no difficulty in listening to either speech at will and "rejecting" the unwanted one. Note that aural directivity does not arise here; the earphones are fixed to the head in the normal way. To use a loose

---

[4] Some of Cherry's further experiments are reported in Cherry and Taylor, 1954.

expression, the "processes of recognition may apparently be switched to either ear at will." This result has surprised a number of listeners; although of course it is well known to anyone who has made hearing tests. It may be noteworthy that when one tries to follow the conversation of a speaker in a crowded noisy room, the instinctive action is to turn one ear toward him, although this may increase the difference between the "messages" reaching the two ears.

The subject is instructed to repeat one of the messages concurrently while he is listening (Broadbent, 1952) and to make no errors. Surprising as it may seem this proves easy; his words are slightly delayed behind those on the record to which he is listening. One marked characteristic of his speaking voice is its monotony. Very little emotional content or stressing of the words occurs at all. Subjectively, the subject is unaware of this fact. Also he may have very little idea of what the message that he has repeated is all about, especially if the subject matter is difficult. But he has recognized every word, as his repeating proves.

But the point of real interest is that if the subject is subsequently asked to repeat anything of what he heard in his other (rejected-message) ear, he can say little about it at all, except possibly that sounds were occurring.

Experiments were made in an attempt to find out just what attributes, if any, of the "rejected" message are recognized.

LANGUAGE OF "REJECTED" EAR UNRECOGNIZED

In a further set of tests the two messages, one for the right ear and one for the left, started in English. After the subject was comfortably repeating his right-ear message, the left-ear message was changed to German, spoken by an Englishman. The subject subsequently reported, when asked to state the language of the "rejected" left-ear message, that he "did not know at all, but assumed it was English." The test was repeated with different, unprepared listeners; the results were similar. It is considered unfair to try this particular test more than once with the same listener.

It was considered that a further series of tests might well indicate the level of recognition which is attained in the "rejected" ear, raising the questions, Is the listener aware even that it is human speech? male or female? and the like.

WHAT FACTORS OF THE "REJECTED" MESSAGE ARE RECOGNIZED

In this series of tests the listening subjects were presented at their right-hand ears with spoken passages from newspapers, chosen carefully to avoid proper names or difficult words, and again instructed to repeat these passages concurrently without omission or error. Into their left ears were fed signals of different kinds, for different tests, but each of which started and ended with a short passage of normal English speech in order to avoid any troubles that might be involved in the listener's "getting going" on the test. The center, major, portions of these rejected left-ear signals thus reached the listener while he was steadily repeating his right-ear message.

Again no one listening subject was used for more than one test; none of them was primed as to the results to be expected. The center, major, portions of the left-ear signals for the series of tests were, respectively:

(a) Normal male spoken English—as for earlier tests.
(b) Female spoken English—high-pitched voice.
(c) Reversed male speech (i.e., same spectrum but no words or semantic content).
(d) A steady 400-cps oscillator.

After any one of these tests, the subject was asked the following questions:

(1) Did the left-ear signal consist of human speech or not?
(2) If yes is given in answer to (1), can you say what it was about, or even quote any words?
(3) Was it a male or female speaker?
(4) What language was it in?

The responses varied only slightly. In no case in which normal human speech was used did the listening subjects fail to identify it as speech; in every such instance they were unable to identify any word or phrase heard in the rejected ear and, furthermore, unable to make definite identification of the language as being English. On the other hand the change of voice—male to female—was nearly always identified while the 400-cps pure tone was always observed. The reversed speech was identified as having "something queer about it" by a few listeners, but was thought to be normal speech by others.

The broad conclusions are that the "rejected" signal has certain statistical properties recognized, but that detailed aspects, such as the language, individual words, or semantic content, are unnoticed.

Experiments and Early Theories

Cherry's research has introduced a new phenomenon and a new experimental technique. Let us review this technique briefly, for it will play an increasingly important role in later sections of this chapter. The technique is to require a subject to repeat a message that is presented to him—to *shadow* the message—while at the same time he is presented with other material, either auditorally or visually. Cherry reports that the task of shadowing is easy, but also that "one marked characteristic of (the subject's) speaking voice is its monotony. Very little emotional content or stressing of the words occurs at all . . . he may have very little idea of what the message that he has repeated is all about." Cherry's description of the subject's tone of voice and inability to remember what had been shadowed suggests a difficult task. Actually, the task of shadowing can be made either easy or difficult, depending upon the details of the way it is performed.

The critical variables involved in shadowing are of two forms: the instructions given to the subject and the type of material that is being shadowed. The type of material is important, for if a passage of prose is selected from a novel, the task is easier than if the material is from a technical work. Both these selections are grammatical; the shadowing task becomes even more difficult if the material consists of randomly arranged English words; harder yet are nonsense words. The importance of the grammatical aspects of the material cannot be overemphasized. The first part of Cherry's paper shows that even in the absence of physical cues, two different speeches mixed together can be disentangled if there are sufficient grammatical constraints involved. When the grammatical constraints are relaxed by using speeches constructed of clichés or nonmeaningful phrases, separation of the messages becomes very difficult or impossible. Even when the speeches to be separated are accompanied by physical cues, such as being presented to different ears or being read in separate voices, grammatical structure plays an important role in the ability to attend to one while rejecting the other. We would not survive at the cocktail party were the speech of the participants completely devoid of grammatical structure or meaning. We shall return to this issue later, for the structure imposed on verbal messages by the rules of grammar and meaning play an important role in recent theories of attention.

Cherry reports that his subject's "words are slightly delayed behind those on the record to which he is listening." We call this type of behavior *phrase shadowing*, and it simplifies the task for the subject. Indeed, skilled typists, readers, or Morse code receivers learn to type, speak, or write with a considerable lag between what they produce and what they receive or see. The lag needs to be long enough to take advantage of the structure of language, but not so long as to impose a memory burden. We can tremendously increase the difficulty involved in shadowing by instructing subjects to stop phrase shadowing and start *phonemic shadowing*. In phonemic shadowing, the subject is required to repeat each sound as he hears it, without waiting for the completion of a phrase, or indeed, without waiting for the completion of a word. Phonemic shadowing is difficult to do; it takes a lot of practice for subjects to learn how, and even then they usually cannot do it without error.

Shadowing, then, is a powerful but complicated experimental task.

It has many problems as a laboratory tool in the study of attention because it is difficult to measure just how much effort the subject uses in performing the shadowing. The list of variables that influence shadowing illustrates that a simple tabulation of how accurately the subject's spoken words agree with the presented material does not even begin to tell us how much attention is diverted to the task. Cherry suggests some of the other measures we might have to use. Is not the inability of subjects to remember the content of the shadowed message a statement of its difficulty? Here the act of shadowing must have interfered only with memory, not perception, because the fact that the shadowing was accurate proves that every word of the passage was perceived properly. Why, then, is there little memory for it? The fact that Cherry's subjects used phrase shadowing indicates that memory was involved; some memory had to store each word between the time it arrived at the ears and the time it was spoken by the subject. Phrase shadowing implies that there is a grammatical analysis of the material being processed. With all this memory and analysis, we must conclude, surprisingly enough, that although Cherry places maximum emphasis on the "rejection" of information from the nonshadowed channel, material that was shadowed is also "rejected," at least to some extent.

When Cherry tested subjects on their ability to recognize the language of the material presented on the "rejected" channel, he stated that "it is considered unfair to try this particular test more than once with the same listener." Unfair? If shadowing truly diverts the attention from the material presented on the other channel, why should it be unfair to use listeners in the same test several times? Is it unfair because after a while the listeners would be able to say what language had been presented? If so, just what is taking place when subjects shadow? Can they selectively accept or reject other material?

This discussion should not be read as a criticism of Cherry's experiments. The discussion is only intended to emphasize some of the difficulties involved in doing research on attention and to spell out some new theoretical issues. The effects Cherry reports are dramatic ones. In a later series of experiments, the psychologist Moray (1959) tried to determine exactly how much information humans retain of the rejected channel. He found that even when English words were repeated as many as 35 times in the rejected ear, there was absolutely no retention of them. Even when the subjects were told that they were later to be tested on their retention of material from the nonshadowed ear, it made little difference; the task of shadowing was so difficult that it completely distracted their attention from other material.

There are several possible explanations of these results. The inability of subjects to recall much information about material on the nonshadowed channel might be the result of masking: the sounds of the message to be shadowed combined with the subject's voice as he repeats that message drown out or mask the voice speaking the other message. There are several reasons, however, why this is probably not correct. The simplest reasons (though by no means all that might be given) come from the introspections of subjects and from a simple logical analysis of the experiment.

The logical analysis proceeds as follows: we can present the speech from both information channels over one loudspeaker. When we do this, the word that is about to be shadowed is interfered with by both the word coming from the other, nonshadowed speech and the word being spoken by the subject. The word in the nonshadowed message is, similarly, interfered with by both the voice of the subject and the word being spoken on the message to be shadowed. Thus, the total amount of interference is the same for both channels, yet one channel is perceived—the subject shadows it properly—and the other channel is not—the subject recalls very little about its properties.[5]

The easiest way to dispel any possible alternative explanation for the result is to try the task. The impression you receive is quite clearly that of a limited ability to process the material. It is as if you attend to the total speech input only in order to latch on to the desired speech. Then, you dare not release your attention from the message you are shadowing even for an instant, for if you do, you will not be able to maintain perfect shadowing. Even though the sounds and words from the nonshadowed message are heard, they pass by without leaving any lasting impression.

There is still one other difficulty with the observation that little or nothing is remembered of the nonshadowed task. Both Cherry and Moray waited a while before asking their subjects how much they remembered of the nonattended material. James hints at the problem when he tells us that "an object once attended to will remain in the memory, whilst one inattentively allowed to pass will leave no traces behind." Does that mean that even the object that receives no attention is remembered briefly before its traces disappear? To answer this question is simple; we need only interrupt the subject while he is shadowing and quickly demand of him what was presented on the ear he was not shadowing. This is what we might call the "what-did-you-say" phenomenon. Often when someone to whom you were not "listening" asks a question of you, your first reaction is to say, "Uh, what did you say?"

---

[5] This argument neglects the effect of grammatical context on the ease with which a message can be perceived, even with interference. It is easier to understand material that fits within a grammatical context than ungrammatical material. The shadowed message presumably is a grammatical message, whereas the nonshadowed message, in the absence of effort to understand it, is essentially a list of isolated words, poorly remembered. Nonetheless, the masking argument is not very convincing.

But then, before the question is repeated, you can dredge it up yourself from memory. When this experiment was actually tried in my laboratory (Norman, 1969) and repeated by Glucksberg and Cohen (1970), the results agreed with intuitions: there is a temporary memory for items to which we are not attending, but, as Cherry, James, and Moray point out, no long-term memory.

The first complete theory of attention came in 1958 by Donald Broadbent, from the psychological laboratories in Cambridge, England. Broadbent developed a series of experiments, the most famous involving simultaneous memorization of two simultaneously presented sequences of digits.[6]

When Broadbent presented his subjects with three pairs of digits dichotically, so that one set of three digits read serially was heard at one ear at the same time that a second set of digits was heard at the other ear, he found surprising results. First, his subjects could barely recall 4 or 5 digits, whereas in more normal situations people have little trouble in remembering a string of 7 to 10 digits. Second, subjects preferred to organize their output by ears, rather than by the apparently more natural order, the order in which they heard the digits. That is, if the right ear has presented to it the digits 1, 7, 6 at the rate of one digit every half-second and the left ear the digits 8, 5, 2, the actual order of presentation of the digits is by the three pairs 1-8, 7-5, and 6-2. The preferred order of recall, however, is to give one ear's sequence first and then the other's: 1, 7, 6 and then 8, 5, 2. Usually, subjects get all the digits correct from the first ear, but make errors in the other sequence.

What can we make of these results? Broadbent concluded that they illustrated the properties of selective attention; selection was made on the basis of the physical channels by which the digits were presented. After considering a large set of experimental findings of various sorts, including the dichotically presented digits and Cherry's results, Broadbent put together a theoretical structure which he felt represented the underlying processes.

---

[6] A glossary of terminology might be appropriate here. In experiments involving auditory information presented to the two ears, it is necessary to distinguish among the various ways in which that information might be presented.

Consider two sources of sounds, *A* and *B*, which we wish to present simultaneously to a listener. If *A* and *B* are both presented to one ear only (through an earphone) we say that the presentation is *monaural*. If *A* and *B* are mixed together and then presented to both ears, so that both ears hear exactly the same material, we say the presentation is *binaural*. If the two channels are fed into separate ears, so that the left ear hears only *A* and the right ear only *B*, we say the presentation is *dichotic*. Finally, if we feed *A* through one loudspeaker and *B* through another placed nearby in such a way as to recreate the sound patterns resulting when two persons might simultaneously take the part of *A* and *B*, we say the presentation is *stereophonic*. Similar distinctions can be made for visual material: *monoptic, dioptic, stereoscopic*.

The Filter Model

Broadbent was attempting to piece together a model of human capability that would account for a wide variety of data, not just those from experiments in attention. Basically, Broadbent suggested that the limit to our ability to perceive competing messages is perceptual; we are able to analyze and identify only a limited amount of the information that arrives at our sensory inputs. He proposed that the brain contains a "selective filter" that can be "tuned" to accept the desired message and reject all others. The filter thus manages to block undesired inputs, reducing the processing load on the perceptual system. In the following excerpt from his book, Broadbent summarizes the model and tries to show how it is compatible with the evidence from a rather wide variety of psychological tasks. His model is important, for it shaped the direction for further research in attention. It is appropriate that we review it now, before we examine other, later experiments.

*Perception and Communication**

DONALD E. BROADBENT

SUMMARY OF PRINCIPLES

(a) A nervous system acts to some extent as a single communication channel, so that it is meaningful to regard it as having a limited capacity.

(b) A selective operation is performed upon the input to this channel, the operation taking the form of selecting information from all sensory events having some feature in common. Physical features identified as able to act as a basis for this selection include the intensity, pitch, and spatial localization of sounds.

(c) The selection is not completely random, and the probability of a particular class of events being selected is increased by certain properties of the events and by certain states of the organism.

(d) Properties of the events which increase the probability of the information, conveyed by them, passing the limited capacity channel include the following: physical intensity, time since the last information from that class of events entered the

* Donald E. Broadbent. Perception and Communication. *London: Pergamon Press, 1958. Pages 297–300. Copyright © 1958 by D. E. Broadbent. With permission of author and publisher.*

limited capacity channel, high frequency of sounds as opposed to low.

— — —

(h) Incoming information may be held in a temporary store at a stage previous to the limited capacity channels: it will then pass through the channel when the class of events to which it belongs is next selected. The maximum time of storage possible in this way is of the order of seconds.

(i) To evade the limitations of (h) it is possible for information to return to temporary store after passage through the limited capacity channel: this provides storage of unlimited time at the cost of reducing the capacity of the channel still further and possibly to zero. (Long-term storage does not affect the capacity of the channel, but rather is the means for adjusting the internal coding to the probabilities of external events; so that the limit on the channel is an informational one and not simply one of a number of simultaneous stimuli.)

(j) A shift of the selective process from one class of events to another takes a time which is not negligible compared with the minimum time spent on any one class.

— — —

An information-flow diagram incorporating the more probable principles is shown in Fig. 2.1.

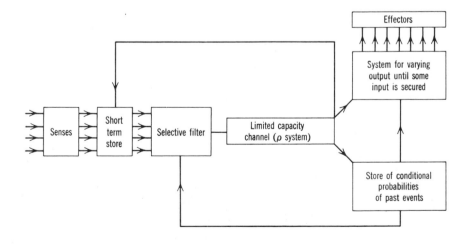

Fig. 2.1. A tentative information-flow diagram for the organism, as conceived at the present time.

— — —

Major Implications of These Principles

Now that these principles are stated thus boldly, it may be urged that they are not particularly surprising. Do we not know that attention is limited, that noises distract us, that we consciously rehearse any matter which must be remembered for a short period, and so on? What gain is there from putting these everyday experiences into this stilted language? They have already been formulated by the classical introspective psychologists: why is time and effort wasted on rephrasing them?

These are two answers to this objection. First, it is indeed true that the principles lead to no prediction which is contrary to everyday observation. It would be a poor set of scientific principles which did do so: though it is not uncommon for psychologists to feel that they ought to contradict common beliefs about behaviour.

But secondly, as a matter of history it is not true that these principles are obvious nor that they were adequately formulated by classical psychologists. It is quite possible to say that mentalistic statements are consistent with them: to say that our limited capacity single channel is to be equated with the unitary attention of the introspectionists. Indeed, the writer believes that the one is simply a more exact version of the other. But a view of attention as unitary might also be taken to mean that a man cannot perform two tasks at once: which experimental evidence shows to be untrue. A view of noise as distracting might be taken to mean that card-sorting or mental arithmetic will be worse performed in noise, which they are not.

Broadbent provides us with a complete structure for selection and attention which agrees with intuition and with the facts known at that time (1958). Basically the hypothesis can be summarized by saying that a limited-capacity processor deals with but one channel of information at a time. The human selects among the various sources of information impinging on his sense organs on the basis of the physical characteristics of the information. When necessary, he switches attention among the various input sources. A short-term memory system prevents loss of information about the immediate past history of the unselected channels.

The Filter Model Fails and Is Modified

Broadbent's theory indicated a specific theoretical structure that, in turn, had strong implications on how people behave. Some of these implications were tested and proved wrong. One method of probing the theoretical structure is by means of the question raised earlier with Cherry's paper: how are we able to switch our attention among inputs if we are unaware of the content of unselected inputs?

A crucial experiment on this point was done by two undergraduates at Oxford University, Gray and Wedderburn (1960). They rejected the idea that attention was based on the physical characteristics of sensory channels and suggested that psychological attributes played an important role in selection. Their experiments were simple in concept, but the results were devastating to Broadbent's theory. Suppose we listened to one word so divided that different syllables of the word are presented alternately to different ears. At the same time, another word is decomposed in a similar fashion and presented to the complementary ear. Would not the attention switch from ear to ear and thus re-create each word correctly, rather than stick to one physical channel and get a nonsensical mixture of syllables? If this is so—and Gray and Wedderburn showed that it is—the attention mechanism must be able to extract the meaning of information from the two ears in order to know which to choose. But Broadbent's system (Fig. 2.1) requires attention to be switched at an early stage in the processing of sensory information, much before any of the meaning has been extracted.

The distinction between selection on the basis of physical or sensory analyses and selection on the basis of a more thorough analysis of meaning is very important. Broadbent's theoretical scheme makes good sense; we would not like to discard the overall structure. Yet it is clear from even the simple points raised by Gray and Wedderburn that something is wrong. A much more complete discussion of this problem was put forth by Anne Treisman in her doctoral dissertation at Oxford University in 1961. Treisman examined the role of verbal and linguistic features on her subjects' ability to select one message from among several. In particular, she hoped to test Broadbent's suggestion that "classes" of words may behave in the same way as sensory channels do by presenting messages in different languages. Certainly a difference in language is an extreme case of a verbal distinction between two messages without any general differences in physical characteristics. In addition, she examined the role of familiarity, redundancy, meaningfulness, and similarity.

Treisman evaluated Broadbent's theory of a selective filter by continuing and elaborating on Cherry's experimental methods. The technique of this research is to keep the subject occupied performing a shadowing task while various types of competing messages and signals are presented to him. It has been found that if the subject manages to keep up the shadowing task, gross physical changes of the nonshadowed message are noticed (change from a man's voice to a woman's), simple changes are not noticed (changes in the language of the nonshadowed message), and "important" words on the nonshadowed ear are often noticed (the subject's name or material that would be relevant within the context of the shadowed material).

The problem discussed for the rest of the chapter deals with the way in which our ability to perceive material is limited. The selective filter proposed by Broadbent works to minimize the amount of processing that must be performed by more complex, higher-level processes. Broadbent evidently had in mind an ascending chain of complexity with some central mechanism performing the final analysis on incoming information. In this scheme one wants to eliminate irrelevant messages from the central mechanism. The problem, as we shall see, is that the properties required of the filter became so complex that the filter seemed to be almost as complicated as the final mechanism it was attempting to serve.

In her experiments, Treisman studied selective attention to one of two competing messages, presented binaurally. The messages were created by varying a number of different attributes. The irrelevant material was sometimes read with the same voice as the relevant material (female) and sometimes in a different voice (male). The nature of the irrelevant material also varied, sometimes being a technical discussion, other times passages from novels, and sometimes passages from the same novel as the relevant channel. Finally, the language of the irrelevant passage varied from English to Latin, French, German, and Czech (with a deliberate English accent), to English played backward over the tape recorder, and even to a French translation of the English shadowed message. The subjects' job was to shadow the relevant channel and ignore entirely the irrelevant material. As we can guess from Cherry's study, this is an easy task when the voices and materials used for the two messages are different, but a difficult task when the same voices and similar materials are used.

The aim of these studies, remember, was to determine at what level the selection of relevant from irrelevant material was made. Broadbent postulated selection almost entirely based on sensory features. Treisman hoped that by using a variety of irrelevant material she could distinguish between the relative effects of cues based entirely on sensory features and cues that required the determination of familiarity and meaning. Her experiments showed that sensory cues alone were not sufficient. She summarized her results and put forth a hypothesis to account for the types of errors made by her subjects (Ss).

Verbal Cues in Selective Attention*

ANNE M. TREISMAN

(1) It was shown that a difference in voice (male vs. female) and a difference in language have quite different effects on tasks requiring selective

* Anne M. Treisman. Verbal cues, language and meaning in selective attention. American Journal of Psychology. 1964, 77, 215–216. Copyright © 1965 by Karl H. Dallenbach. With permission of author and publisher.

response to one of two messages. The dlifference in voice allows the irrelevant message to be rejected much more efficiently, and this probably takes place at an earlier stage in the perceptual analysis of inputs. (2) When two messages share the same general physical characteristics, a difference in language allows some selection between them; however this seems more similar to selection between two English messages on the basis of subject matter than to the efficient performance obtained with different voices. Thus, complete rejection of one language as such appears to be impossible. (3) Phonetic cues make an unknown foreign language less distracting than a message which is phonetically similar to English (the Czech nonsense), and allow the Ss to name the irrelevant foreign language. Reversed speech however, causes a relatively high degree of interference. (4) The Ss' knowledge of the language affects the amount of interference it produces. In most cases, however, little of the content of the rejected message can be reported. Many Ss failed to notice that the Czech was not normal English and not all the Ss, even among those who knew the language fluently, realize that a rejected French message was a translation of the selected English one. While similarity of the languages at the phonetic level makes selection more difficult (as with the Czech), similarity of meaning (with the French translation) produced no general increase in interference. (5) Finally, when both messages are in the same language and same voice, selection is based chiefly on transitional probabilities between words and its efficiency varies with the degree of contextual constraint within both the selected and irrelevant messages. This is the only condition in which a considerable number of overt intrusions from the irrelevant message is made.

These findings are relevant to the following problems: (1) Are both messages fully analyzed before one is selected to determine the responses? (2) If not, at what stage in the analysis is one of the two discarded? (3) What determines selection and switching between messages? How does this depend on the familiarity and phonetic structure of the languages and on the transitional probabilities between words?

(1) Analysis of irrelevant message. For the following reasons, it seems unlikely that both messages are always fully analyzed and that selection takes place only for the overt responses: (a) less than half the Ss recognized either the French translation or the Czech nonsense, although this would have added no more load to response or memory than noticing the male voice. Those who did identify these messages may have done so by switching to the irrelevant message.

— — —

(2) Stage at which selection is made. The question then arises: at what stage is one of the two messages rejected from further analysis? It does not seem possible to reject or filter out irrelevant messages which differ only in verbal characteristics in the same efficient way as those which differ in general physical features.

— — —

If this early selection were possible between messages in the same voice but different languages, known and unknown languages should cause equal interference and both should be easier to reject than a message in the same language as the selected message. Neither of these predictions was confirmed by the results.

The results thus suggest that features of incoming messages are analyzed successively by the nervous system, starting with general physical features and proceeding to the identification of words and meaning, and that selection between messages in the same voice, intensity, and localization takes place during, rather than before or after, the analysis which results in the identification of their verbal content. It seems to be at this stage that the information-handling capacity becomes limited and can handle only one input at a time, either keeping to one message where possible, or switching between the two. Broadbent's suggestion that one may think of classes of words as constituting separate "input channels" which can be rejected, as such, is not supported by these results.

(3) *Factors determining selection and switching between messages.* What, then, determines selection and switching when both messages arrive on one input channel? The irrelevant messages seem to fall into two main classes: (*a*) those which the Ss potentially could identify; and (*b*) those whose verbal content they could never identify at all, because the language was unknown or the tape played backwards.

(*a*) When the irrelevant message was in a known foreign language or in English, the interference often took the form of making the Ss shift their attention to the wrong message and lose the correct message altogether for a time. The results with the statistical approximations suggest that the Ss repeat the correct message until its transitional probabilities fall to a low value. Differences in the competing messages do not affect the point at which they switch, but do affect their subsequent performance. Having switched, the Ss have two decisions to make: whether to repeat aloud what they hear, or to switch back. The instructions were to repeat as much as possible, rather than remaining silent when in doubt. This would encourage the Ss to make overt responses until they switched back, except when these were obvious errors, such as words in a different language.

We can now try to interpret these experiments and hypothesize what must be happening. To summarize Treisman's results once more, she found a graded effect on the ability of her subjects to reject an irrelevant message. When there was a distinct physical difference between relevant and irrelevant channels, subjects had no difficulty in shadowing one without being bothered by the other. When the messages had similar physical characteristics but belonged to different languages, they were much less successful. The better the subjects knew the irrelevant languages, the more it interfered. The most difficult task was to maintain shadowing one message when both were read in the same language and spoken with the same voice.

To explain these results, Treisman postulates an analytical mechanism that performs a series of tests on incoming messages. The first tests distinguish among the inputs on the basis of sensory or physical cues; later tests distinguish among syllabic patterns, specific sounds, individual words and, finally, grammatical structure and meaning. The sequence of tests can be thought of as a tree, with incoming sensory information starting at the bottom and working its way up to a unique end point, with tests at each spot where there is a choice of branches that might be taken. Moreover, Treisman suggests that the tests be flexible, so that if a particular word is expected, all the tests relevant to selecting that word might be prebiased or presensitized toward it. Thus, analysis is much simplified for items that are expected to occur.

If channels have physical distinctions, then at a very early stage of testing it will be possible to separate one from the other. This is done by attenuating the irrelevant channel so that it no longer interferes with the later testing procedure. Thus, words that appear on the irrelevant channel will be severely attenuated because they fail the physical test. If, however, a word on the irrelevant channel fits within the context of the material which has just been analyzed, it might very well be detected because the sensitization of each test toward the expected event would tend to cancel the effects of the attenuation of the irrelevant channel. Note, by the way, that by this model we ought to make mistakes, often claiming to have heard an item that was not actually presented. These false recognitions are a result of the lowered decision criteria for the tests relevant to expected events. Thus, although this presensitization makes detection of the correct event more likely, it also increases the likelihood that similar sounding items will pass the test incorrectly.

Treisman moves us one step further in the specification of the level at which attention becomes selective. She suggests that all incoming signals are analyzed to some extent by a sequence of operations. Signals are separated from one another by their physical features when that is possible and by their grammatical features when that becomes necessary. Grammatical information is used to bias or sensitize the criterion for identifying certain signals. Thus, in the middle of a sentence we might expect a certain grammatical class of words to occur, so we presensitize our analytical mechanisms for the possibility. This explains why we are sometimes able to pick out material presented in competing messages when that material appears to be relevant to the context to which we are primarily attending. The details of this procedure are left unexplained. Obviously, it implies that all signals, whether thought to be relevant or irrelevant, must receive a good deal of analysis, if only so that they may be discarded with some certainty. The infrequent relevant signal from interfering channels would never get through the attention mechanism had it not received some identification before the final selection process took place.

Early versus Late Selection

Our neat, pretty picture of an attention mechanism has disappeared. William James described how one stream of thought was separated from all possible ones. It appeared that this was an automatic process, requiring but little mental effort and resulting in a major simplification of duties for higher level processes. But now the story is not so simple. Evidently, we choose among incoming channels of information on the basis of rather complex analyses of the incoming signals. We had assumed that the purpose of selective attention was to allow a central mechanism to concentrate its efforts on analyzing and responding to one problem at a time. But now it appears that selection among alternative channels itself requires complex processing. What have we gained by the concept of a selective mechanism?

The main argument against Treisman's explanation concerns the complexity of the operations she proposes. Presumably, the selective nature of attention serves the purpose of reducing the amount of analysis that some central device must perform on incoming information by feeding it only one signal at a time. This concept is fine as long as the selection can be performed by looking for simple, physical differences among the signals. It is very easy to conceive of a system that separates a man's voice from a woman's or a voice on the left from one on the right. As soon as we are forced to use the meaning of signals to aid us in our selection, the problem becomes very complex. The meaning of the peculiar sound waveform that comprises a word cannot be determined without extensive analysis of the signal, an analysis that must use information stored in memory. At this point the whole purpose of a selective mechanism seems to disappear, for if we need to extract the meaning of all incoming signals to determine what to attend to, how does the selectivity help us?

An alternative theory of selective attention requires us to move the selection mechanism back a bit. That is, suppose we admit that every incoming signal does indeed find its match in memory and receive a simple analysis for its meaning. Let the selective attention mechanism take over from there. We still save some work because there is a lot more to understanding the meaning of the sequence of signals arriving on an information channel than simply looking up each one in memory. By this procedure, however, we have to assume that the way by which a sensory signal gets to memory is done automatically and by means of the sensory features of the signal alone. This has important implications for a theory of memory, as well as for the theory of attention and selection.

The general framework for this type of theory of attention was first stated in 1963 by the psychologists J. Anthony Deutsch and Diana Deutsch, then at Oxford, England (Deutsch and Deutsch, 1963). The Deutsches' theory was elaborated in a way not unrelated to the suggestion of Treisman by Norman (1968). Consider the scheme outlined in Fig. 2.2.

All signals arriving at sensory receptors pass through a stage of analysis performed by the early physiological processes. The parameters extracted from these processes are used to determine where the representation of the sensory signal is stored. Thus, as shown in Fig. 2.2, all sensory signals excite their stored representation in memory. Now, at the same time, we assume that an analysis of previous signals is going on. This establishes a class of events deemed to be *pertinent* to the

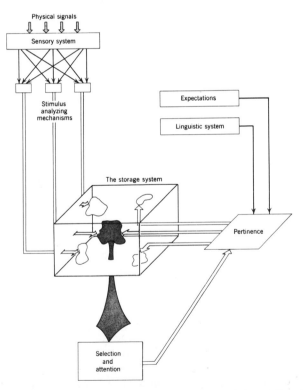

Fig. 2.2. The selection process. Both the physical inputs and the pertinence of information determine what will be selected for further processing. Physical inputs pass through the sensory system and stimulus-analyzing mechanisms before exciting their representation in the storage system. Simultaneously, the analysis of previously encountered material, coupled with the history of expectations and the rules of perception, determine the class of events assumed to be most pertinent at the moment. The material that receives the greatest combined excitation is selected for further attention.

ongoing analysis. The set of pertinent items also excites their representation in memory. The item most highly excited by the combination of sensory and pertinence inputs is selected for further analysis (the shaded item in Fig. 2.2.).

CHOOSING BETWEEN APPROACHES

Since 1968, much of the research on attention can be characterized as studies of two models. One model tends to favor early selection of incoming information, with the site of the attentional restriction early in the stages of processing. The other model tends to favor late selection of incoming information, with the site of attentional restriction late in the stages of processing. In the years since 1968, there has been increasing evidence favorable to both notions. Unfortunately, there has also been evidence that does not support either notion.

Suppose subjects are asked to shadow material presented to one ear, but also to push a button every time they hear a critical word (perhaps the word "tap") in either ear. Proponents of late selection would say that responses to the word "tap" should be equally good regardless of to which ear it is presented, for it has equal "pertinence" in all cases. Proponents of early selection say that if subjects are forced to attend to one sensory channel by the attentional demands of the shadowing task, then they will respond well to the word "tap" when it is in the same ear as the material to be shadowed and poorly otherwise. Indeed, when Treisman and Geffen (1967) did this study, the results supported the Treisman model of early selection and could not be easily explained by the model of late selection.

Suppose that while subjects listen to and shadow sentences presented to one of their ears, words semantically related to the shadowed sentences are presented to their other ears. In the early selection models, there should be no effect of the semantic relationship between unattended words and the attended message. But the late selection model predicts that the two sources of meaning will interact with one another. Notice that here we are talking about an interaction of meaning, not simple signals. It takes a considerable amount of processing to extract the meaning of a word from its sound.

Several studies have shown that the meaning of "unattended" words does affect performance on the "attended" task. Lewis (1970) showed that shadowing of the message on the attended ear was delayed when the word presented to the unattended ear was a synonym of the word in the attended one. McKay (1973) had subjects shadow sentences such as:

(a) "They threw stones toward the bank yesterday."

The word presented in the unattended ear was either "river" or "money."

Then, when presented with a recognition test for the meaning of the sentence to which they had attended, subjects were asked to choose between:

(b) "They threw stones toward the side of the river yesterday."
(c) "They threw stones toward the savings and loan association yesterday."

Subjects who had the word "river" presented to the unattended ear tended to select (b) as their choice for the meaning, whereas subjects who had the word "money" in the unattended ear tended to select (c). Moreover, the subjects did not remember what word had been presented to the unattended ear, although it obviously must have been processed to some considerable amount in order to influence the results.

Von Wright, Anderson, and Stenman (1975) tried a different approach. They presented an electric shock to their subjects (at a strength judged to be "very unpleasant") when one of a set of critical words was spoken to them. In one such training session, subjects were allowed to escape the shock if they depressed a switch within a half second of the start of the word. In such a procedure, subjects become conditioned to the word-shock combination, and presentation of a critical word causes a slight decrease in the skin resistance (probably caused by a slight amount of sweat secretion). Thus, one can detect whether the subject has responded to the word by measuring the skin resistance: This is called the GSR measure (galvanic skin response). After the conditioning had been successfully established, subjects shadowed a message presented to one ear while a list of words was presented to the other ear. In the unattended list, there were some neutral words, some of the critical words that had been conditioned to the shock, and both synonyms and homonyms of the critical words. (The study was done in Finland, and all the words were two-syllable Swedish words, accented on the first syllable.) Despite the fact that *no* shocks were ever given in the experiment itself, there was an appreciable GSR to the critical words presented in the unattended ear, and a lesser, though still substantial, response to the homonyms and synonyms. Again, this pattern of results supports the suggestion that information in the unattended channel is processed reasonably deeply. Thus, these experiments support the model that proposes late selection and are not easily explained by models proposing early selection. (This experiment is similar to one performed earlier by Corteen and Wood, 1972.)

All these studies have some problems not entirely answered by the experiments. In particular, one never knows whether or not subjects deliberately monitored the "unattended" channel occasionally, perhaps switching to it on an infrequent basis. One theorist, Neville Moray, argued that all the attention experiments can be characterized by a continual, rapid switching of attention among the different signals. In fact, Moray has shown that there are some types of experiments that cannot be accounted for by either of these theories.

Moray studied how well subjects could detect tones presented to them in the two ears. In some conditions, tones occurred only in one ear, in other conditions both. In the conditions where the tones were presented to both ears, there were two types of trials. In one, tones could sometimes occur simultaneously in both ears. In the other, two tones would never simultaneously occur at the two ears. All these conditions allow for detailed examination of the interactions among the tones and the subjects' ability to detect them. The argument can obviously get a bit complicated, but the effort is worthwhile.

Moray named the various conditions according to how many signals the subject was listening for. Consider the cases where the subject was listening for signals in both ears. If there could actually be a signal in either the left or the right ear, but never in both ears at the same time, Moray called it the XOR condition, for *exclusive or*. If the signal could be in either the left or the right or both, this was called IOR, for *inclusive or*. Cases where the signal occurred in both ears simultaneously are called the AND condition.

Attention: Selective Processes in Vision and Hearing*

NEVILLE MORAY

Tone bursts of 3000 Hz were delivered to one ear and tone bursts of 2111 Hz to the other ear of observers. The onset and offset of the tone bursts were exactly simultaneous on the two ears, and controlled through a two-channel electronic switch.[7]

— — —

Subjects were required to press a left hand button when they heard an increment in their left ear, a right hand button when they heard an increment in their right ear, and a central button when they heard an increment in both ears. Four conditions of presentation were used. These were Single Mode (in which only one ear was used, the other being silent throughout); Select Mode (in which both ears received tone bursts, but the listener was

* N. Moray. Attention: Selective processes in vision and hearing. *New York: Academic Press, 1970. Pages 184–218. Copyright © 1970 by Neville Moray. Reprinted by permission.*

[7] Hz is the unit of frequency. It is an abbreviation for Hertz, the name of the great German physicist Heinrich R. Hertz (1857–1894). One cycle per second is called one Hz. Frequencies of 2111 and 3000 Hz are very high in pitch, close to the highest notes on the piano keyboard. 2111 Hz is very close to the C one octave below the highest note on the piano; 3000 Hz is approximately three notes higher—the highest F on the piano.

to ignore one ear completely and only respond to the other); XOR Mode (in which both ears received tone bursts, but targets never occurred simultaneously); and IOR Mode (in which targets could occur either on the left ear or on the right ear, or simultaneously on both, the last condition being a logical AND Mode). In addition a control was run using IOR presentation Mode but requiring the listener to ignore the single targets and respond only to the simultaneous pairs with the AND response.

It is rather curious that so little attention has been paid to the AND mode of presentation (simultaneous targets). Most of the experiments have been either Select Mode in which the listener accepts one message and rejects the other or, more rarely, XOR in which responses are made to targets in two messages, but targets are never simultaneous (Treisman and Geffen, 1967, for example). Indeed, while Deutsch and Deutsch's model clearly predicts that the AND condition will show severe interference between the messages, Treisman's model makes no explicit prediction about AND signals. Treisman says that in the XOR condition and the Select Mode the listener can attenuate an unwanted message (but there is no indication how rapidly such attenuation could be redirected in the XOR Mode). However, for the AND case, it is not clear that a listener should attenuate one and reject the other rather than rejecting both, or for that matter accepting both, since the theory only says that the Select Mode *can* result in the attenuation of one message, not that in all competitive situations attenuation of all except one message must occur.

— — —

The Table [2.1] shows that Treisman's model will not fit the facts. Notice the last three rows of data. AND is the percentage of ANDs (simultaneous targets) which were correctly detected in the IOR presentation mode. AND* is where IOR presentation was used with AND response only (other targets being ignored). Here again responses to ANDs are extremely poor . . . NAND is the percentage of single responses made either to a left target, or a right target, or to what was really an AND.

TABLE 2.1.

Mode of Attention	Mean Percentage of Detections of Signal
Single	58.8
Select	67.9
XOR	54.4
IOR	52.1
AND	30.6
NAND	70.8
AND*	42.0

(Adapted from Table 5 of Moray (1970, Page 187).

Now, if Treisman's model says that an observer sharing his attention equally between two messages attenuates neither, ANDs should equal Singles. They do not. If he attenuates both messages when sharing equally between the two, NAND responses should be no better than AND responses, but they are. If the listener attenuates one channel and listens only to the other, given that attention wandered from side to side the observed results could be obtained; on the basis of the shadowing work Treisman maintains that information about crude physical characteristics is available from both messages even in Select Mode. But the data on AND responses shows that this is not true.

— — —

Treisman's model does not then fit the data, and needs more elaboration to state explicitly what the predictions are from it about performance in the AND Mode.

How does Deutsch and Deutsch's model fare? The crucial condition here appears to be XOR. The listeners in Moray's experiments were clearly told that the two messages were equally important. There was no *a priori* difference in the importance of the two signals. There are no simultaneous targets in the XOR Mode; therefore even though the listeners were monitoring both channels there could never be competition for responses since at any given time only the one or the other response was required. Yet performance on the XOR condition was significantly worse than on the Single Mode or the Select Mode, at least in some subjects. There is some effect of response selection, since AND* shows that when only ANDs are to be detected (single right or left targets being ignored), performance was better than when AND responses are made in the full IOR response mode. However the low level of performance in the XOR Mode, which is much more apparent when the data is available subject by subject rather than pooled (see the original papers), would not be predicted by the Deutsch model.

Now where are we? First, we have at least two theories, each better than the other for some class of conditions, but each with its own difficulties. Moreover, there are some results not easily accountable by either. What do we do now? Whenever a situation like this occurs, it is usually wise to back up a bit and review what we are trying to do. These theories all have served a valuable purpose in guiding us to a good understanding of some phenomena, but if we go back and look at what is really meant by attention, we see that we have only scratched the surface. Another look at the phenomena might help us take a different view, one that might be more successful. Indeed, this is a useful tactic in scientific research in general. After awhile, theories and experiments tend to get lost, buried in the fine details of experimental techniques and results. The overall broad picture can be forgotten. We must remember that we are attempting to understand the wide range of human cognitive phenomena, and a new look at those phenomena might be rewarding, especially because of the tantalizing nature of our theories— so near, but yet not quite there.

At this point in this story, it is time again to take a diversion, to explore another aspect of information processing: the acquisition of information. The one thing that must of certainty be true of the study of attention is that it cannot be divorced from the study of other cognitive phenomena. Attention is at the heart of the organism's activity in interpreting, understanding, and reacting to information both externally and internally generated. It is clear that one's knowledge greatly influences the processing of information, just as it is clear that the incoming information must ultimately influence one's knowledge. Somehow, in the mix of interactions between internal information (knowledge) and external information, some choices and decisions must be made. This chapter has shown the importance of arousal, mental effort, and conscious awareness on attentional processes, as well as several possible theoretical approaches to an understanding of attentional phenomena. But until we get more of the story of the processing of information, and most especially of the acquisition of information, it is best to postpone the final description of the attention mechanism.

The rest of this book is concerned with topics in perception and memory. These topics are intimately related to our study of attention, and it is not possible to understand one without understanding the others. If some mechanism is able to assess the relative worth of different sensory messages, leaving one or a limited number for further processing, then it can do so only through an analysis that must include information stored in memory. We need information about the past in order to interpret the present. The interactions of sensory inputs with pattern recognition and memory are essential parts of human information processing.

Let us look now at the way we interpret incoming sensory information: the problem of pattern perception of that incoming information. The attention mechanism cannot select intelligently among alternative channels of information unless it can first make a basic identification of the nature of the information. Suppose we hear several voices in the same ear. If we are to select one speaker, we must be able to extract from the complex acoustical waveform resulting from the combined voices the features corresponding to each voice. This problem is one of pattern recognition, and it has been studied more by specialists in computers, automata theory, and artificial intelligence than by psychologists. In the next chapter we review pattern recognition and the process of acquiring information. We then return to an examination of attentional mechanisms and to the consideration of some new theoretical approaches that seem capable of resolving the difficulties described in this chapter, thus providing a start toward describing more of the phenomenological properties and clinical studies.

SUGGESTED READINGS

This chapter has only introduced the story of attention. It ended with the problems stated, but unsolved. The next chapter provides new material that helps our understanding of the processes involved in making sense out of the information that arrives at the sensory systems. Chapter 4 then goes back to the phenomena of attention, examines some new issues, and then puts the whole story together, using some of the tools introduced both in this chapter and in Chapter 3.

Because this chapter is just the start of the story, it is premature to suggest readings. Thus, suggestions for further readings on attention are postponed until the end of Chapter 4. (In addition, there are suggestions for further readings at the end of Chapter 3 for the topics discussed in that chapter.)

3
The Acquisition of Information

One common view of human information processing suggests that the sense organs serve only as transducers, changing physical energy to some physiological representation. An attention mechanism then selects interesting aspects of the physiological image of the world for further processing by a central system. According to this viewpoint, the sensory system is something like a television channel, conveying information about the environment by encoding the visual and acoustical information received in as complete and undistorted a fashion as possible. This description is wrong.

Stimulus-Analyzing Mechanisms

The picture that has emerged from the results of an increasingly large number of experiments in psychology, physiology, neurology, and the communication sciences implies that the nervous system performs substantial alterations of the physical image received by the sense organs. These transformations extract information about color, enhance contours, determine size and direction of movement of visual images, extract the pitch and loudness of acoustical images, and determine the spatial and temporal relationships of visual and acoustical signals. These transformations are of great use to the nervous system because they simplify tremendously the information that must be transmitted to higher–level analyzing systems. This, in turn, simplifies the job of analyzing the sensory inputs. Transformations lose information, however, for aspects of the signal that are combined with one another at one level of processing cannot be separated at higher levels.

Thus, information about incoming signals is abstracted by a number of different analyzing mechanisms. As this information is processed by the nervous system, the outputs of the analyzers may be successively combined, forming a hierarchical process whereby the outputs of one level of analyzers are analyzed by yet another. Presumably the types of analyzers are limited, but the ways in which they can be combined are not.

It is not yet possible to determine how stimulus recognition is accomplished. It is possible, however, to review a number of possible mechanisms and determine what demands and implications they have for the processes of attention and memory. In this chapter the primary emphasis is on the *psychology* of perception. We start where the physiologists leave off, trying to determine how humans work with and manipulate the messages sent over the sensory pathways. The basic problem is to determine how we match the complex sensory waveforms with material stored in memory.

The problem can be illustrated most easily by an analysis of speech. The acoustical waveform of speech is very complicated. Yet we are able to transform this waveform into meaningful messages at a very rapid rate. This transformation requires us to decompose the speech into its basic linguistic components, match what we hear to information already stored in long-term memory, and perform the necessary syntactic and semantic analysis in order to determine the meaning of the message. Several stages of processing are necessary in doing this analysis. First, we must transform the sensory waveforms into some physiological representation. Then, in order to interpret the incoming sensory message, we must get both it and the material stored in memory into the same type of physiological coding. Even this obvious step is extremely difficult. Spoken words have to reduce to a common format that is independent of accents and peculiarities of the individual speaker. Indeed, visually presented words must end up in a similar format to auditorally presented words, for we make no distinction in meaning based on the difference between speaking and writing.

DATA DRIVEN AND CONCEPTUALLY DRIVEN PROCESSING

We can classify processing systems into two major types, differing by how the operations are guided. The systems described in the previous section can be classified as driven by the data, analyzing the input information with ever-increasing levels of sophistication. Thus, speech analysis starts with the sensory coding and works its way to the interpretation of the meaning of the utterance. In a similar way, a visual input starts as an image within the eye and proceeds through various physiological stages that locate lines, movements, colors, and contours. Then, special mechanisms recognize particular combinations of features. The process continues until the analysis has reached a specific classification or recognition of the incoming signals. Any sequence of operations that proceeds from the incoming data, through increasingly sophisticated analyses, is called *data driven* or *bottom-up* analysis. The phrase "bottom-up" refers to the fact that if we draw a picture of the processing levels, putting the incoming data on the bottom of the picture with the increasingly more sophisticated levels of analysis drawn in successive layers above, then the flow of analysis proceeds from the bottom (the incoming data) to the top (the final recognition of the input).

There is a different way to do the processing. Bottom-up systems do not take account of expectations. The human system seems to be guided by conceptualizations of the incoming information. That is, it is also necessary to consider processes that start at the top and work down. This can be called a *conceptually driven* or a *top-down* system. A top-down system for visual signals might start with the highest-level expectation of an object that is further refined by analyses of the context to yield expectations of particular lines in particular locations. Top-down, conceptually driven systems can be powerful, but their success depends heavily on their ability to make intelligent choices of what objects to expect.

The differences between top-down and bottom-up analyses are less than might seem by these descriptions. Indeed, the remaining part of this chapter will demonstrate that the human processing system cannot be explained by either system alone; both processes are essential. Both top-down and bottom-up processing must take place simultaneously, each assisting the other in the completion of the overall job of making sense of the world.

THE IMPORTANCE OF CONTEXT

The most persuasive evidence for the existence of top-down, conceptually driven systems for analysis comes from considerations of the importance of context on the process of pattern recognition. With a bottom-up system of pattern recognition, once the various mechanisms have been set up, incoming sensory signals go through a sequence of fixed neurological processes, and, *voila!* they come out identified, labeled, and tagged. The problem with such a system is that our interpretation of sensory signals depends on the whole environment in which they are imbedded. Thus, ambiguous perceptions get interpreted in completely unambiguous ways, depending on the context surrounding them. All of us must have had the experience of misreading a word or failing to see an indistinct or distant object. Yet, when told what the word or object really was, we looked again and suddenly it was clear and distinct. Why did we have trouble in the first place? Evidently we are able to change the rules of pattern recognition as we go along, dynamically adjusting to our expectations.[1]

Contextual information is of great importance in perceptual processing. The average skilled reader, for example, is able to process between 300 to 600 words each minute. In order to do this, he must be able to identify as many as 10 words and, presumably, 50 to 70 letters, each second. This is faster than the recognition process can operate on isolated letters or words. This high rate is illusory, however, because grammatical text has many constraints on it. From any point of view, language is highly redundant. Our language habits impose severe restraints on the possible and likely sequences of letters that can appear within a word, the sequence of words that can appear in any sentence, and the way ideas are introduced on a page. It is possible to take advantage of all these aspects of language so that, in order to read, only a little information need be extracted from individual letters or words. In fact, most of the letters and many of the words in a text can be skipped without any loss in intelligibility.[2]

A simple experiment can illustrate many of these points. Try to read material held upside down. (It is better to start with highly redundant material, such as a light novel or a child's book, rather than something technical.) Practice reading for a while, perhaps as much as an hour. As your practice, you will note a dramatic increase in your rate of reading. At first you will have trouble with individual letters, but soon you will ignore the letters and read words, then finally, whole phrases. As you read in this unusual way you are able to notice habits of which you were unaware in normal reading. You don't see all of a word: you tend to guess. You find yourself reading a long phrase quite rapidly, but only because you knew it was likely to have occurred in the context of the passage. The process is quite automatic and not nearly so conscious and deliberate as this description would imply. In fact, the way

---

[1] This phenomenon is so dramatic that it provides a useful demonstration for lectures. All one has to do is to play a recorded song to the audience. The record must be selected to be one with relatively unintelligible words, and one that is unfamiliar to most of the audience (rock music is ideal). Simply ask the audience to identify the words. They will fail. Then project a printed version of the words on a screen and play the recording again. This time the words will be "heard" distinctly. (This demonstration was suggested by the British psychologist, John Morton.)

[2] This discussion has ignored the performance obtained with special speed-reading techniques. Although these techniques apparently allow individuals to "read" material at rates measured in the thousands and tens of thousands of words per minute, this remarkable speed need not be primarily a result of an increased rate of processing individual words. The speed reader can improve his rate by taking full advantage of the redundancy of the written language, eliminating wasted eye movements (such as regressions), and skipping much irrelevant material. Thus, the speed reader is one who **has** tremendously *increased* his reliance on conceptually guided processing.

to discover what you are doing is to make a mistake: realize that those last few words don't make sense in the context of the sentence, or that the ending "ing" just doesn't belong to the word you read. Then, once the mistake is made, it is often possible to go back and re-create what must have happened. (Further descriptions of this process are provided by Kolers and Perkins, 1975.)

Reading upside down is a convenient way of slowing down the normal process so that we can introspect about our operations. It is a rather convincing demonstration of the complexity of normal reading and the efficient way in which we use clues to avoid having to process every aspect of the printed page.

Some of the same points can also be illustrated by speeding up the normal process. Read a page of text while timing yourself. Then read it two more times, first very slowly—word by word—then once more, moderately slowly. Now read the entire passage as rapidly as you can, timing your rate of reading. You should be able to double your reading speed this way. Now read the passage once more, again while timing yourself. You should still be improving, but the last reading is approaching the speed reached by speed-reading techniques, although you probably move your eyes very inefficiently. (Obviously, this is not the technique used by speed readers, although it is not a bad training method.) Note that you did not read the material as much as you confirmed it; the prior knowledge of the contents of the material was essential to the success of the trial.

Decision Units

The perception of printed words has much in common with the perception of speech. A good deal of the work on pattern recognition devices has dealt with speech recognition. We can recognize speech under very poor conditions; the speech waveform may be distorted, mixed with noise, fragmented, and be, in general, a very poor representation of the sounds actually spoken by the talker. In speech recognition we do several things that have not usually been considered necessary for pattern recognition. First, we use the habits of the speaker to help decode his words. We always do better at understanding speech after we have listened to the speaker for a while. This implies that we change the characteristics of our analyzing mechanisms to match the characteristics of the speaker. Second, we use the grammar of language to help us. We do better at recognizing material when the number of possible words is limited, but adding grammatical constraints improves our performance even more. Use of these rules lets us reject possibilities that do not fit into the rule. Note that general linguistic rules are required, not a dictionary of possibilities. Systems that store all possible words (in the case of speech), or all possible combinations of two words, or of three words, and so on, hoping to decode speech by matching each set of physical signals against a possible stored representation, are doomed to failure, if only because the size of the dictionary they must maintain will increase without limit. There is no grammatical rule that limits the size of sentences. Moreover, almost every sentence we hear, read, or speak is novel and differs in some way from all other sentences we have previously encountered. A pattern recognition device hoping to take advantage of the statistics of spoken speech is going to have trouble with all these unique arrangements.

Third, we do not recognize speech at the same time as we hear it. Rather, we tend to hang back, delaying the decoding process for a syllable or two, waiting to get more information about the signal. This tactic of delay is very important and common. As we discussed in Chapter 2, the skilled receiver of Morse code or the stenographer writes down the message with a rather large delay after its actual reception. When we read aloud or type (skillfully), our eyes examine the manuscript quite far in advance of the part that we actually speak or type.

These properties of human performance are stressed in the next selection. George Miller believes that artificial pattern recognition devices are probably using the wrong information for their decisions. He suggests that automatic speech recognizers could learn from the techniques used by humans.

The Perception of Speech*

GEORGE A. MILLER

It is often assumed that when we are listening to speech we are making phonetic decisions, phonemic decisions, syntactic decisions, semantic decisions—all more or less simultaneously. Since the decision units involved in these hypothetical decisions are hierarchically related, one might expect that decisions would be made first at the lowest level, then the outcome would provide a basis for decisions at the next higher level, etc. No doubt this approach is reasonable and could be made the basis for a device to recognize speech, but there are several reasons for doubting if it describes the way people naturally operate. One of the strongest criticisms is a subjective one: Phenomenologically, it seems that the larger, more meaningful decisions are made first, and that we pursue the details only so far as they are necessary to

* George A. Miller. Decision units in the perception of speech. IRE Transactions on Information Theory. 1962, IT-8, 81–83. Copyright © 1962 by The Institute of Radio Engineering (now called the Institute of Electrical and Electronics Engineers, Inc.) With permission of the author and the Institute of Electrical and Electronics Engineers.

serve our immediate purposes. The ancient belief that perceptual wholes are compounded by associating independent elements of sensation has a very poor reputation among modern psychologists, and any attempt to give priority to the molecular processes is likely to encounter considerable scepticism.

But let us pursue this model a bit further. If the small details of input are discriminated first, how is it possible to take advantage of the redundancy of the message? Presumably, the sequence of preceding decisions must be stored and used to limit the set of alternatives among which the next decision is to be made. Such a Markovian mechanism, however, would lead to compound errors. Once a mistake occurs, the incorrect context so created tends to cause further mistakes until the process of recognition becomes stalled. A reasonable answer to this objection, however, is that we must regard the decisions reached at the lower levels as tentative and subject to revision pending the outcome of decisions made at some higher, more molar level. Once this tentative character is admitted, of course, it becomes necessary to continue storing the original input until the molar decisions have been reached.

However, if complete storage is necessary even after the lower-level decisions have been tentatively reached why bother to make the lower-level decisions first? Why not store the message until enough of it is on hand to support a higher-level decision, then make a decision for all levels simultaneously?

One advantage of a delayed-decision strategy is that the decision rate is reduced. Consider the rates we must cope with: In order to comprehend messages spoken at 150 words/minute, we would presumably have to make about a dozen phonemic decisions every second, and perhaps 100 phonetic decisions. To say that people can make decisions at such rates is to extend the concept well beyond its usual psychological range. Many psychologists have measured the time required to make a decision among several alternatives; reaction times in the neighborhood of 0.2 to 0.5 seconds are commonly obtained. The exact value, of course, depends upon the exact conditions of measurement. An important point for the present argument, however, is that for highly practiced subjects the time required to make a choice reaction may *not* increase as a function of the number of alternatives that can occur (Mowbray, 1960). The time required to decide between two alternatives is effectively the same as that required for 30 alternatives. This fact is important for the present discussion, since it means that a single delayed decision would require far less time than would a series of immediate decisions. Our limited decision rate imposes a much stronger constraint on our channel capacity than does our limited ability to discriminate accurately among many alternatives.

Of course, the rates that psychologists have measured have generally been close to the maximum. It seems plausible that ordinary conversation would put less strain on us. Perhaps we make about one decision per second in ordinary listening. If we accept this as a rough estimate, it suggests that the phrase—usually about two or three words at a time—is probably the natural decision unit for speech.

Miller, Heise, and Lichten (1951) reported that words spoken in the context of a sentence can be identified more accurately than the same words spoken in isolation, but in haphazard order. This result supports the assumption that decisions about smaller units can be more accurate when they occur in a redundant context. But how do listeners take advantage of this redundancy? Miller, Heise, and Lichten attributed the superior intelligibility to the fact that the sentence context reduces the number of alternative words among which a listener must decide. "The effect of the sentence is comparable," they wrote, "to the effect of a restricted vocabulary, although the degree of restriction is harder to estimate. When the talker begins a sentence, 'Apples grow on . . . ,' the range of possible continuations is sharply restricted. This restriction makes the discrimination easier and lowers the threshold of intelligibility."

This explanation may be logically correct, but it carries an implication that listeners make successive decisions about words while they are listening to sentences. In view of the present argument, however, we question whether a decision could be made about word N fast enough to limit the alternatives considered for word $N + 1$.

In order to test whether words heard in sentences are more intelligible because the number of alternative words is reduced or because sentences permit a delayed decision, an experiment was conducted that held the number of alternatives constant but varied the sequential properties of the test lists. A vocabulary of 25 monosyllabic English words was selected and organized into five subvocabularies of five words each, as shown in Table 3.1. Intelligibility tests were conducted at several signal-to-noise ratios with each of the five subvocabularies and with the entire vocabulary of 25 words. In these tests a list of 100 consecutive words was read at a rate of about 1.5 words/sec. Listeners repeated what they heard into a dictating machine. In order to maintain synchrony, the talker paused slightly after every fifth word.

It was found, as anticipated, that a word is more often heard correctly when the listener expects it as one of five alternatives than when he expects it as one of 25. The more interesting conditions, however, were the following:

TABLE 3.1. Five Subvocabularies Used to Explore the Perceptual Effects of Grammatical Content

1	2	3	4	5
Don	Brought	His	Black	Bread
He	Has	More	Cheap	Sheep
Red	Left	No	Good	Shoes
Slim	Loves	Some	Wet	Socks
Who	Took	The	Wrong	Things

One type of test list was constructed by randomly choosing the first word from subvocabulary 1, the second from subvocabulary 2, the third from 3, the fourth from 4, the fifth from 5, the sixth from 1 again, etc. The reader should verify for himself that the result of this procedure is to generate English sentences: "Slim loves more wet sheep" and "He has the wrong socks" are typical examples. Then, to contrast with the sentences, test lists consisting of pseudo-sentences were formed by selecting the words in reverse order: "Sheep wet more loves slim" and "Socks wrong the has he" illustrate the result obtained here.

The important feature of test lists constructed in this manner is that each successive word is one of five possibilities—the number of alternatives is the same—but in one case a listener can use his grammatical habits to form longer units, whereas in the other case grammar is no help and he must make an immediate decision about each word as it occurs.

The results of these tests are plotted in Fig. 3.1. The tests with sentences and with the 5-word vocabularies gave the same results, so the experiment verifies the claim that the sentence context effectively reduces the number of alternatives from 25 to 5. However, pseudo-sentences, which also involved five alternatives, gave the same function—perhaps slightly lower—as did the tests with a 25-word vocabulary. The listeners were unable to take advantage of the reduced number of alternatives in the pseudo-sentences—presumably because they could not shift rapidly enough from one subvocabulary to the next when the shifts occurred in a nongrammatical order—and so they treated each word as if it could have been any one of the 25 in the total vocabulary.

It should be noted that the test lists were read at a relatively rapid pace and without significant pauses. When the lists were read at a rate of one word

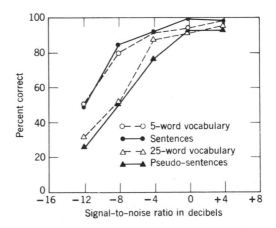

Fig. 3.1. Grammatical context improves intelligibility, but ungrammatical context does not—even though the number of alternative words that could occur was the same in both cases.

every two seconds, pseudo-sentences were heard just as well as were the sentences or the tests using 5-word vocabularies. Indeed, even when the pseudo-sentences were read at regular conversational speeds, but with a 10 second pause between successive pseudo-sentences, they were heard almost as well as are the 5-word tests. In order to demonstrate that the pseudo-sentences were more difficult than grammatical sentences, it was necessary to read them rapidly and continuously so that delayed decisions were truly impossible.

We can describe this experiment in slightly different terms, as follows: The basic *vocabulary* from which the test lists were constructed was a set of 25^5 sequences of five words. For some lists, subvocabularies consisting of 5^5 alternative sequences were selected. When these subvocabularies were selected by reducing the number of different words that could occur in the tests, or by making the sequences conform to grammatical rules, the listener's task was easier. But when the subvocabulary consisted of 5^5 alternative sequences selected by nongrammatical rules, the listener was not able to take advantage of it.

When the experiment is described in this way, the result seems wholly in line with what one might expect on the basis of the well-established principal that smaller vocabularies make easier listening. The important thing to notice, however, is that 5^5 is a large vocabulary and five syllables is a long delay. If we accept this principle in general we shall be faced with a much larger dictionary of decision units than our usual dictionaries would lead us to expect.

An engineer hoping to build devices that will recognize speech has a right to be discouraged with this result. His machines are much better at lightning fast decisions among relatively few alternatives, whereas people are better at making slow decisions about relatively large amounts of information. Presumably there is quite a lot of rapid, parallel processing going on in the brain, even though the decision mechanism itself seems to be the sluggish serial device we have already described.

There is no *a priori* reason to insist that recognition devices must work on the same principle as does the human being. It should be borne in mind, however, that speech is uttered for human ears. If people do in fact follow a strategy of delayed decisions in listening to the on-going flow of speech, then there is no guarantee that a speech signal must always contain the kind of information needed to support a sequence of immediate decisions. It may yet prove necessary to use our perceptual and grammatical knowledge, before we succeed in building reliable speech recognizers.

Miller elegantly illustrates that we use grammatical information obtained from the structure of a sentence to improve our perception of the individual words of that sentence. The grammatical information improves performance simply because it limits the number of alternative words we must consider when trying to understand speech. Miller argues, however, that humans normally cannot make decisions as rapidly as their performance in perceiving sentences would imply; hence, he suggests that we hang back, postponing interpretation of individual sounds until a reasonable sample has been assembled.

A SPEECH-UNDERSTANDING SYSTEM

One thing seems clear: the human uses all possible sources of information in making sense of the information presented through the sense organs. A major task is to determine just how the interactions of different sources of knowledge take place. One important source of ideas comes from the attempts of people working in the field of computer science and artificial intelligence to construct artificial systems capable of understanding speech. By the very nature of the task, these researchers are forced to consider explicit mechanisms for allowing the interactions.

In this section we examine a computer system that is being developed at the Carnegie-Mellon University in Pittsburgh. The system is called *Hearsay*. The main point of interest to us is how their system handles the interactions among different knowledge sources. The particular problem we examine is that of recognizing chess moves. That is, a person is playing chess with a computer. Instead of actually moving pieces on the board, he speaks them to the Hearsay system. Imagine, if you will, that the game is being played over the telephone, and so the Hearsay system plays the part of one of the opponents. Why chess? As Reddy and Newell put it:*

Voice-chess was chosen as one of the first tasks for the Hearsay system, not because it is important to play chess with a computer over the telephone, but because chess provides a good environment to evaluate the ideas about the role of various sources of knowledge in speech perception. Chess plays the role in artificial intelligence that the fruit fly plays in genetics. Just as the genetics of *drosophila* are studied not to breed better flies, but to learn the laws of heredity, so we study chess to understand the laws of artificial intelligence. In Hearsay, chess was chosen as a task because the syntax, semantics, and vocabulary of discourse are well defined and are amenable to systematic study.

Reddy and Newell work in the fields of computer science, artificial intelligence, and psychology, a cross-fertilization of disciplines that is becoming increasingly common and productive. The Hearsay project

* R. Reddy and A. Newell. Knowledge and its representation in a speech understanding system. *Knowledge and Cognition.* L. W. Gregg (Ed.). Potomac, Md.: Lawrence Erlbaum Associates. 1974. Page 256. Copyright © 1974 by Lawrence Erlbaum Associates, Inc. With permission of authors and publisher.

represents the joint efforts of a large group of investigators, and the several excerpts here will only touch briefly on the overall system. (More complete reference to their works is provided in the Suggested Readings section of this chapter.)

Knowledge and Its Representation in a Speech Understanding System*

RAJ REDDY AND ALLEN NEWELL

The model consists of a set of cooperating independent knowledge processes that are capable of helping in the decoding of a spoken utterance either individually or collectively. Each process uses some source of knowledge (possibly different representations of the same source of knowledge) to determine whether it has anything interesting to contribute in a given context (of a partially recognized utterance) and to generate, reject, or rank order hypotheses in that context. Knowledge processes communicate with each other by writing (or modifying) hypotheses on a "blackboard." Since knowledge processes speak different languages, e.g., knowledge at the acoustic-phonetic level is of a different type than that at the semantic level, mechanisms are provided to translate hypotheses between levels. Since the role of a knowledge process is to generate or verify hypotheses, the system can continue to function even in the absence of one or more of these sources of knowledge, as long as there are some generators and some verifiers in the aggregate.

KNOWLEDGE AT THE SEMANTIC LEVEL

There are several sources of knowledge at the semantic level: the knowledge about the task domain, the current state of the conversation, a model of user behavior, knowledge about (meaningful use of) language and so on. The notions of "apriori semantics of the task" and "situational semantics of the conversation" help to define the microworld and the situation. Having investigated several tasks, we find the identification and representation of these types of knowledge are difficult and imprecise. However, in the case of voice-chess, these knowledge sources are well defined and contribute significantly to the reduction of search space. The "apriori semantics of the task" are given by the rules of the chess game. The "situational semantics of the conversation" are given by the current board position. The rules of chess and the board position are used to formulate a list of legal moves which represent plausible hypotheses for what might be taken by the user next. Fig. 3.2. gives an example of a board position in which the user has to make a move. Fig. 3.3. gives a list of legal moves for this situation. This list

* *R. Reddy and A. Newell,* op. cit. *1974. Pages 256–260, 267–272, 280–281.*

Fig. 3.2. Example of a board position in chess.

```
KN/KN1−KB3
KN/KN1−K2
QB/QB1−KB4
QB/QB1−K3
QB/QB1−KN5
QB/QB1−Q2
QN/QB3−Q5
KBP/KB2−KB4
KBP/KB2−KB3
QR/QR1−QN1
KP/K4−K5
QB/QB4−Q5
K/K1−KB1
K/K1−Q1
QB/QB4−Q3
K/K1−Q2
QN/QB3−QN5
QB/QB4−QN5CH
QB/QB4−K2
KRP/KR2−KR4
KN/KN1−KR3
QNP/QN2−QN4
QRP/QR2−QR4
QRP/QR2−QR3
KRP/KR2−KR3
KNP/KN2−KN3
QNP/QN2−QN3
QB/QB4−QN3
QB/QB4−KB1
QN/QB3−K2
KNP/KN2−KN4
QN/QB3−Q1
QN/QB3−QR4
QN/QB3−QN1
QB/QB4XKBP/KB7C
QB/QB1−KR6
QB/QB4−K6
QB/QB4−QR6
```

Fig. 3.3. Possible legal moves in the board position given in Fig. 3.2., rank ordered according to the goodness of move.

is used by the Hearsay system in restricting the plausible utterances to 40 or so moves. These sources of knowledge are represented in Hearsay as a program (Gillogly, 1972).

The notion of a "user model" is used to represent the psychological state of the user (Newell et al., 1973, page 85) and a model for predicting his behavior in a given state. For the voice-chess task, the user model is the same for all users and primarily incorporates the notions of goodness of a move as indicated by piece advantage, and so on. It does not at present include the discovery of the strategy being pursued by a given user. Fig. 3.3. gives a rank ordering of the legal moves based on the goodness of move evaluation procedure in TECH (Gillogly, 1972).

Given a task, a situation, and user model, all of which may be used to predict what the user might say next, there is still a great deal of variability possible. This essentially depends on the linguistic performance of the user. In the chess situation given in Figs. 3.2. and 3.3. and given that the user has decided to use the move "B-QN3," Fig. 3.4. gives some of the 108 ways he can utter this move.

Neely (1973, pp. 73–79) shows how knowledge about the partially recognized utterance is used to constrain the variability in linguistic performance of the user. Basically, given that a word such as "captures" or "takes" appears in the partial sentence hypothesis, this knowledge can be used to further restrict the search to the capture moves in that board position. This restricted set of moves is used to give high semantic preference to the key content words that may occur in the predicted option word list.

— — —

1. BISHOP TO KNIGHT THREE
2. QUEEN BISHOP TO KNIGHT THREE
3. QUEEN'S BISHOP TO KNIGHT THREE
4. BISHOP ON BISHOP FOUR TO KNIGHT THREE
5. BISHOP ON QUEEN BISHOP FOUR TO KNIGHT THREE
6. BISHOP ON QUEEN'S BISHOP FOUR TO KNIGHT THREE

   .
   .
   .

64. QUEEN'S BISHOP ON BISHOP FOUR GOES TO QUEEN'S KNIGHT THREE

   .
   .

69. QUEEN'S BISHOP ON QUEEN'S BISHOP FOUR GOES TO QUEEN KNIGHT THREE
70. QUEEN'S BISHOP ON QUEEN BISHOP FOUR GOES TO QUEEN'S KNIGHT THREE
71. QUEEN BISHOP ON QUEEN'S BISHOP FOUR GOES TO QUEEN'S KNIGHT THREE
72. QUEEN'S BISHOP ON QUEEN'S BISHOP FOUR GOES TO QUEEN'S KNIGHT THREE

   .
   .

107. QUEEN BISHOP ON QUEEN'S BISHOP FOUR MOVES TO QUEEN'S KNIGHT THREE
108. QUEEN'S BISHOP ON QUEEN'S BISHOP FOUR MOVES TO QUEEN'S KNIGHT THREE

Fig. 3.4. Many different ways of saying "B-QN3" in the Hearsay system.

THE USE OF KNOWLEDGE IN THE RECOGNITION PROCESS

Here we will illustrate the operation of the Hearsay system and the use of various sources of knowledge by considering in detail the recognition process of an utterance. The utterance to be recognized is "bishop to queen knight three" given in Fig. 3.5. This utterance is a legal move in the context of the board position given in Fig. 3.2. The speech input from the microphone is passed through five band pass filters and through an unfiltered band.

— — —

Fig. 3.6. shows a plot of these as a function of time for the utterance given in Fig. 3.5. The top line of text indicates where the word boundaries were marked during the manual segmentation process. (This permits manual verification of the accuracy of the machine recognition process in the later stages —naturally it is not used in recognition.)

— — —

THE RECOGNITION PROCESS

— — —

Fig. 3.6 shows the first cycle of the recognition process. At this point none of the words in the sentence have been recognized and the processing begins left to right. The syntax module chooses to hypothesize and generates 13 possible option words, implying that the sentence can begin with "rook's," "rook," "queens," etc. The ACO module which incorporates the acoustic-phonetic and lexical knowledge rejects two possible realizations of "bishop" and "bishops" as being inconsistent with the acoustic-phonetic evidence. Since the word "bishop" may be pronounced in several ways (in reduced and nonreduced vowel form), another realization of "bishop" is in fact accepted. The semantics module rejects "castle" and "castles" as being illegal in that position. The remaining words are rated by each source of knowledge. The composite rating and the word beginning and word ending markers for the eight best words are shown in Fig. 3.6. The word "rook's" gets a rating of 425, "rook" a rating of 443, and so on. "Bishop," the correct word, gets the highest rating of 553. These words are then used to form the beginning sentence hypotheses, which are shown with their ratings at the bottom of Fig. 3.6.

Fig. 3.7 shows the second cycle of the recognition process. The top sentence hypothesis is "bishop. . . ." An attempt is being made to recognize the word following "bishop." Again syntax hypothesizes. Given that "bishop" is the preceding word, the syntactic source of knowledge proposes only seven option words out of the possible 31 words in the lexicon—a reduction in the search space by a factor of 4. Of these possible seven words, the acoustics module rejects words such as "takes," "on," etc., and semantics rejects none. The remaining words are rated by each of the sources of knowledge and a

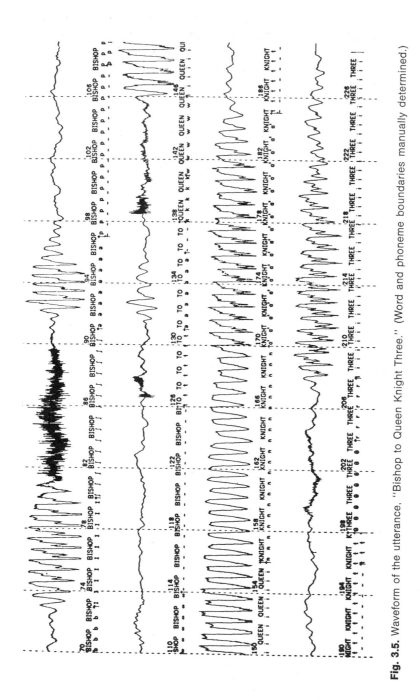

Fig. 3.5. Waveform of the utterance, "Bishop to Queen Knight Three." (Word and phoneme boundaries manually determined.)

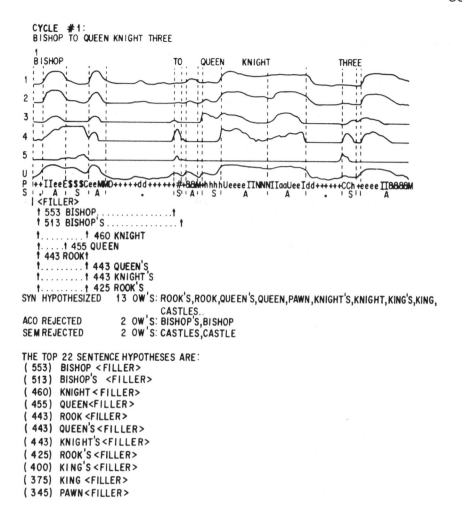

```
CYCLE #1:
BISHOP TO QUEEN KNIGHT THREE
```

Fig. 3.6. First cycle of the recognition process.

composite rating along with word boundaries is shown in Fig. 3.7 for each of the acceptable words. The correct word, "to," happens to get the highest rating of 553. The new top sentence hypothesis is "bishop to . . ." with a composite rating of 553. Notice the growth of the sentence hypothesis list. All the acceptable sentence hypotheses are rank ordered. The top sentence hypothesis of Fig. 3.6 has now branched into three new sentence hypotheses, most of which have higher ratings than the sentence hypotheses generated during the preceding cycle.

— — —

In this section, we have demonstrated how knowledge processes communicate and cooperate with each other in the recognition process by illus-

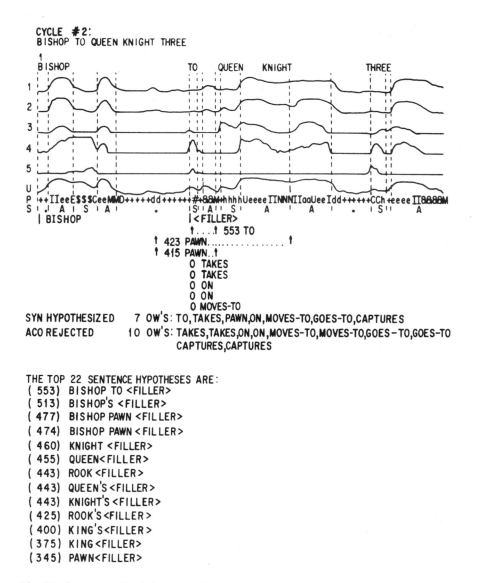

CYCLE #2:
BISHOP TO QUEEN KNIGHT THREE

SYN HYPOTHESIZED   7 OW'S: TO,TAKES,PAWN,ON,MOVES-TO,GOES-TO,CAPTURES
ACO REJECTED   10 OW'S: TAKES,TAKES,ON,ON,MOVES-TO,MOVES-TO,GOES-TO,GOES-TO
                          CAPTURES,CAPTURES

THE TOP 22 SENTENCE HYPOTHESES ARE:
(553) BISHOP TO <FILLER>
(513) BISHOP'S <FILLER>
(477) BISHOP PAWN <FILLER>
(474) BISHOP PAWN <FILLER>
(460) KNIGHT <FILLER>
(455) QUEEN<FILLER>
(443) ROOK <FILLER>
(443) QUEEN'S <FILLER>
(443) KNIGHT'S <FILLER>
(425) ROOK'S<FILLER>
(400) KING'S<FILLER>
(375) KING<FILLER>
(345) PAWN<FILLER>

Fig. 3.7. Second cycle of the recognition process.

trating the step-by-step use of knowledge in the recognition of an utterance. We notice substantial reductions of the search space are achieved by the use of knowledge in generating hypotheses, and verifying them. The knowledge-generated rank ordering of the hypotheses provides the necessary focus of attention for probabilistic tree searching.

Let us now consider the contribution of each of the sources of knowledge toward the recognition of the utterance. Fig. 3.8 illustrates the respec-

Task: Chess
Vocabulary size: 31
Speaker: JB
No. of Utterances: 21
No. of Words: 105

Knowledge Sources Used	Accuracy	
	% Words Recognized Correctly	% Sentences Recognized Correctly
Acoustic-Phonetics only	40%	0%
Acoustics and Syntax	65%	14%
Acoustics, Syntax and Semantics	88%	46%

Fig. 3.8. Contributions of acoustics, syntax, and semantics as sources of knowledge in the accuracy of recognition.

tive contributions of semantics, syntax, and acoustic-phonetics in the recognition of 19 utterances (containing 101 words) from the voice-chess task with a vocabulary of 31 words. The accuracy at the word level is 40% when only acoustic phonetic knowledge is used. This increases to 65% with the addition of syntactic knowledge and 88% with the addition of both syntactic and semantic knowledge. The effect of multiple sources of knowledge at the sentence level is more dramatic—the accuracy increases from 0% to 46%. The exact percentages of accuracy are irrelevant; as the knowledge present in the system grows so will the accuracy. What is important to note is that with the effective use of all the sources of knowledge, the recognition processes will not only be more accurate but also faster and more economical.

There are problems with the Hearsay system. One major issue is that there is a lack of balance between the parts of the system that perform the analysis of the speech waveform and the parts that perform the generation of hypotheses. The analysis of the speech waveform is simply insufficient; only a limited set of features is extracted from the waveforms; the human auditory system does a much better job. The human can recognize words spoken out of context, or words that do not fit Mexico with a simple contextual scheme. But in Hearsay, the conceptual analysis is so overbearing that the system will simply not recognize utterances unless it believes them to be plausible. Thus, the word "Mexico" inserted into the text two sentences ago would completely stymie a system that worked like the Hearsay system. Similarly, in interpreting chess moves, if the chess player suggests an illegal move, then the system will not "hear" it, but instead will interpret it as best it can as one of the possible legal moves. These errors in Hearsay are not without redeeming features; they are exactly the sorts of errors that humans tend to make. If this text had been read aloud, many listeners would not have "heard" the word "Mexico." But Hearsay overdoes it. In the terminology introduced earlier, Hearsay overemphasizes top-down analysis at the expense of bottom-up analysis. (These deficits should not overshadow the importance of the work in showing how different sources of knowledge interact in the process of speech recognition. Moreover, the deficits discussed here are recognized by the people working on Hearsay, and apply only to the first system, Hearsay I. A new system, Hearsay II, is designed to overcome some of the criticisms.)

The importance of the Hearsay work lies in its demonstration of how different sources of knowledge can each contribute to the overall processing of sensory data. The details of Hearsay are probably irrelevant for an understanding of psychological processing, but the spirit is not. Interaction of knowledge must be a critical and essential component of any psychological theory that attempts to understand the analysis of information. The "blackboard" of the Hearsay system is one possible mechanism for this important interaction to occur.

INTERACTIONS BETWEEN DATA DRIVEN AND CONCEPTUALLY DRIVEN PROCESSING

The important point about human pattern recognition is that it proceeds by means of all possible sources of information at the same time. There is an interaction of data driven and conceptually driven processes. The arrival of sensory information triggers an automatic series of analyses, starting at the sensory organs and continuing far up the chain of processing stages. Simultaneously, the context in which the sensory events are embedded triggers expectations based on past experience and general knowledge. These expectations produce conceptually driven processing, top-down processes that eventually merge with the bottom-up processes in competing the task.

The interactions between conceptually driven and data driven processing occur as a general principle of human information processing. For example, it occurs in the processing of visual information, so that many visual scenes can be recognized only because of the combination of both types of information. Steve Palmer, working at the University of California, San Diego, developed several compelling visual phenomena that demonstrated the interactions. Here is Palmer's analysis:

The Parsing Paradox: Bottom-Up or Top-Down*

STEPHEN E. PALMER

If perceptual interpretation is a matter of mapping sensations onto structural schemata, which happens first: interpreting the whole or interpreting the parts? How can someone recognize a face until he has first recognized the eyes, nose, mouth, and ears? Then again, how can someone recognize the eyes, nose, mouth, and ears until he knows that they are part of a face? This is often called the parsing paradox. It concerns the difficulties encountered with either a pure "bottom-up" (part-to-whole) or a pure "top-down" (whole-to-part) strategy in interpretive processing.

The solution I propose is that, under most circumstances, the interpretation of parts and wholes proceeds simultaneously in both bottom-up and top-down directions. The final interpretation is reinforced by consistency between a number of levels in the structural schema. For an example of the interactions of part-to-whole and whole-to-part strategies, consider without context the differences between how well a nose must be drawn to be recognizable when it is shown in the context of a face and when it is shown by itself. Most any sort of bump is adequate when it is part of a profile (see Fig. 3.9A)—if it is in the appropriate position. But the same bump will not suffice when it is shown alone (Fig. 3.9B). It is obvious from Fig.

* S. E. Palmer. Visual perception and world knowledge. D. A. Norman, D. E. Rumelhart, and the LNR Research Group. Explorations in Cognition. San Francisco: Freeman. 1975. Pages 295–296. Copyright © 1975 by W. H. Freeman. Reprinted by permission.

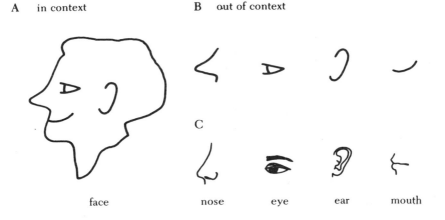

A   in context   **B**   out of context

C

face   nose   eye   ear   mouth

Fig. 3.9. An illustration of part-whole context. Facial features recognizable in the context of a profile (A) are not recognizable out of context (B). When the internal part structure of the facial features is differentiated (C), however, the features become recognizable out of context.

3.9B that the same is true for other parts of the face. In context, all that is needed is a hint of the overall structure of the facial features and the proper spatial relationships between them. Alone, however, the internal part structure of the facial feature must be represented (Fig. 3.9C). A similar demonstration can be made for the head itself. In order to be recognized, it must be seen either as part of a person's body (that is, along with other body parts in the proper spatial relationships) or with its own part structure clearly represented. Now, if one can recognize a nose when it is part of a face, and a face when its part structure is represented, then one can recognize both nose and head without further information. This simple example illustrates the interdependence of part-whole structure in a particularly illuminating way, and emphasizes the sufficiency of just a few structural levels for interpretation.

We now can see an alternative explanation to the problem described by George Miller in the passage on speech understanding ("slim loves more wet sheep"). In our example from Miller's work on the recognition of meaningful sentences, we saw that the grammatical structure of the sentences aided the understanding of the individual words to a considerable extent. Miller suggested this was so because the listener delayed interpreting the sounds until several words had been heard, and delayed the analysis until some grammatical phrases were present. This interpretation seems strange, for when we listen to speech, we do not normally feel that we hang back, delaying the understanding of what we hear. Rather, the feeling is of an immediate understanding. Indeed, one often believes that the words can be predicted even before they are said.

A simpler explanation for Miller's results comes by realizing that both data driven and conceptually driven processes can operate simultaneously. With simultaneous operation, no lag in analysis is necessary. The data driven process completes as much of its operations as is possible, while the conceptual analysis simultaneously puts together as much of the grammatical information as it can. The two processes working together will produce the experimental results reported by Miller. When random words are presented, the conceptually driven analysis plays a minimal role, and it is primarily the data driven processes that operate. This leads to the decrement in performance that Miller observed.

SUGGESTED READINGS

Pattern Recognition

A useful summary of work on the acquisition of information is the book by Stephen Reed, *Psychological Processes in Pattern Recognition* (1973). A good collection of papers on speech recognition is the set edited by Reddy (1975), which includes further discussions of "blackboards" and the Hearsay system (along with others).

Work in the engineering and computer science literature on pattern recognition is well summarized in a book by Duda and Hart (1973); the analyses in Chapter 12 of that book are especially important to psychology. Those interested in the engineering side will find the review by Kanal (1974) to be useful. Other work from computer science and its subdiscipline, artificial intelligence, can be found in either the journal *Artificial Intelligence* or the *Proceedings of the International Joint Conferences on Artificial Intelligence.* These proceedings (from IJCAI-I through IJCAI-IV) may be difficult to find, but they contain an extremely valuable set of materials on advanced work in all phases of artificial intelligence (and theoretical psychology).

The journals *Perception and Psychophysics* and *Journal of Experimental Psychology: Human Perception and Performance* (which split off from the *Journal of Experimental Psychology* with Vol. 105 in 1975) can be expected to provide good sources for new work. The *IEEE Transactions on Audio and Electroacoustics,* the *IEEE Transactions on Acoustics, Speech, and Signal Processing,* and the *IEEE Transactions on Information Theory* are good sources for the engineering literature.

More discussions of the bottom-up, top-down analysis of perceptual processing can be found in the chapter by Palmer (1975) and in the paper by Norman and Bobrow (1976).

Reading

One major area of experimentation has been the study of reading. It has been found that a single printed letter can sometimes be perceived better when it is part of a word than when it is seen all alone (Reicher, 1969; Wheeler, 1970). Studies of this phenomenon have therefore led to discussions very closely related to the discussions in this chapter. Does one read by deciphering the letters and then constructing the words or by interpreting the features of the entire word at once? This question, of course, asks whether reading is more a bottom-up or a top-down process. The answer is most likely to be that it is both. With familiar words or typefaces, we might proceed top-down, using expectations to bias the selection of words, using features of the whole words to interpret the individual letters. With difficult material, we probably resort to bottom-up processes, deciphering the letters, putting them together into units (perhaps pronounceable units), and then determining the word. But these are only the two extremes of the process. Normal reading probably takes place as a combination of these processes, with some bottom-up analyses of the letters suggesting possible words, and with conceptualization of the reading material adding further information. Reading is simply too complex a topic to be treated fairly in this book. The all-time best treatment is by Huey (1908/1968). F. Smith (1971) provides an excellent introduction. Good reviews can be found in Bradshaw (1975) and Smith and Spoehr (1974). An excellent treatment of the theoretical issues of reading, quite complementary to the treatment presented here, is given by Rumelhart's book (in press); this book also gives a good treatment of pattern recognition in general. Krueger's review (in press) of the effect of familiarity in visual perception is also a good source of information. Rumelhart and Siple (1974) present an elegant description of how context influences the perception of words.

The Stroop Phenomenon

Automatic data driven processing in the human is responsible for a fascinating psychological phenomenon. In 1935 Stroop discovered that semantic information can interfere with a person's performance on a task, even when the person tried hard not to interpret the information. The original Stroop effect resulted from printing the names of colors in inks of other colors. The word "blue" might be printed in red ink and the word "green" in blue ink. The task was to name the color of the ink, with the printed word causing interference. Long considered simply an amusing, quaint accident, the Stroop phenomenon has recently been recognized as an important indicator of automatic (data driven) processing. A number of recent studies have explored the Stroop phenomenon, especially in attention, and we can expect to see an increasingly large number of studies using this effect. A review of the earlier part of the revival of interest is provided by Dyer (1973). Cohen and Martin (1975) provide a fascinating and typical illustration of the use of this technique.

4
Attention, Effort, and Resources

"Everyone knows what attention is." So said William James and so began Chapter 2. But does everyone know? Moray (1970) proposed six different meanings. Posner and Boies (1971) suggested three different components. Everyone may know what it is, but maybe it is more than one thing.

What is attention? Consider again the subjective feeling. When you get deeply engrossed in a task, so deeply engrossed that the world closes in and only the central task that is being performed is in focal awareness, then the rest of the world might as well not exist; we characterize that feeling as that of being in a highly attentive state. It is like a trance. When the state ends, there is often a feeling of exhaustion, as if a good deal of mental effort had been expended. In fact, attentional states are a key part of meditative techniques and many religious ceremonies.

Emotion and Arousal

Consider the plight of a diver, weighted down with equipment and faced with danger. The diver equipped with a self-contained underwater breathing apparatus (SCUBA), diving in cold water, may be heavily burdened by all the paraphernalia of that sport. He or she is probably wearing a bulky sponge-rubber wet suit, including a hood over the head, an air tank (weighing around 35 pounds) strapped to the back, perhaps 15 pounds of lead weights on a belt around the waist, fins, gloves, mask, snorkle, knife, depth gauge, compass, watch, decompression meter, air regulator and mouthpiece, air pressure meter, and some type of buoyancy compensator (inflatable life vest). It should come as no surprise that a person encumbered this way is not very agile. Suppose that after 60 minutes of diving in very cold water, the diver is chilled, perhaps to the point of slight trembling. Now suppose the air tank and hose get tangled in the kelp (large seaweed). Such occurrences, though reasonably uncommon, should be of little concern to the well-trained diver. It is possible to remove the tank, and there are several well-known ways to get back to the surface without an air supply. Indeed, there is too much air, because the air in the lungs will expand as the diver rises to the surface.) But there is danger. So we have a tired, cold, and apprehensive diver about to perform a straightforward but dangerous task.

The psychological result of these conditions is to cause a state of high arousal. The diver will be anxious, under high stress. A number of different activities must be attended to, seemingly all at the same time. Failure to do them properly before exhausting the air supply could lead to injury or death. The result of such conditions seems to be the focusing of attention on a more and more narrow set of tasks. The result can often be tragic:

> The question of panic occurs throughout the accounts of the diving accidents, panic that seems to override certain aspects of training even in divers who have had formal instruction. For example, it has been reported that in all of the deaths attributed to diving in California the diver was found still wearing his weight belt despite the attempts in diving courses to make jettisoning of the weight belt automatic in emergencies. The death of a young woman in Tucson a couple of years ago is illustrative. This woman, enrolled in a diving course but lacking experience, was reported to have surfaced in panic and drowned while diving for golf balls in a twelve-foot trap in dark water. When her body was recovered, she was wearing her weight belt, and in addition, was still clutching a heavy bag of golf balls.
>
> **(Bachrach, 1970, Page 122; also see Egstrom and Bachrach, 1971)**

In general, it has been found that when humans become aroused, their performance on a task changes. If we draw a graph, plotting performance on the vertical axis and amount of arousal on the horizontal axis, the shape of the curve looks like an inverted U. At first, increases in arousal lead to improved performance, but then, as arousal builds up to its highest level, performance deteriorates. This relation has been named the Yerkes-Dodson law after its discoverers (Yerkes and Dodson, 1908). An explanation that seems both intuitively satisfying and supported by observations goes like this. As arousal level increases, attention becomes more narrowly focused. Attention to peripheral tasks decreases while attention to the central task increases; this improves performance. With ever-increasing levels of arousal, attention becomes more and more narrowly focused. This excessive narrowing eventually proves detrimental. Attention tends to focus entirely on one detail of the task, a detail that may be irrelevant. (This explanation is essentially a modern restatement of the position suggested by Easterbrook, 1959).

The role of arousal on attention, and thereby on performance, plays an important part of our everyday concept of attention. Most of us have probably noticed the relative narrowing or focusing of attention when apprehensive, or when a dangerous situation appears near. Instructors of sports such as underwater diving, flying, or parachute jumping try to combat the effects of anxiety on performance by *overtraining*. The goal is to make the appropriate responses to different situations become so automatic that they require no conscious attention. Automatic, nonconscious actions seem to be less susceptible to disruption by level of arousal.

AUTOMATICITY

Suppose we are active at several things at once: reading this book, eating, scratching, and tapping with one foot. It is easy to imagine reading this book while walking, book in one hand, apple in the other. Do we attend to all the things we do? Certainly, there would have to be more attention paid to the reading, less to the scratching, tapping, or walking. But is not some attention required to walk, to avoid obstacles, to keep in balance? The answer depends on one's view of attention. Some would equate attention with conscious awareness, and in this case it might only be the reading that is receiving attention. Others might equate attention with the general distribution of mental effort or mental resources to the various activities being performed. In this case, all the tasks receive some amount of attention, but the reading receives the most. Both those views, therefore, lead to similar interpretations.

A general rule appears to be that when a skill is highly learned—perhaps because it has been practiced for years and years—then it becomes automated, requiring little conscious awareness, little allocation of mental effort. Thus, how many tasks it is possible to do at once depends more on the level of training than on the task itself. A novice driver cannot both drive and talk, whereas a skilled driver can easily do both. Similarly, almost everyone can read while walking about. But if the passage being read requires deep thought, quite often the walking will stop. Highly skilled tasks seem to become automated, and thereby not as susceptible to disruption by withdrawing attention. The relationship between automatic processing and attentional control is so strong that one researcher, David LaBerge, has stated that

> *. . . to describe theoretically how automaticity develops is tantamount to describing the gradual elimination of attention in the processing of information. For example, imagine learning the name of a completely unfamiliar letter. This is much like learning the name that goes with the face of a person recently met. When presented again with the visual stimulus one recalls a time-and-place episode which subsequently produces the appropriate response. With further practice, the name emerges almost at the same time as the episode. This "short circuiting" is represented by the formation of a direct line between the visual and name codes. The process still requires attention, so this line is dashed, and the episodic code is used now more as a check on accuracy than as the mediator of the association. As more and more practice accumulates, the direct link becomes automatic (Mandler, 1954), represented by the solid line joining a letter with its name. At this point the presentation of the stimulus evokes the name without any contribution by the Attention Centre. Indeed, in such cases, we often observe that we cannot prevent the name from "popping into our head."*
>
> **(LaBerge, 1975, Page 58)**

LaBerge has shown how it is possible to disrupt tasks not yet fully automated by diversion of attention away from them. Remember the diver who, in panic, drowned in relatively shallow water, still clutching a heavy bag of golf balls and wearing her weight belt? Diving instructors worry about this problem. How do you train someone so they will perform the proper actions, even when in panic? The solution is to overtrain anyone who performs dangerous tasks. Make all actions become automated. Practice the set of possible responses to any situation over and over again. In this way, a minimum of attention is required, and in time of danger, the appropriate sequences get performed automatically. The trouble is that such training is hard to give and hard to take. The person being overtrained in some activity gets bored and wonders what all the fuss is about. Practicing the release of one's weight belt over and over again while diving in a swimming pool seems a pointless exercise to the student. But if that task can be made so automatic that it requires little or no conscious effort, then on the day that the diver needs to act under stress, the task may get performed successfully in spite of the buildup of panic.

For a task to be automated, the necessary components must flow readily from the memory system to whatever mechanism controls actions. In order to say more about the relation between practice and automatization, we need to know more about the way that information is represented within memory. Thus, we postpone further discussion of this issue until we have completed our survey of memory. Chapter 9 is devoted to this problem: the relationship between practice, automatization, and memory.

Mental Pathologies

Disruption of normally automated behavior such as walking or sitting sometimes occurs in mental pathologies. Consider the following description of schizophrenic patients, taken from the book by McGhie on *Pathology of Attention*. Here McGhie is reporting on a schizophrenic patient's description of his difficulties. The passage is taken from McGhie's book, but McGhie is quoting the description from an earlier study (McGhie and Chapman, 1961).

*Pathology of Attention**

ANDREW McGHIE

> *I'm not sure of my own movements any more. It's very hard to describe this but at times I'm not sure about even simple actions like sitting down. It's not so much thinking out what to do it's the doing of it that sticks me . . . I found recently that I was thinking of myself doing things before I would do them. If I'm going to sit down for example, I've got to think of myself and almost see myself sitting down before I do it. It's the same with other things like washing, eating, and even dressing—things that I have done at one time without even bothering or thinking about at all . . . I take more time to do things because I am always conscious of what I am doing. If I could just stop noticing what I am doing, I would get things done a lot faster.*
>
> *I have to do everything step by step now, nothing is automatic. Everything has to be considered.*

One patient who had been a keen athlete prior to his illness declared "when I am racing and am ready to get off the mark I have to think of putting my hands down in front of me and how to lift my legs before I can start. People just do things but I have to watch first to see how they do things. I have to think out most things first and know how to do things before I do them."

— — —

* A. McGhie. Pathology of Attention. *Baltimore: Penguin Books, 1969. Pages 44–48. Copyright © 1969 by Andrew McGhie. Reprinted by permission.*

In his analysis of normal skill, Welford (1958) suggests that the decision mechanism of consciousness is concerned with "the resolution of uncertainty." Economy of mental effort is achieved by many actions being so thoroughly learned that their operation becomes automatic and no longer requires conscious intervention. The reports of schizophrenic patients suggest that the former certainty in well-rehearsed skills has broken down; everything is now uncertain and requires conscious attention and decision making.

— — —

A common stereotype of the schizophrenic patient is that he is an individual who lives in a completely self-contained, phantasy world of his own making —"a dreamer in a world awake" whose attention is withdrawn from external reality and directed inwards. However, this stereotype is flatly contradicted by clinicians who have made intensive studies of schizophrenic patients. Bleuler (1911) described disturbances of attention in schizophrenic patients as follows:

> At the one extreme patients are easily distractible, seem to lack directives of their own and depend entirely on outer impressions; . . . at the other extreme they are undistractible and even the strongest stimuli will fail to influence their train of ideas or arouse their attention . . . lack of distractibility may appear to spring from the patient's lack of interests: as if they care about nothing, nothing can influence their behaviour. But it can be shown that the same patients understand very well what goes on about them, even when they pay no active attention.

He also noted that "even although uninterested and autistically encapsulated patients appear to pay little attention to the outside world, they register a remarkable number of events of no concern to them. The selection which attention exercises over normal sensory impressions may be reduced to zero, so that almost everything that meets the senses is registered." Schilder (1951) described schizophrenic patients as unable to pursue "the determinative idea" in so far as they were constantly at the mercy of ideas subsidiary to the mainstream of their thinking. In a series of clinical studies of chronic schizophrenic patients Freeman, Cameron, and McGhie (1958) described a state of undifferentiated attention which causes the patient to confuse internal mentality and external reality. In a later study by Freeman, Cameron, and McGhie (1966) it was suggested that impaired capacity to sustain attention was one of the most distinctive features of schizophrenic patients.

Vivid illustrations of disturbed attentional behaviour were provided by another systematic study, in which young schizophrenic patients described the difficulties they encountered during the early stages of their illness (McGhie and Chapman, 1961).

When these patients were encouraged to describe recent changes in their own experiences their reports referred most frequently to a disturbance in the normal process of selective attention. Although patients described their difficulties in different ways the following extracts are typical:

> "I can't concentrate. It's diversion of attention that troubles me . . . the sounds are coming through to me but I feel my mind cannot cope with everything. It is difficult to concentrate on any one sound . . . it's like trying to do two or three different things at the one time."
>
> "It's as if I'm too wide awake—very, very alert. I can't relax at all. Everything seems to go through me. I just can't shut things out."
>
> "Everything seems to grip my attention although I am not particularly interested in anything. I'm speaking to you just now but I can hear noises going on next door and in the corridor. I find it difficult to shut these out and it makes it more difficult for me to concentrate on what I am saying to you. Often the silliest things going on seem to interest me. That's not even true; they won't interest me but I find myself attending to them and wasting a lot of time this way. I know that sounds like laziness but it's not really."

Many of the patients also described allied perceptual changes, such as a heightening of sensory vividness; involuntary awareness of features in the perceptual field which had hitherto occupied a background position. The following few comments are again illustrative of the general pattern:

> "During the last while back I have noticed that noises all seem to be louder to me than they were before. It's as if someone had turned up the volume . . . I notice it most in background noises—you know what I mean, noises that are always around you but you don't notice them. Now they seem to be just as loud and sometimes louder than the main noises that are going on . . . it's a bit alarming at times because it makes it difficult to keep your mind on something when there's so much going on that you can't help listening to."
>
> "Have you ever had wax in your ears for a while and then had them syringed? That's what it's like now, as if I

*had been deaf before. Everything is much noisier and it
excites me."*

*"The colours of things seem much more clearer and
brighter . . . maybe it's because I notice so much more about
things and find myself looking at them for a long time. Not
only the colour of things fascinates me but all sorts of little
things, like markings on the surface, pick up my attention
too."*

Attention is a central concept in human behavior. It is a general,
global aspect of human cognition, intimately connnected to one's state
of self-awareness, of consciousness. We see that highly learned, automated activities may require little or no conscious attention to be performed. These highly automated activities can be disrupted, and when
that happens they require conscious control, often to the detriment of
their normal performance. In cases of mental pathologies and everyday stress some learned skills appear to break down, again requiring
conscious control, thereby disrupting a person's normal life. In situations of high arousal, activities do not get performed properly, even when
the failure to perform a simple act can lead to death. Thus, conscious
attention to activities is a critically important aspect of the human mind,
yet such conscious control can disrupt performance. The whole situation
is well summarized by the old doggerel:

A centipede was happy quite until a frog in fun,
Said, "Pray which leg comes after which?"
This raised her mind to such a pitch,
She lay distracted in the ditch,
Considering how to run.

[Anonymous]

A CAPACITY MODEL OF ATTENTION

Now it is time to combine our studies of pattern recognition with
our understanding of the phenomena of the attentional processes. In
our study of attention, we saw that attention to one task appeared to
limit the performance on other tasks, and the natural quesion to ask
was, "at what stage in the processing does this limit occur?" But the
very nature of the question implies a certain picture of the stages of
information processing, one that we now see may not be an accurate
characterization of the processing. When we ask about processing
stages, we are thinking primarily of a bottom-up analysis of stimulus
information, going from initial stages of sensory transduction, through

the extraction of critical features, to the recognition of the input. But the various papers we have examined on pattern recognition show us that the process is more complex than that. Different sources of knowledge converge to aid the process of acquiring information. The system seems to be not a simple sequence of stages, but rather a set of interacting mechanisms, all working together to produce the final result.

The limit on attentional capacity appears to be a general limit on resources, not necessarily a blockage at any particular stage in the processing. Daniel Kahneman, an Israeli psychologist working at the Hebrew University in Jerusalem, suggests that attention and mental effort are intimately correlated, and that the major limitation on processing is in fact a limit of resources. Kahneman suggests that arousal can increase the amount of resources available to the subject. Here is his description of the processes:

Attention and Effort*

DANIEL KAHNEMAN

The completion of a mental activity requires two types of input to the corresponding structure: an information input specific to that structure, and a nonspecific input which may be variously labeled "effort," "capacity," or "attention." To explain man's limited ability to carry out multiple activities at the same time, a capacity theory assumes that the total amount of attention which can be deployed at any time is limited.

— — —

A model of the allocation of capacity to mental activity is shown in Fig. 4.1. The model should be read beginning with the boxes labeled Possible Activities. These boxes correspond to structures that have received an information input (not shown in the model). Each such structure can now be "activated," i.e., each of the possible activities can be made to occur, by an additional input of attention or effort from the limited capacity. Unless this additional input is supplied, the activity cannot be carried out. Any type of activity that demands attention would be represented in the model, since all such activities compete for the limited capacity. Activities that can be triggered by an information input alone are not considered in the model.

Different mental activities impose different demands on the limited capacity. An easy task demands little effort, and a difficult task demands much. When the supply of attention does not meet the demands, performance falters,

* D. Kahneman. Attention and Effort. Englewood Cliffs, N.J.: Prentice-Hall, 1973. Pages 9–11. Copyright © 1973 by Prentice-Hall, Inc. Reprinted by permission.

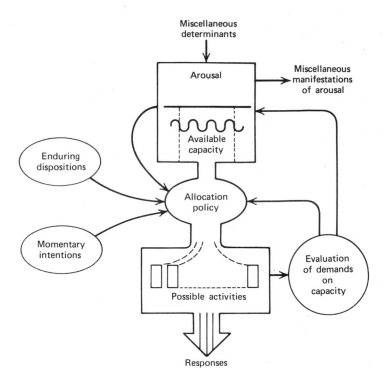

Fig. 4.1. A capacity model for attention.

or fails entirely. According to the model, an activity can fail, either because there is altogether not enough capacity to meet its demands or because the allocation policy channels available capacity to other activities. In addition, of course, an action can fail because the input of relevant information was insufficient. Thus, we may fail to detect or recognize a signal because we were not paying attention to it. But there are signals so faint that no amount of attention can make them plain.

A capacity theory must deal with three central questions: (1) What makes an activity more or less demanding? (2) What factors control the total amount of capacity available at any time? (3) What are the rules of the allocation policy?

— — —

The key observation that variations of physiological arousal accompany variations of effort shows that the limited capacity and the arousal system must be closely related. In Fig. 4.1, a wavy line suggests that capacity and arousal vary together in the low range of arousal levels. In addition, arousal and capacity both increase or decrease according to the changing demands of current activities.

The two central elements of the model are the allocation policy and the evaluation of demands on the limited capacity. The evaluation of demands is the governor system that causes capacity (or effort) to be supplied, as needed by the activities that the allocation policy has selected. The policy itself is controlled by four factors: (1) Enduring dispositions which reflect the rules of involuntary attention (e.g., allocate capacity to any novel signal; to any object in sudden motion; to any conversation in which one's name is mentioned); (2) Momentary intentions (e.g., listen to the voice on the right earphone; look for a redheaded man with a scar); (3) The evaluation of demands: there appears to be a rule that when two activities demand more capacity than is available, one is completed; (4) Effects of arousal.

— — —

The present chapter has illustrated two types of attention theories, which respectively emphasize the structural limitations of the mental system and its capacity limitations. Both types of theory predict that concurrent activities are likely to be mutually interfering, but they ascribe the interference to different causes. In a structural model, interference occurs when the same mechanism is required to carry out two incompatible operations at the same time. In a capacity model, interference occurs when the demands of two activities exceed available capacity. Thus, a structural model implies that interference between tasks is *specific,* and depends on the degree to which the tasks call for the same mechanisms. In a capacity model, interference is *nonspecific,* and it depends only on the demands of both tasks. Both types of interference occur. Studies of selective and divided attention indicate that the deployment of attention is more flexible than is expected under the assumption of a structural bottleneck, but it is more constrained than is expected under the assumption of free allocation of capacity. A comprehensive treatment of attention must therefore incorporate considerations of both structure and capacity.

The aim of cognitive processes is to form a meaningful interpretation of the world. Sensory information at any moment must be gathered together and interpreted in terms of a coherent framework. Past experience has created a vast repertoire of knowledge. Assume that this knowledge is organized into structural *frames* or *schemas* that can be used to characterize any experience. The problem of the perceptual processes is to determine the appropriate schema to match the present occurrences. When there are discrepancies, either a new schema must be selected or the current one must be reorganized.

Assume that when sensory information enters through the sensory system, the processes operating on it do so automatically, up through the extraction of features. Then as a result of these processes, the sensory memory is active, with different regions representing the different feature sets. Imagine, if you will, a memory space with regions of activity flourishing here, fading away there. Each new sensory input starts up new activity, and the system must attempt to organize the structures that have been activated into some meaningful schema. This is a bottom-up, data driven analysis: analysis driven by the sensory input.

There are other ways to analyze things. Consider a schema that has been activiated because it is suggested by an input or from context. What else does this schema require? Use the requirements as a guide in the search for the feature space. Does the schema require a contour to the left? Ask if any procedure can provide data about one. Does the system postulate that it is perceiving a room? Then look for corners, walls, a ceiling. Ask if the feature space is consistent with the interpretation. These are top-down, conceptually driven analyses: analyses driven by the conceptual organization.

Kahneman's suggestion that the total resources available to a system are limited is a valuable one. It can be extended to a detailed analysis of processing mechanisms. To see this, follow the analysis presented by Norman and Bobrow:

On Data-Limited and Resource-Limited Processes*

DONALD A. NORMAN AND DANIEL G. BOBROW

RESOURCE-LIMITED PROCESSES

Consider the problem of performing a complex cognitive task. Up to some limit, one expects performance to be related to the amount of resources (such as psychological effort) exerted on the task. If too little of some processing resource is applied (perhaps because processing resources are limited by competition from other tasks being performed at the same time) then one would expect poor performance. As more resources are applied to the task, then presumably better and better performance will result. Whenever an increase in the amount of processing resources can result in improved performance, we say that the task (or performance on that task) is *resource-limited*.

The principle of continually available output allows an increased use of computational resources to be reflected in an improvement in performance. If a process using a fixed strategy did not provide an output until it was finished, then increasing resources would simply shorten the time required to get some output. But, if the process continually makes available its prelimi-

*D. A. Norman and D. G. Bobrow. On data-limited and resource-limited processes. Cognitive Psychology. 1975, 7, 44–64. Copyright © 1975 by Academic Press, Inc. Reprinted by permission.

nary results, higher-level processes can continually be making use of them. As increased resources allow the process to upgrade the quality of its output, the improvement can be immediately used by any other processes for which the output is relevant. In a similar fashion, processing overloads need not cause calamitous failure, but simply a decrease in performance.

DATA-LIMITED PROCESSES

Consider the task of detecting a superthreshold sound: for example, the sound made by striking a piano key in a quiet room. The detection task is straightforward: the processing is limited by the simplicity of the data structure. Consider now the task of determining whether or not a particular signal has occurred within a background of noise. Suppose the recognition mechanism uses all the most powerful techniques at its disposal—matched filters, correlated techniques, and so on. In either of these two tasks, once all the processing that can be done has been completed, performance is dependent solely on the quality of the data. Increasing the allocation of processing resources can have no further effect on performance. Whenever performance is independent of processing resources, we say that the task is *data-limited*.

In general, most tasks will be resource-limited up to the point where all the processing that can be done has been done, and data-limited from there on.

The implications of this argument are easy to derive, with one digression. First, we must consider how any process is affected by the resources given to it. In general, if a process is resource-limited, then the more resources allocated to it, the better the performance. If the process is data-limited, then its performance is not affected by resources: The graph detailing the relationships between performance and resource is shown in Fig. 4.2.

Most processes have both data-limited regions and resource-limited regions. Whenever some medium range of resources is allocated to a group of processes, some will appear to be always data-limited, others will appear to be always resource-limited, and still others will seem to be in the transition stage between resource-limited and data-limited, the exact status depending on how much processing resource is allocated.

Norman and Bobrow discuss central processing:

LIMITED CAPACITY CENTRAL PROCESSING*

When several active processes compete for the same limited resource, then the performance-resource functions of these processes become critically

---

* Norman and Bobrow. *op. cit.* 1975. Pages 49–50; 57–59.

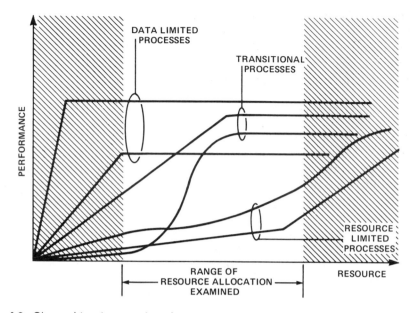

Fig. 4.2. Observable classes of performance-resource functions. When processes are examined only over a limited range of resource allocation, some will appear to be independent of resources (because they are data-limited in the region under consideration), others will appear to require indefinite amounts of resources (because they are resource-limited within this region), and others will be in a transition between data- and resource-limited operation.

important in determining just what effects will be observed. We assume that there is a fixed upper limit on available processing resources: Let the limit be signified by L. Operations which share the same limited capacity mechanism will not interfere with one another until the total processing resources required by all exceeds L. Moreover, in any given range of resource allocation, one process may interfere with others, but the others need not interfere with it. Just what kind of interference effects are found depends upon the particular form of the performance-resource function for each process. Interference can only be observed when a process is operating within its resource-limited region. Note, therefore, that the effects of interference need not be symmetrical. If task A interferes with task B, but not the reverse, then it would be incorrect to conclude that one of these tasks does not require processing capacity from the same central pool as the other. On the contrary, interference in either direction implies that both tasks draw resources from the same common pool. The asymmetry in effect results when one task is data-limited while the other is resource-limited. The symmetry or asymmetry of interference between two tasks is likely to depend in large part upon task instructions and subject strategy—upon which of the competing tasks receives first priority. The high-priority task will tend to be data-limited, and the low-priority task resource-limited.

Selective Attention

The literature on selective attention provides a rich set of data to be analyzed. Consider the experiment in which a subject is presented with two channels of spoken information by having two voices played to him over earphones, one voice to each ear. He is asked to repeat aloud the words that he hears on one channel (the procedure is called "shadowing") while the experimenter manipulates what happens on the other channel. In the literature the channel that is to be shadowed is called the *primary* channel and the other the *secondary* one.

In one such experiment, performed by Treisman and Geffen (1967), special target words were inserted into either the primary or secondary channels and subjects were instructed to tap the desk with a ruler whenever they detected a target word, no matter on which channel the target had occurred.

For the purposes of this experiment, we must compare the recognition of words on the primary channel with the recognition of words on the secondary channel. Processing resource is divided into two parts, with R_P going to the primary channel and $R_s = L - R_p$ going to the secondary channel. The relevant performance-resource functions are shown in Fig. 4.3. The perform-

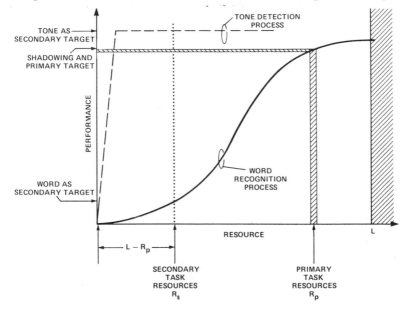

Fig. 4.3. The performance-resource function for a shadowing task. When the primary task is to shadow, sufficient resources must be allocated to keep performance relatively high. As a result, performance on a secondary task that is governed by a similar performance-resource function must appear to be "attenuated" (most secondary tasks that are verbal meet this criterion). A task operating on a much simpler performance-resource function will still be performed at a high level despite the simultaneous performance of the primary task. (This is illustrated with a data-limited function, corresponding to the task of detecting an auditory tone.)

ance on the primary task—shadowing—is determined by the instructions to the subject. Its level is high, yielding a reasonably high accuracy. The shadowing level tells us something of the performance level and thereby allows us to determine the primary processing resource, R_p. That being known, the maximum value that the secondary processing resource, R_s, can take on is $L - R_p$. Figure 4.3 shows that this guarantees a low level of performance for the detection of words on the secondary channel.

Suppose the target signal were an auditory tone instead of a word. Presumably the process necessary to detect a superthreshold tone and to discriminate it from speech sounds is rather simple, implying that it becomes data-limited at low resource values. Thus, as shown in Fig. 4.3, a tone should always be detectable on the secondary channel, even with very high performance levels on the primary channel. This is essentially the result found by Lawson (1966).

The analysis presented here is quite consistent with the idea that unattended inputs are "attenuated." The difference is that we are stating how a division of processing resource might force a process lower down on its resource-limited function, thereby essentially "attenuating" its analysis. The notion of "attenuation" is thus seen to depend critically upon the principle of continually available output in the operation of the relevant processes.

A THEORY OF ATTENTION

The picture we now have of attentional processes is the same as our earlier one, and yet it is quite different. If there really are simultaneous processes working, performing bottom-up, data driven analyses as well as top-down, conceptually driven ones, then the major limitation on what we can perform depends on how many resources are used.

Now we can begin to make sense out of a lot of the literature on attention. Since we no longer need ask the question about the location of a critical attentional bottleneck in the stages of processing, the earlier debate about the locus of attention is no longer relevant. Instead, we ask exactly what resources are demanded by a task and see if the demand exceeds the supply. If we assume that well-learned tasks are those that have become "automated," thus requiring little conscious control and few resources, then we can see why we can perform several well-learned tasks simultaneously, but only one or just a few poorly learned ones. When we first learn to drive a car, we cannot both drive and talk, and the task of driving seems difficult and mentally tiring. Later on, driving experience reduces the resources required, and we can drive, talk, sing, and still have excess capacity.

A good example of the nature of resource limits comes from the results of an informal experiment. While visiting the laboratory of William Johnston at the University of Utah, in Salt Lake City, I acted as a subject in Johnston's experiment on attention. Johnston presented two different passages of text to his subjects over earphones. Both passages were spoken in the same male voice, and both were about scientific topics (one was about psychology, the other about some other, unrelated topic). Both passages were presented to both earphones, so both appeared to be localized in the middle of the head. The only way to tell the passages apart was by topic. One passage started slightly before the other, and the subject was asked to attend to it, for he would be asked questions about it at the end. This task is very difficult. When both passages occur at the same location in space, read by the same voice, it is very difficult to keep the two separated, but it can be done.

Now, in addition, a light in front of the subject occasionally increased in intensity for a brief period. Whenever the subject saw the light flash, he was to push a button. The amount of time that it took to respond to the light flash was taken as a measure of the attentional load on the subject.

The interesting part of the experiment came when one of the two passages was a familiar one. One passage was made familiar by playing it to the subject many times prior to the start of the experiment. After each playing, the subject was asked a question about its contents. When the experiment was performed, if the passage that was to be attended to was the familiar one, it was easy to follow the proper text, and the amount of time needed to respond to the light flash was reasonably short. When the task was reversed, so that the passage to be followed was unfamiliar while the passage to be ignored was familiar, then things were much more difficult. When I acted as a subject, I found it very difficult to concentrate on the proper passage, for phrases of the other one kept breaking through, automatically, despite my attempts to prevent it.

The most interesting result, however, came when the light flashed. Even when I had managed to get going properly and was listening to the unfamiliar passage, each time the light flashed and I made my response, the effort of making the response seemed to stop the listening process. I would lose my place and would have to start over from the beginning. The task seemed only barely possible, and even the very slight amount of processing necessary to respond to the light was sufficient to drive me close to the limit of my resources for performing the listening task. Needless to say, Johnston found that the reaction time to respond to the light in this condition was increased for all his subjects (Johnston and Heinz, 1974).

The word "attention" refers to a variety of concepts, each differing in meaning, but each overlapping the other. The consideration of mental resources adds a unitary concept to the nature of attention. A person can direct processing resources in many different ways, concentrating sometimes on some aspect of the sensory input through the sense organs, sometimes on deep processing of internally generated ideas, and sometimes on preparing for a forthcoming activity. Moreover, the processing system is continually attempting to combine all sources of information at its disposal into a unified, understandable picture. Many different knowledge sources all interact. Some processing proceeds from the input signals, a bottom-up, data driven sequence of processing. Other processing proceeds from internally generated hypotheses or conceptualizations, a top-down, conceptually driven sequence of processing. Above all, there is some limit on how much processing can be performed at any one time.

In Chapter 2 we saw that the phenomena of attention studied in the experimental laboratory seemed to lead toward two conflicting models of the attentional process. Moreover, although each model had its virtues, each was also unable to explain some experimental results. From this chapter, we begin to see that perhaps both models were equally correct, but both were incomplete. Models of attention that postulate early selection can probably be compared with models of top-down processing. Both kinds of processing occur, and both models are correct.

If different knowledge sources interact with one another, and if the system can drive itself by both data driven and conceptually driven processes, then we can see how things fit together to make sense of the original efforts to piece together a theory of attention. When attention is concentrated on incoming sensory information, then the system is one that emphasizes data-driven, bottom-up analyses; it therefore looks as if it were an early-selection device. With other tasks, the system can be one that emphasizes conceptually driven, top-down processing and therefore can look as if it were a late-selection device. But other modes of operation are also possible, and these give rise to some of the other aspects of attentional phenomena.

The trail of the theoretical understanding of attention has been long and tortuous. You are forgiven if you think it to be muddled, full of confusions and contradictions. Such is the way of science. The early theories are absolutely necessary, for they combine the existing phenomena in useful ways, giving insights and helping to generate intelligent new experiments. These experiments lead to reconsideration of the theoretical picture. New, competing theories often emerge, but because each theory is constructed intelligently, each is correct for some things, wrong for others. Eventually, some new approach provides a way of incorporating all the previous results (and theories), and a new step of progress has been completed. You might think of a scientific theory as providing conceptually driven guidance to the field and of experiments as providing data-driven guidance. Both are necessary.

Beware. The resolution of the attentional processes presented here is not the final word. In the coming years we will learn more about the human information processing system. Some of the new evidence will present puzzles, strange anomalies that refuse to fit comfortably into our understanding of processing structures. But eventually some new formulation will come along, and the new data will then fit nicely with the old. A new stage will have been reached.

SUGGESTED READINGS

General Reading in Attention

The periodic conferences on *attention and performance* provide a convenient access to a large body of experimental literature on attention. Most of the workers on attention from the world gather together periodically at these symposiums, and the proceedings are an excellent place to start. See Sanders (1967, 1970) for symposiums I and III; Kornblum (1973) for IV; and Rabbitt and Dornic (1975, in press) for V and VI. (Symposium II was on reaction time, not on attention.)

Three major recent books on attention are Broadbent's *Decision and Stress* (1971), which reviews a huge body of experimental literature, Kahneman's *Attention and Effort* (1973), and Moray's book (1970). In addition, Treisman's article in the journal *Psychological Review* (1969) is an important discussion of the flexibility of attentional mechanisms. Posner and Boies treat the different components of attention in *Psychological Review* (1971), and Posner (1969) has contributed a good deal of our knowledge about the early stages of attention and pattern recognition. Keele (1973) provides a good introduction. Posner's short introduction to cognition (1973) is an excellent book, although the treatment of attention itself is minimal. The effects of practice on performance are discussed in Chapter 9 of this book. Also, see the papers by LaBerge (1975) and LaBerge and Samuels (1974).

Other Aspects of Attention

It is possible to measure brain potentials (evoked potentials) from the scalp of a person performing a task on attention; although this physiological research is just in its infancy, there is every hope that it will add to our complete understanding of attention. The papers by Hillyard, Hink, Schwent, and Picton (1973) and by Picton and Hillyard (1974) provide a review of this literature. The related paper by Picton, Hillyard, Krausz, and Galambos (1974) should also be consulted. These are advanced papers, however, and the reader is expected to know quite a bit about physiological recording techniques. The *Psychological Review* paper by Walley and Weiden (1973) presents a neuropsychological theory of attention. Similarly, the *Psychological Review* article by Pribram and McGuinness (1975) provides a thorough review of the physiological literature relevant to attention, but this is also a difficult paper to read. Perhaps a better starting point is the review by Naatanen (1975).

Interesting and relevant introductions to the literature on abnormalities of attention are provided by several sources. The book by G. Reed (1972) probably provides the best introduction. It is readable and provocative. McGhie's book (1969) on the pathology of attention is also a good one, and Chapman and Chapman (1973) review thought processes in schizophrenia, with some treatment of attention. Baddeley (1972) provides a useful and readable review of the effects of emotional arousal on selective attention. Mandler (1975*b)* provides a more thorough treatment of the entire role of emotional factors in human action.

Finally, the role of attention plays a major role in many meditative or religious ceremonies and practices. Interesting analyses of the role of attention in these situations are provided by Ornstein (1972) in his book on the psychology of consciousness, and by the tales of Carlos Casteneda of his encounters with Don Juan. (*Tales of Power,* 1974, is probably the most relevant for the topics discussed in this book; see especially pages 225–254, "The Strategy of a Sorcerer"). Castaneda's works can be disputed, and it certainly is not clear whether they are fact, fiction, or fancy. But no matter. The works contain interesting insights into the nature of attention and consciousness and, if you will, the relationship between the information provided by the senses (data driven processing) and the interpretation one places on them (conceptually driven processing). Even fiction can be illuminating. The best review of all, however, is provided by Adam Smith in his semi-scholarly, highly readable treatment of mind, consciousness, and meditation (Smith, 1975).

5
Short-Term Memory

Neither attention nor pattern recognition operates in isolation. Both require that incoming sensory messages be interpreted with the aid of the context of the messages and their past history. Both context and history can be relevant only through the action of memory. To determine the immediate context of events, we need, at the least, a temporary storage system to keep a memory of the recent past. To examine the entire past history of an event requires a permanent storage system.

Studies of attention, pattern perception, and memory are usually considered to be different and independent, but all three areas must eventually be combined into one picture of information processing. We have already examined attention and pattern recognition. What can we say about memory?

MEMORY OF THE PRESENT

We start our study of memory with the most direct and immediate source, our introspections. There appear to be several types of memories differing in their completeness, their duration, and the manner by which we get material in and out of them. We are continually aware of events that are just now happening, but this sense of the immediate present fades into a hazy recollection of the past. Is the distinction between our clear memory of the present and our vague memory of the past real or is it an illusion? Again, the best clear statement of these different aspects of memory comes from William James.[1]

---

[1] William James. *The Principles of Psychology,* Vol. 1. New York: Henry Holt and Co., 1890. Pages 643–647. (Republished by Dover, 1950.)

The stream of thought flows on; but most of its segments fall into the bottomless abyss of oblivion. Of some, no memory survives the instant of their passage. Of others, it is confined to a few moments, hours, or days. Others, again, leave vestiges which are indestructible, and by means of which they may be recalled as long as life endures. Can we explain these differences?

— — —

Well, the first manifestation of elementary habit is the slow dying away of an impressed movement on the neural matter, and its first effect in consciousness is this so-called elementary memory. But what elementary memory makes us aware of is the just past. The objects we feel in this directly intuited past differ from properly recollected objects. An object which is recollected, in the proper sense of that term, is one which has been absent from consciousness altogether, and now revives anew. It is brought back, recalled, fished up, so to speak, from a reservoir in which, with countless other objects, it lay buried and lost from view. But an object of primary memory is not thus brought back; it never was lost; its date was never cut off in consciousness from that of the immediately present moment. In fact it comes to us as belonging to the rearward portion of the present space of time, and not to the genuine past.

James distinguished between our immediate knowledge of the past and what he called "properly recollected objects." Our knowledge of the psychological present is too direct, immediate, and without conscious effort to be called a true memory, said James. True recollection from memory requires effort and the knowledge that what we are recovering differs from what we are presently experiencing. To distinguish these two phenomena, James proposed that the first, more immediate, memory be called *primary,* and the second, more indirect, *secondary.*

What relation does attention bear to recent memories? We have previously seen that the way in which we can divert our attention to events appears to require that all sensory events be analyzed in sufficient detail to determine their immediate relevance, a level of analysis that presumably involves memory. If this is so, our primary memory ought to contain a complete record of all events that have just occurred, not just those to which we are attending at the moment. James agreed, and found his proof in the following passage by Exner, a Viennese psychologist.[2]

---

[2] *Ibid.* Page 646. James is quoting from Exner in L. Hermann, *Handbuch der Physiologie,* Vol. 2. 1880. Page 282.

Impressions to which we are inattentive leave so brief an image in the memory that it is usually overlooked. When deeply absorbed, we do not hear the clock strike. But our attention may awake after the striking has ceased, and we may then count off the strokes. Such examples are often found in daily life. We can prove the existence of this primary memory-image, *as it may be called, in another person, even when his attention is completely absorbed elsewhere. Ask someone, e.g., to count the lines of a printed page as fast as he can, and whilst this is going on walk a few steps about the room. Then, when the person has done counting, ask him where you stood. He will always reply quite definitely that you have walked. Analogous experiments may be done with vision. This primary memory-image is, whether attention have been turned to the impression or not, an extremely lively one, but is subjectively quite distinct from every sort of after-image or hallucination. . . . It vanishes, if not caught by attention, in the course of a few seconds. Even when the original impression is attended to, the liveliness of its image in memory fades fast.*

Let us continue the study of immediate memories; how much do we retain of events that have just previously occurred? Our intuition suggests we keep a very accurate record. When I shut my eyes for an instant, I can still picture the disarray on my desk with what appears to be perfect accuracy. But is the impression of complete recollection of just-experienced events accurate?

When we try to determine exactly how much is retained of an immediate memory, we find very little. If a person is asked to name what he has just seen, he stumbles, able to recall but a handful of items. In fact, the results of a large number of carefully controlled experiments indicate that humans can usually recall only a very limited number of items which have just been presented to them—from as few as four to, perhaps, ten items. The rather low limit on the number of new (and unrelated) items we can recall after a single exposure is one of the puzzles of memory. Meaningful material is relatively easy to learn, but we have trouble with isolated items. The contents of our immediate recall of unrelated material is commonly called the memory span, but this is a misleading phrase; it should be called the memory limitation. Why is there this apparent contradiction between the richness of our impressions of recent events and the sparseness of our recall of those impressions?

One reason for the apparent discrepancy is that the very act of recalling one event may cause us to forget others. It was not until 100 years after Exner that this notion was tested, and even then, the experiments only began to answer the puzzle. Let us look at one such study, performed in the late 1950s at Harvard University by George Sperling.

The Information in Brief Presentations*

GEORGE SPERLING

How much can be seen in a single brief exposure? This is an important problem because our normal mode of seeing greatly resembles a sequence of brief exposures. Erdmann and Dodge (1898) showed that in reading, for example, the eye assimilates information only in the brief pauses between its quick saccadic movements. The problem of what can be seen in one brief exposure, however, remains unsolved. The difficulty is that the simple expedient of instructing the observer of a single brief exposure to report what he has just seen is inadequate. When complex stimuli consisting of a number of letters are tachistoscopically presented, observers enigmatically insist that they have seen more than they ·an remember afterwards, that is, report afterwards. The apparently simple question: "What did you see?" requires the observer to report both what he remembers and what he has forgotten.

The statement that *more is seen than can be remembered* implies two things. First, it implies a memory limit, that is, a limit on the (memory) report. Such a limit on the number of items which can be given in the report following any brief stimulation has, in fact, been generally observed; it is called the span of attention, apprehension, or immediate-memory (cf. Miller, 1956). Second, *to see more than is remembered* implies that more information is available during, and perhaps for a short time after, the stimulus than can be reported. The considerations about available information are quite similar, whether the information is available for an hour (as it is in a book that is borrowed for an hour), or whether the information is available for only a fraction of a second (as a stimulus which is exposed for only a fraction of a second). In either case it is quite probable that for a limited period of time more information will be available than can be reported. It is also true that initially, in both examples, the information is available to vision.

In order to circumvent the memory limitation in determining the information that becomes available following a brief exposure, it is obvious that the observer must not be required to give a report which exceeds his memory span. If the number of letters in the stimulus exceeds his memory span, then he cannot give a whole report of all the letters. Therefore, the observer must be required to give only a partial report of the stimulus contents. Partial reporting of available information is, of course, just what is required by ordinary schoolroom examinations and by other methods of sampling available information.

An examiner can determine, even in a short test, approximately how

* G. Sperling. *The information available in brief visual presentations.* Psychological *Monographs.* 1960, 74, 498, 1–2. Copyright © 1960 by the American Psychological Association. Reprinted by permission.

much the student knows. The length of the test is not so important as that the student not be told the test questions too far in advance. Similarly, an observer may be "tested" on what he has seen in a brief exposure of a complex visual stimulus. Such a test requires only a partial report. The specific instruction which indicates which part of the stimulus is to be reported is then given only after termination of the stimulus. On each trial the instruction, which calls for a specified part of the stimulus, is randomly chosen from a set of possible instructions which cover the whole stimulus. By repeating the interrogation (sampling) procedure many times, many different random samples can be obtained of an observer's performance on each of the various parts of the stimulus. The data obtained thereby make feasible the estimate of the total information that was available to the observer from which to draw his report on the average trial.

The time at which the instruction is given determines the time at which available information is sampled. By suitable coding, the instruction may be given at any time: before, during, or after the stimulus presentation. Not only the available information immediately following the termination of the stimulus, but a continuous function relating the amount of information available to the time of instruction may be obtained by such a procedure.

In his experiments, Sperling presented visual arrays of English letters briefly to his subjects and then asked for only partial reporting of the image. Basically, he presented a set of 12 letters, arranged in 3 rows of 4 letters. Then, after a brief exposure, Sperling signaled which letters were to be recalled by presenting an acoustical tone of high, medium, or low frequency. A high tone, for example, meant that the top row would be reported. By controlling both the component of the image to be reported and the delay between presentation of the letters and the tone, Sperling was able to minimize the detrimental effect of early reports on later ones, while getting a systematic measure of the rate of decay of the sensory image. The sampling procedure ensured that subjects were tested over all parts of the sensory image, so it was possible to infer the total capacity of the sensory memory from the repeated partial reports. Not surprisingly, Sperling found that the sensory image does in fact contain much more information than had previously been reported.

Sperling argued that the contradiction between what we see and what we recall is based simply on the problems of testing human subjects. The act of recall causes forgetting. Actually, then, Sperling is proposing a more complex system than we envisaged before. He suggested that there are at least *three* stages of memory. The first is a complete sensory image of just-occurring events, the second is an immediate or short-term memory that contains the limited information we are able to extract from the rapidly decaying, sensory image, and the third (implied, but not mentioned) is a permanent or long-term memory with a large capacity. Sperling talked only about the first of the memories, the system now called *visual short-term memory* or *sensory information store*. What about other memory systems?

The study of memory is not quite as simple as it might appear. It has a surprising number of tricks and twists to its functioning. Actually, this should not be a surprise, for human memory is perhaps our most important cognitive capacity. Without memory there would be no intellectual functioning. We could not learn from experience or recognize anything. We could only do those things for which the nervous system had been prewired. Language would disappear, and so too would most meaningful communication. Memory processes are a critical part of intellectual behavior. It is not surprising that we are far from unravelling its secrets.

When modern research on memory began, initial progress was smooth and rapid. Psychologists peeled away layers of memory functioning. First there was a visual short-term memory, then a short-term memory, then a long-term memory. In addition, there seemed to be the equivalent of the visual short-term memory for the other sensory systems as well, certainly for touch and hearing. As investigations gradually expanded to more and more phenomena, the story became more complex. Indeed, the rest of this book will be devoted primarily to unravelling the story of human memory. It will be an interesting story, even though it will not present the final resolution. Let us look first at the early days of investigation, when discoveries were exciting and simple, and it appeared that researchers were on the final path to unveiling the picture of the many stages of memory processing.

In the early 1950s, the mathematical theory of information played an important role in the thoughts, theories, and experiments of psychologists. The reasons are fairly obvious. Communication engineers had developed a formal structure for discussing the effects of channel capacity, noise, and transmission rate on the amount of information that any message could contain. Psychologists realized that the human could be viewed as an information-processing device, reducing and transmitting the information contained in the environment through the sensory system and into some encoding in memory. Thus stated, the psychologists and engineers were studying similar problems. Limitations on memory capacity could be interpreted as limitations on the ability to receive information.

THE MAGICAL NUMBER PROBLEM

George Miller summarized a good deal of the early research on memory and processing limits in a paper that has since become widely known as "the 7 ± 2" paper. In this paper, Miller discussed the application of the concept of channel capacity to studies of memory and absolute judgments. His discussion of the memory problem is directly relevant to our discussion here, so we start with a brief look at Miller's explanation of information theory followed by his discussion of memory.

The Magical Number Seven, Plus or Minus Two*

GEORGE A. MILLER

My problem is that I have been persecuted by an integer. For seven years this number has followed me around, has intruded in my most private data, and has assaulted me from the pages of our most public journals. This number assumes a variety of disguises, being sometimes a little longer and sometimes a little smaller than usual, but never changing so much as to be unrecognizable. The persistence with which this number plagues me is far more than a random accident. There is, to quote a famous senator, a design behind it, some pattern governing its appearances. Either there really is something unusual about the number or else I am suffering from delusions of persecution.

I shall begin my case history by telling you about some experiments that tested how accurately people can assign numbers to the magnitudes of various aspects of a stimulus. In the traditional language of psychology these would be called experiments in absolute judgment. Historical accident, however, has decreed that they should have another name. We now call them experiments on the capacity of people to transmit information. Since these experiments would not have been done without the appearance of information theory on the psychological scene, and since the results are analyzed in terms of the concepts of information theory, I shall have to preface my discussion with a few remarks about this theory.

INFORMATION MEASUREMENT

The "amount of information" is exactly the same concept that we have talked about for years under the name of "variance."[3] The equations are dif-

---

* G. A. Miller. *The magical number seven, plus or minus two: some limits on our capacity for processing information.* Psychological Review. 1956, 63, 81–97. *Copyright © 1956 by the American Psychological Association. With permission of the author and publisher.*

[3] "Variance" here refers to the statistical concept of the amount of dispersion or variability there is in a set of measurements. People unfamiliar with the concept will find it satisfactory to substitute the word "variability" every place that Miller uses "variance." To state Miller's point in terms of variability: if everybody in the world had exactly the same height, then a new measurement of that height would convey no new information. If heights vary, however, the measurements are meaningful and convey information. In fact, the more unexpected the result (the greater the variability), the more information contained in the measurement. Variability (and variance) is always stated in the units of the thing being measured. Thus, we might say that the variability of heights is plus or minus so many inches.

ferent, but if we hold tight to the idea that anything that increases the variance also increases the amount of information we cannot go far astray.

The advantages of this new way of talking about variance are simple enough. Variance is always stated in terms of the unit of measurement—inches, pounds, volts, etc.—whereas the amount of information is a dimensionless quantity. Since the information in a discrete statistical distribution does not depend upon the unit of measurement, we can extend the concept to situations where we have no metric and we would not ordinarily think of using the variance. And it also enables us to compare results obtained in quite different experimental situations where it would be meaningless to compare variances based on different metrics. So there are some good reasons for adopting the newer concept.

The similarity of variance and amount of information might be explained this way: When we have a large variance, we are very ignorant about what is going to happen. If we are very ignorant, then when we make the observation it gives us a lot of information. On the other hand, if the variance is very small, we know in advance how our observation must come out, so we get little information from making the observation.

— — —

If the human observer is a reasonable kind of communication system, then when we increase the amount of input information the transmitted information will increase at first and will eventually level off at some asymptotic value. This asymptotic value we take to be the *channel capacity* of the observer: it represents the greatest amount of information that he can give us about the stimulus on the basis of an absolute judgment. The channel capacity is the upper limit on the extent to which the observer can match his responses to the stimuli we give him.

Now just a brief word about the *bit* and we can begin to look at some data. One bit of information is the amount of information that we need to make a decision between two equally likely alternatives. If we must decide whether a man is less than six feet tall or more than six feet tall and if we know that the chances are 50-50, then we need one bit of information. Notice that this unit of information does not refer in any way to the unit of length that we use—feet, inches, centimeters, etc. However you measure the man's height, we still need just one bit of information.

Two bits of information enable us to decide among four equally likely alternatives. Three bits of information enable us to decide among eight equally likely alternatives. Four bits of information decide among 16 alternatives, five among 32, and so on. That is to say, if there are 32 equally likely alternatives, we must make five successive binary decisions, worth one bit each, before we know which alternative is correct. So the general rule is simple: every time the number of alternatives is increased by a factor of two, one bit of information is added.

There are two ways we might increase the amount of input information. We could increase the rate at which we give information to the observer, so that the amount of information per unit time would increase. Or we could ignore the time variable completely and increase the amount of input information by increasing the number of alternative stimuli. In the absolute judgment experiment we are interested in the second alternative. We give the observer as much time as he wants to make his response; we simply increase the number of alternative stimuli among which he must discriminate and look to see where confusions begin to occur. Confusions will appear near the point that we are calling his "channel capacity."

Miller summarized a number of studies on absolute judgments and memory and found "a clear and definite limit to the limit with which we can identify absolutely the magnitude of a unidimensional stimulus variable." The limit is called the span of absolute judgment, and it usually lies somewhere in the neighborhood of seven. Increased accuracy of judgments over that can be obtained by a number of techniques. "The three most important of these devices are (a) to make relative rather than absolute judgments; or, if that is not possible, (b) to increase the number of dimensions along which the stimuli can differ; or (c) to arrange the task in such a way that we make a sequence of several absolute judgments in a row."

The span of immediate memory behaves differently than does our ability to make absolute judgments. Immediate memory appears to be limited by the number of items, regardless of the information content of the items. Because of this, Miller found that the apparent memory span could be increased by a recoding process. Normally, when we try to remember a list of items, we can immediately recall about seven of them. If, however, we were first to learn a code word for every possible pair of items we could easily retain a string of seven code words. Thus, without overloading our normal memory span of seven, we could fool an observer into thinking that our span was actually 14 items. This process of increasing the memory span by efficient grouping of old items into new items, Miller called *chunking*. Miller concludes:

RECODING

In order to speak more precisely, therefore, we must recognize the importance of grouping or organizing the input sequence into units or chunks. Since the memory span is a fixed number of chunks, we can increase the number of bits of information that it contains simply by building larger and larger chunks, each chunk containing more information than before.

A man just beginning to learn radio-telegraphic code hears each *dit* and *dah* as a separate chunk. Soon he is able to organize these sounds into letters and then he can deal with the letters as chunks. Then the letters organize themselves as words, which are still larger chunks, and he begins to hear whole phrases. I do not mean that each step is a discrete process, or that plateaus must appear in his learning curve, for surely the levels of organization are achieved at different rates and overlap each other during the learning process. I am simply pointing to the obvious fact that the dits and dahs are organized by learning into patterns and that as these larger chunks emerge the amount of message that the operator can remember increases correspondingly. In the terms I am proposing to use, the operator learns to increase the bits per chunk.

In the jargon of communication theory, this process would be called *recoding*. The input is given in a code that contains many chunks with few bits per chunk. The operator recodes the input into another code that contains fewer chunks with more bits per chunk. There are many ways to do this recoding, but probably the simplest is to group the input events, apply a new name to the group, and then remember the new name rather than the original input events.

Since I am convinced that this process is a very general and important one for psychology, I want to tell you about a demonstration experiment that should make perfectly explicit what I am talking about. This experiment was conducted by Sidney Smith and was reported by him before the Eastern Psychological Association in 1954.

Begin with the observed fact that people can repeat back eight decimal digits, but only nine binary digits. Since there is a large discrepancy in the amount of information recalled in these two cases, we suspect at once that a recoding procedure could be used to increase the span of immediate memory for binary digits. In Table 5.1 a method for grouping and renaming is illustrated. Along the top is a sequence of 18 binary digits, far more than any subject was able to recall after a single presentation. In the next line these same binary digits are grouped by pairs. Four possible pairs can occur: 00 is renamed 0, 01 is renamed 1, 10 is renamed 2, and 11 is renamed 3. That is to say, we recode from a base-two arithmetic to a base-four arithmetic. In the

TABLE 5.1. Way of Recoding Sequences of Binary Digits

Binary Digits (Bits)		1	0	1	0	0	0	1	0	0	1	1	1	0	0	1	1	1	0
2:1	Chunks	10		10		00		10		01		11		00		11		10	
	Recoding	2		2		0		2		1		3		0		3		2	
3:1	Chunks	101			000			100			111			001			110		
	Recoding	5			0			4			7			1			6		
4:1	Chunks	1010				0010				0111				0011				10		
	Recoding	10				2				7				3						
5:1	Chunks	10100					01001					11001					110			
	Recoding	20					9					25								

recoded sequence there are now just nine digits to remember, and this is almost within the span of immediate memory. In the next line the same sequence of binary digits is regrouped into chunks of three. There are eight possible sequences of three, so we give each sequence a new name between 0 and 7. Now we have recorded from a sequence of 18 binary digits into a sequence of 6 actual digits, and this is well within the span of immediate memory. In the last two lines the binary digits are grouped by fours and by fives and are given decimal-digit names from 0 to 15 and from 0 to 31.

It is reasonably obvious that this kind of recoding increases the bits per chunk, and packages the binary sequence into a form that can be retained within the span of immediate memory. So Smith assembled 20 subjects and measured their spans for binary and octal digits. The spans were 9 for binaries and 7 for octals. Then he gave each recoding scheme to five of the subjects. They studied the recoding until they said they understood it—for about 5 or 10 minutes. Then he tested their span for binary digits again while they tried to use the recoding schemes they had studied.

The recoding schemes increased their span for binary digits in every case. But the increase was not as large as we had expected on the basis of their span for octal digits. Since the discrepancy increased as the recoding ratio increased, we reasoned that the few minutes the subjects had spent learning the recoding schemes had not been sufficient. Apparently the translation from one code to the other must be almost automatic or the subject will lose part of the next group while he is trying to remember the translation of the last group.

Since the 4:1 and 5:1 ratios require considerable study, Smith decided to imitate Ebbinghaus and do the experiment on himself. With Germanic patience he drilled himself on each recoding successively, and obtained the results shown in Fig. 5.1. Here the data follow along rather nicely with the results you would predict on the basis of his span for octal digits. He could remember 12 octal digits. With the 2:1 recoding, these 12 chunks were worth

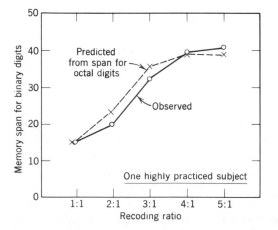

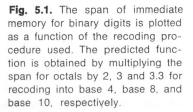

Fig. 5.1. The span of immediate memory for binary digits is plotted as a function of the recoding procedure used. The predicted function is obtained by multiplying the span for octals by 2, 3 and 3.3 for recoding into base 4, base 8, and base 10, respectively.

24 binary digits. With the 3:1 recoding they were worth 36 binary digits. With the 4:1 and 5:1 recodings, they were worth about 40 binary digits.

It is a little dramatic to watch a person get 40 binary digits in a row and then repeat them back without error. However, if you think of this merely as a mnemonic trick for extending the memory span, you will miss the more important point that is implicit in nearly all such mnemonic devices. The point is that recoding is an extremely powerful weapon for increasing the amount of information that we can deal with. In one form of another we use recoding constantly in our daily behavior.

In my opinion the most customary kind of recoding that we do all the time is to translate into a verbal code. When there is a story or an argument or an idea that we want to remember, we usually try to rephrase it "in our own words." When we witness some event we want to remember, we make a verbal description of the event and then remember our verbalization. Upon recall we recreate by secondary elaboration the details that seem consistent with the particular verbal recoding we happen to have made. The well-known experiment by Carmichael, Hogan, and Walter (1932) on the influence that names have on the recall of visual figures is one demonstration of the process.

The inaccuracy of the testimony of eyewitnesses is well known in legal psychology, but the distortions of testimony are not random—they follow naturally from the particular recoding that the witness used, and the particular recoding he used depends upon his whole life history. Our language is tremendously useful for repackaging material into a few chunks rich in information. I suspect that imagery is a form of recoding, too, but images seem much harder to get at operationally and to study experimentally than the more symbolic kinds of recoding.

It seems probable that even memorization can be studied in these terms. The process of memorizing may be simply the formation of chunks, or groups of items that go together, until there are few enough chunks so that we can recall all the items. The work by Bousfield and Cohen (1955) on the occurrence of clustering in the recall of words is especially interesting in this respect.

SUMMARY

I have come to the end of the data that I wanted to present, so I would like now to make some summarizing remarks.

First, the span of absolute judgment and the span of immediate memory impose severe limitations on the amount of information that we are able to receive, process, and remember. By organizing the stimulus input simultaneously into several dimensions and successively into a sequence of chunks, we manage to break (or at least stretch) this informational bottleneck.

Second, the process of recoding is a very important one in human psychology and deserves much more explicit attention than it has received. In particular, the kind of linguistic recoding that people do seems to me to be the very life blood of the thought processes. Recoding procedures are a constant concern to clinicians, social psychologists, linguists, and anthropologists and yet, probably because recoding is less accessible to experimental manipulation than nonsense syllables or T mazes, the traditional experimental psychologist has contributed little or nothing to their analysis. Nevertheless, experimental techniques can be used, methods of recoding can be specified, behavioral indicants can be found. And I anticipate that we will find a very orderly set of relations describing what now seems an uncharted wilderness of individual differences.

Third, the concepts and measures provided by the theory of information provide a quantitative way of getting at some of these questions. The theory provides us with a yardstick for calibrating our stimulus materials and for measuring the performance of our subjects. In the interests of communication I have suppressed the technical details of information measurement and have tried to express the ideas in more familiar terms; I hope this paraphrase will not lead you to think they are not useful in research. Informational concepts have already proved valuable in the study of discrimination and of language; they promise a great deal in the study of learning and memory; and it has even been proposed that they can be useful in the study of concept formation. A lot of questions that seemed fruitless twenty or thirty years ago may now be worth another look. In fact, I feel that my story here must stop just as it begins to get really interesting.

And finally, what about the magical number seven? What about the seven wonders of the world, the seven seas, the seven deadly sins, the seven daughters of Atlas in the Pleiades, the seven ages of man, the seven levels of hell, the seven primary colors, the seven notes of the musical scale, and the seven days of the week? What about the seven-point rating scale, the seven categories for absolute judgment, the seven objects in the span of attention, and the seven digits in the span of immediate memory? For the present I propose to withhold judgment. Perhaps there is something deep and profound behind all these sevens, something just calling out for us to discover it. But I suspect that it is only a pernicious, Pythagorean coincidence.

The differences between our ability to make absolute judgments and to retain things in immediate memory result from differences in the types of information processing involved. When we try to make an absolute judgment we are trying to encode information. That is, we are trying to categorize the stimulus input according to previously learned classifications. The span of immediate memory, however, is a measure of our ability to retain material that has already been encoded; this is a very important distinction. The limit on span seems to be determined by the number of items we are trying to retain; the limit on absolute judgments seems to be determined by the number of judgments we are trying to make.

By the time something gets into immediate memory it has already received a good deal of processing. For one thing, it seems to have been translated into meaningful units. It makes sense that the number of meaningful components we can retain is not related to the amount of information contained in the original stimulus material. It also makes sense that we can improve our apparent memory span by recoding or "chunking" the items we are trying to remember. After all, any meaningful item ought to be just as difficult to remember as any other meaningful item, regardless of the number of physical attributes actually represented. In fact, it would be surprising if the limit of immediate memory were related to stimulus parameters. Meanings attached to words have little relationship to the sound or shape of what we speak or write (with the special exception of onomatopoeic words), so why should our memory for these meanings have any relationship to simple stimulus parameters?

The immediate memory we are discussing here is quite different from the visual information storage discussed earlier in this chapter. The visual storage maintained an image of the stimulus for a duration sufficient to let the encoding of visual shapes into meaningful components take place. The output of visual short-term memory enters the immediate memory that we have just been discussing.

The important question we must ask about immediate memory concerns the limit on its span. Why seven items? Why a limit at all? This limited memory is very strange because there does not seem to be any limit on the amount of material that we are able to learn: we can retain millions, even billions of things. How do we learn those millions of items if we have such a small capacity in immediate memory? These issues define the area of study now called "short-term memory." The questions and the area are not new; later we shall read what William James said about it in 1890, but modern concepts of the properties of short-term memory developed about the time that Miller wrote his article on the magical number seven. Before we turn to theories of immediate or short-term memory (later, we also call it "primary memory"), let us detour slightly in order to review the experimental procedures that are in common use.

EXPERIMENTS ON SHORT-TERM MEMORY

Experimental Procedures

There are many ways to test a subject's recollection of previously presented stimulus items. In recent years, however, a fairly standard form of experimental design has been used by those interested in short-term memory. Basically, we present a subject with a set of stimulus items in serial order, one item at a time, for some fixed period of time. After all the items have been presented once, a short period may follow during which he is asked to do some irrelevant task. Then he is given a test to determine his memory of the items.

The purpose of the irrelevant task is to impose a controlled delay between presentation of the stimulus item and its test in order to minimize how much the subject rehearses the items. Typical tasks used in these delay periods include requiring the subject to count backward rapidly from some arbitrary starting point (often he must count backward by threes, e.g., 572, 569, 566, . . .) or to name or write things presented at a rate that is difficult for him to follow. In many experiments the irrelevant task is eliminated completely, and the presentation of later stimulus items acts as an irrelevant task for the retention of the earlier items.

A variety of testing procedures can be used to determine how much a subject remembers about the stimulus list, but they all can be reduced to two basic methods. One, *recall,* is to ask the subject to recite what he remembers of the items shown him, giving him a point for each item that matches one on the stimulus list. The other testing procedure, *recognition,* is to show the subject test items and ask him to decide whether or not they were part of the stimulus list.

These are simplified abstractions of the actual procedures. As might be expected, there are many possible variations: in *free recall,* subjects are allowed to recollect as many items as they can in whatever order they like; in *serial recall,* they must report the items in the same order in which they were presented; in *ordered recall* they can report the items in any order they please, but they must also report the order or position of their presentation; in *probed recall,* the subject is presented with some cue for the proper item, sometimes an associate of the item, sometimes its location in the list, sometimes a neighboring item, and sometimes a portion of the item itself. The list of alternative testing methods using the recall procedure can be extended indefinitely, with today's list being extended by the ingenuity of tomorrow's experimenter.

Th same sort of catalog can be made for recognition tests of memory. The main variations, however, center around two themes: the number of tests that a subject is given for each stimulus list, and the number of items used per test. Thus, in *simple recognition,* one test item is presented and the subject must decide whether or not it appeared in the list. In *multiple alternative* situations, however, the subject is presented with several test items: his job is to decide which one was presented earlier. A recall test of memory can be considered to be a form of multiple alternative tests of memory whenever the subject knows the set of possible answers.

The Study of Errors

How do we determine the properties of stored material? Perhaps the most powerful way to begin is to look at the types of errors that are made in using the information. We assume that an error occurs when only part of the stored representation of an item has been recovered, either because the remainder of the trace has temporarily eluded our attempts to recover it or because it has been lost from the storage. The part that can be recovered tells us something about the organization of the memory. We can examine the relationship of the recovered material to the original: what physical features are still retained; what psychological features; what distortions occur?

A simple question, related to the studies of pattern recognition reviewed in Chapter 3, concerns the manner by which simple objects are represented in storage. For example, in what form do we encode letters of the alphabet? If letters were stored in a form analogous to their visual appearance, then we might suspect that as the memory trace became less distinct, letters that were similar in shape (such as *P* and *F*) might get confused with one another.

In the 1960s, at the Applied Psychology Research Unit in Cambridge, England, Conrad performed a number of experiments to examine the type of errors subjects make in short-term memory tasks using visually presented letters as the items to be remembered (Conrad, 1959, 1962, 1964; Conrad and Hull, 1964). Conrad had to perform several experiments. First, he had to show that the errors observed in his experiments were introduced by the memory rather than the perceptual system. Second, he had to determine the nature of confusions caused by deficits in memory. Third, he had to discover the scheme of storage that would lead to the errors found.

Conrad was able to demonstrate that items recalled incorrectly were acoustically related to the original items, even when the material had been presented visually. Thus, the stored representation was related to the spoken representation. It is as if rehearsal of verbal material were an auditory (or spoken) process, with the memory being for what has been rehearsed rather than for what has actually been presented. Conrad's results have played an important role in the development of theories of memory, as we have seen in earlier chapters and will see again in the next chapter.

The procedures followed in these experiments are fairly straightforward, but the interpretation of the results is not so simple. The basic datum is the *matrix of confusions*: the table that indicates the relative frequency with which each possible letter has been confused with each of the other possible letters. If storage were related to the visual form of letters, we would expect that the letter *E* might sometimes be remembered as an *F* and the letter *C* might be remembered as an *S*. In fact, we often remember an *E* as a *C* and an *F* as an *S*. Although it is very easy to distinguish the matrix resulting from confusions among acoustical representations of letters from that resulting from visual representations, other distinctions are not so easily determined. For example, is the stored representation of letters more closely related to the actual sounds of the spoken letters—an auditory representation—or to the movements or motor commands used to speak the sounds—an articulatory representation? The difference between articulatory and auditory representation is very important in the assessment of theories of speech perception. In order to distinguish among these representations we would need to generate classes of items that differ from one another in one aspect, say articulation, but do not differ much by another aspect, say in their sounds.[4]

Although subtle distinctions are difficult to make from an analysis of confusion in memory, nonetheless, the method has proved to be very powerful in determining many of the characteristics of stored material. This approach has also been used to study the linguistic constituents of spoken sounds (Wickelgren, 1965a, 1966a), to determine how a series of items are stored and linked to one another (Conrad, 1965; Wickelgren, 1965b, 1966a, b, c), and to distinguish the properties of short- and long-term storage (Baddeley, 1966).

The study of errors indicates that when a person is presented with words to remember, the encoding within short-term memory is related to their acoustical properties. This result has attracted a good deal of interest about the storage and rehearsal mechanisms of people who are congenitally deaf and must therefore use some other method of encoding. Bellugi, Klima, and Siple (1975) found that deaf subjects in the United States made errors in memory that reflected the organizational features of American Sign Language (ASL), implying that both encoding and rehearsal took place in a form of mental signing. (Also see the paper by Conrad, 1970.)

The analysis of errors has proved to be a fruitful way of exploring the properties of memory. That acoustic confusions occur in the early stages of the processing of verbal material is established without doubt. But too much should not be made of this fact. It does not mean that we say to ourselves all the material that we intend to learn, for this would be ridiculous. Surely we learn nonverbal experiences without any recourse to words. The verbalization seems to apply only to the learning of verbal material, where there are several good reasons why it should take place. For one thing, it is sensible that the memory system encode equivalent information in the same way regardless of the form in which it is received. Thus, spoken speech and printed words have the same meaning,

---

[4] Throughout this book the terms *"acoustical"* and *"auditory"* are used somewhat interchangeably with reference to the encoding of information in memory. This should be interpreted to mean that the encoding is related to some aspect of speech, but no implication should be drawn about the relative importance of either the speech sounds or the speech articulation in the memory encoding.

so why not have one means of accessing them? Because people learn to hear and speak before learning to read and write, it is sensible that the spoken word be the common base. In addition, we are highly practiced in dealing with written and spoken material, and by the arguments that we presented in preceding chapters, this causes the responses to such material to become automatic. Hence, the Stroop effect, in which verbal responses are made to printed names even when a person wishes not to.

It makes sense that there should be acoustic encoding of verbal material—and thereby acoustic confusions—early in the stages of processing. But meaningful interpretation should also occur, for as we have seen, the actual understanding of incoming sensory information takes place by the interactions of data driven analyses with meaningful, conceptually driven analyses. So we should get some semantic confusion early on as well, as indeed we do (see Shulman, 1970, 1972).

Rehearsal

Rehearsal is a type of inner speech by which we maintain a limited amount of material in memory indefinitely. We all use rehearsal when we remember something, for example, a telephone number, by "saying it to ourselves."

The fact that we act as if we were saying something to ourselves does not necessarily imply that we are actually speaking or even using any of our speech mechanisms. The primary implications of rehearsal lie in its more obvious characteristics. Material that is learned or retained through rehearsal appears to be stored in a form that is related to the way it is performed. Thus, mistakes in retention of words are likely to bear acoustic or phonetic relations to the correct item, even if the material was originally presented visually. Second, rehearsal is a serial process; only one item can be rehearsed at any one time. Third, it is slow; it occurs at the rate of three to six items per second.

It is an easy matter to teach subjects how to rehearse or to give them distracting tasks to do so they cannot rehearse. (A favorite task that seems to prevent subjects from rehearsing previously presented materials is to have them count backward by threes, aloud, and at a rapid rate.) These manipulations change the amount and character of material that can be remembered. Thus, although no one really understands the nature or purpose of rehearsal, it is easy to control the way that subjects do it, thereby controlling the way that material is learned.

Note that the nature of rehearsal is highly dependent on the nature of the items that are being rehearsed. For the normal subject, when the items being retained are words, then rehearsal appears to be vocal in nature. For the congenitally deaf subject, however, words appear to be rehearsed through sign language, and the errors made by the deaf in memory reflect confusions among memories for signs (Bellugi, Klima, and Siple, 1975). When the items to be rehearsed are not words, but are actions, sounds, visual scenes, tastes, or smells, then the rehearsal tends to mimic the properties of these sensory modalities. Almost nothing is known about rehearsal for nonverbal items, but almost everyone has experienced it. In Chapter 9 we will see that professional musicians and sports players often devote hours each day to mental rehearsal. Mentally going through the actions of hitting a ball, or a fancy acrobatic maneuver, or playing a difficult musical passage is thought to improve the performance of these skills. While we will emphasize the rehearsal of verbal material and talk of acoustic confusion in the memory of newly learned items, we should remember that these discussions are relevant only to studies of the learning of words.

Memory for Nonverbal Material

Words have been studied extensively for two rather obvious reasons. First, they provide a convenient source of material. It is easy to explain to the subject what is wanted, and the subject, in turn, finds it easy to work with words. Second, the use of language is of such importance to human communication that the study of all aspects of language—which includes the memory for words—is an obvious step to take.

We must be careful, of course, that our conclusions about memory systems do not become distorted because of the heavy predominance of studies that examine simple verbal materials. It is important that we also examine memory for pictures, for faces, for body movements, and essentially for all types of human experiences. Later in this book we will briefly review some of the results of experiments on memory for other types of materials. At the moment, however, we are faced with the fact that the majority of studies from which we draw our conclusions are studies for verbal material.

There is one more problem with the memory for words that must be considered. When we study a person's memory for a list of words that have just been presented, we really are not studying how well the words themselves are retained, but rather whether the person can remember which words were part of the experimental study. That is, if we present a word list such as

house
cord
limb

pile
dune
beef

to someone saying that we will test the memory later on, we are really not testing whether the words are familiar. All those words are known by subjects. What we really are testing is whether the subject remembers that they appeared in a particular list.

For another example of the same point, suppose we do an experiment on the recognition of people. We take 25 people who are completely unknown to the subject and parade them before him, one at a time, 10 seconds per person. Then, later, we mix those 25 people with 25 new ones. Now, we parade each of these 50 people before our subject, one at a time. As each person comes into view, the subject is asked to judge whether that person is one of the people seen earlier.

This experiment is a true test of memory. It gets at how well faces are learned and retained. It is not the same as an experiment performed with a list of 25 words, in which each word is shown to the subject for 10 seconds and then combined with 25 other words and re-presented to the subject. With words, all the items were already familiar to the subject; with people, none of the items were familiar. When we tested for memory of the people, the question was:

Have you ever seen this person before?

When we tested for the memory of the words, we could not ask

Have you ever seen this word before?

because all were common words that had been seen many times before. Instead, we had to ask where the word had been encountered:

Was this one of the words that was just shown to you?

One question requires pure recognition, the other episodic recognition. That is, asking whether a person recognizes an item is asking whether it has ever been experienced before, without regard to when or where. Asking if an item was one seen in a particular time or context is asking for memory of the episode in which it was experienced. Later on, in Chapter 8, we see that the distinction between these two issues is an important aspect of the representation of information within memory, a distinction discussed as the difference between *semantic* and *episodic* *memory.*

EARLY THEORIES OF SHORT-TERM MEMORY

The recent view on the nature of immediate memory is that it represents a temporary storage device that can retain a small, limited amount of material. Almost every designer of modern information processing devices has discovered that it is necessary to have temporary storage units at all places that communicate with the environment (i.e., on all input-output lines). These storage units or buffers are necessary because the mode and speed at which information processes can take place within the device differ from the mode and speed at which information can be received from or transmitted to the environment. The arguments saying that these buffers are necessary on man-made equipment are very general ones; they apply to anything attempting to perform logical operations on information received from the environment. Hence, they should apply to living organisms as well as to artificial ones. Of course, logical arguments about the desirability of a mechanism such as short-term memory are certainly not proof of its existence in humans.

If, for the moment, we accept the argument that special short-term memory does exist, we still have to determine its properties. One of the earliest detailed descriptions of the possible operation of a short-term memory was provided by the English psychologist John Brown, in a series of papers published in 1958 and 1959. He suggested that material in this memory fades away in time unless some effort is made to retain it by means of rehearsal. Rehearsal, he argued, maintains an item in short-term memory by renewing the trace of the item in much the same way that a new presentation of that item would revive it. Once the rehearsal ceases, however, the item decays as if it had just been presented. Thus, in short-term memory, rehearsal serves to prolong a trace, but has no other effect. We must assume, however, that rehearsal of an item would also increase its likelihood of being stored permanently, perhaps in a different memory system. This argument was not stressed by Brown, but it would appear to be a logical extension of his theory. In fact, it is needed by almost any theory of memory because, after all, we do remember some items for very long periods of time. Any theorist who proposes a short-term memory model in which all items eventually decay to nonexistence is obviously restricting himself from considering the properties of long-term memory.

John Brown specified two other things in his theory. One point was the nature of decay. The process of decay was considered to be analogous to the process of adding noise to the memory trace. Thus, the image in memory became less and less distinct over time, with a continual decrease in the number of details that could be recovered. Memory errors increase as the image decays, with the incorrectly recalled items bearing some similarity to the original. The other point Brown made was that an unrehearsed memory trace decayed as a result of the passage of time. This point has been much disputed lately, with an opposing view contending that time has little effect on the material stored in memory. It is, of course, very difficult to distinguish a theory that postulates decay in time from one that postulates decay caused by interference, primarily because it is not possible to do the one critical experiment everyone would accept. The critical experiment would be to present material to a subject, have him do nothing for some period of time, and then test his retention of the items. The interference theorist would predict no loss: the time theorist would predict substantial loss. The catch is that it is not possible for a subject to "do nothing." Rehearsal, thinking, conscious and un-conscious processes all occur continually. There is no simple switch we can throw to turn a subject "off" for a short period of time. Who is to say, then, whether any decay in memory is a result of the passage of time or activity?

The rate of forgetting of poorly rehearsed material was demonstrated by Lloyd and Margaret Peterson at Indiana University in 1959. In order to minimize rehearsal, they had their subjects perform a task that was both irrelevant to the memory task and difficult. The task was to count backward (by threes) from a randomly determined starting point in time with the rhythm produced by a metronome. The memory task itself was to retain a sequence of three consonant letters. Normally, it is not difficult to retain three letters, but in this experiment, the deterioration was almost complete after 18 seconds.

Rapid decay of material from memory occurs only under limited experimental conditions that include the presence of some interfering (or rehearsal-preventing) task. This suggests that the span of immediate memory is limited primarily by the rehearsal process. A possible memory system is one in which the limited capacity of immediate memory is due to difficulty in rehearsing too many items at once. Rehearsal might serve both to maintain material in immediate memory and to help transfer it to a more permanent store. This theory was proposed in 1965 by Waugh and Norman and is stated in the next selection.

Primary Memory*

NANCY C. WAUGH and DONALD A. NORMAN

It is a well-established fact that the longest series of unrelated digits, letters, or words that a person can recall verbatim after one presentation seldom exceeds 10 items. It is also true, however, that one can nearly always recall the most recent item in a series, no matter how long the series—but only if this item may be recalled immediately, or if it may be rehearsed during the interval between its presentation and recall. Otherwise it is very likely to be

* Nancy C. Waugh and Donald A. Norman. Primary memory. Psychological Review. 1965, 72, 89, 92–93. Copyright © 1965 by the American Psychological Association and reprinted with their permission.

lost. If we may assume that attending to a current item precludes reviewing a prior one, we can say that the span of immediate memory must be limited in large part by our inability to rehearse, and hence retain, the early items in a sequence while attempting to store the later ones. Our limited memory span would then be but one manifestation of our general inability to think about two things at the same time.

Why should an unrehearsed item in a list be forgotten so swiftly? Is its physiological trace in some sense written over by the traces of the items that follow it? Or does this trace simply decay within a brief interval, regardless of how that interval is filled?

— — —

We shall assume here that rehearsal simply denotes the recall of a verbal item—either immediate or delayed, silent or overt, deliberate or involuntary. The initial perception of a stimulus probably must also qualify as a rehearsal. Obviously a very conspicuous item or one that relates easily to what we have already learned can be retained with a minimum of conscious effort. We assume that relatively homogeneous or unfamiliar material must, on the other hand, be deliberately rehearsed if it is to be retained. Actually, we shall not be concerned here with the exact role of rehearsal in the memorization process. We are simply noting that, in the usual verbal-learning experiment, the likelihood that an item in a homogeneous list will be recalled tends to increase with the amount of time available for its rehearsal.

— — —

Conversely, material which is not rehearsed is rapidly lost, regardless of the rate at which it is presented. It is as though rehearsal transferred a recently perceived verbal item from one memory store of very limited capacity to another more commodious store from which it can be retrieved at a much later time.

We shall follow James (1890) in using the terms *primary* and *secondary memory* (PM and SM) to denote the two stores. James defined these terms introspectively: an event in PM has never left consciousness and is part of the psychological present, while an event recalled from SM has been absent from consciousness and belongs to the psychological past. PM is a faithful record of events just perceived; SM is full of gaps and distortions. James believed that PM extends over a fixed period of time. We propose instead that it encompasses a certain number of events regardless of the time they take to occur. Our goal is to distinguish operationally between PM and SM on the basis of the model that we shall now describe.

Consider the general scheme illustrated in Fig. 5.2. Every verbal item that is attended to enters PM. As we have seen, the capacity of this system is sharply limited. New items displace old ones; displaced items are permanently lost. When an item is rehearsed, however, it remains in PM, and it

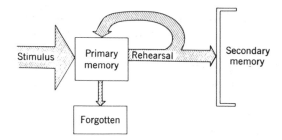

Fig. 5.2. The primary and secondary memory system. All verbal items enter primary memory, where they are either rehearsed or forgotten. Rehearsed items may enter secondary memory.

may enter into SM. We should like to assume, for the sake of simplicity, that the probability of its entering SM is independent of its position in a series and of the time at which it is rehearsed. Thus, it would not matter whether the item was rehearsed immediately on entering PM or several seconds later: as long as it was in PM, it would make the transition into SM with fixed probability.

In their discussions, Waugh and Norman placed heavy emphasis on the role of rehearsal in prolonging the period of storage of material in primary memory and increasing the likelihood of entry into secondary memory. Rehearsal for grammatical material is both a serial and a verbal process. If rehearsal plays the roles suggested, then it may be the key to the relation between attention and memory. We have seen that when one channel of information is being attended to, little information is retained about the properties of the other channel. Even more striking, when subjects shadow verbal material, they have little retention of the material just shadowed, even though this material must have undergone considerable processing by the nervous system in order for it to be heard and repeated verbally. Could it be that the difficulty of performing the shadowing task precludes the possibility of rehearsal, thus minimizing the longer-term retention of the shadowed material?

The picture just presented of memory makes for nice reading, but is it accurate? It will take a while for the slow process of scientific investigation to reach definitive conclusions, but meanwhile it might be wise to review some of the arguments now going on and mention some of the problems not well handled by the sensory-primary-secondary division of memory.

One experimental finding that must be explained by any theory of memory is the serial position effect of recall. The serial position effect refers to the fact that when a list of homogeneous items is learned, best retention will occur for the two ends of the list and poorest retention will be in the middle. The exact shape of the serial position curve depends on a number of experimental variables, but the basic fact that the beginning and end of a list of items show increased retention over the others occurs again and again in a variety of experimental settings.

The relative superiority of items at the end of the list (recent items and, hence, the recency effect) over those at the middle can be accounted for by the primary memory phenomenon. When the list has just been presented, the last items are still in primary memory and can be recalled immediately. Even if immediate recall of last items is prevented, they may still be rehearsed. Since, by definition, no items are presented after the last one, the rehearsal tends to be prolonged and effective. If both immediate recall and rehearsal of the last items of a list are prevented, the recency effect ought to disappear, and indeed it does.

Early items in a list also receive superior recall, and this effect cannot be explained as simply as the recency effect. Waugh and Norman ignored the problem by restricting their analysis to items beyond the first few. Knowledge does not come through ignorance, however, and it is clear that eventually the phenomenon will have to be explained. A possible explanation, compatible with the multiple memory assumption, is that early items in a list received increased attention over later ones and, hence, are more likely to be transferred to longer-term memory systems. By this notion, therefore, the serial position effect in short-term memory experiments is due to increased attention of early items and the easy recall of late items from primary memory. The evidence necessary to support the theory comes from the fact that it is possible to modify the shape of the serial position curve dramatically by instructing the subject how he should spend his time. We can flatten the initial part of the curve by asking the subject to spend "equal amounts of attention on each item." ("Think about each item when it is presented; when a new item is presented, concentrate on it. Do not think of any of the earlier items.") It is also possible to enhance the memory of the first item by suitable instructions. ("Concentrate all your attention on the first item even while the other items are being presented.")

A second theory suggests that transfer from primary to secondary storage is performed by an attention or rehearsal mechanism that can handle only one item at a time. The first item presented in a list automatically receives full attention of the processor. The second and later items must wait until the first item has finished. A queue is formed of items waiting for transfer into longer-term memories. Items toward the end of the list have an increasing probability of being forgotten before their turn comes up.

A different type of theoretical explanation of the increased retention of early items is that of proactive interference. The experimental finding is simple: retention decreases with the number of similar *previous* tasks. The normal explanations for proactive interference are based on an interference theory in which memory traces from earlier learned material become confused with traces from material presently being learned. Early items in a list suffer least from proactive interference effects.

How Many Memories?

A common argument against the existence of several different types of memories is that similar laws apply to phenomena attributed to different systems. The same serial position effect is noticed in studies of short-term memory as in studies of long-term memory, the same type of proactive interference, the same relationship between similarity of items and ease of retention, and the same relationships, in fact, for a long list of psychological phenomena. These similarities of behavior can be taken to imply that there is but one type of memory, with perhaps different modes of excitation. What we have been calling sensory memory may simply represent a rapid decay of traces in the memory; what we have been calling primary memory may be a somewhat slower decay of the traces in the memory; what we have been calling secondary memory might be an even slower decay of the same memory. In fact, one of the parameters of memory might simply be the rate at which stored information is dissipated. According to this argument, then, we are mistaken when we attempt to attribute different rates of decay to different memory systems.

Waugh and Norman were aware of this controversy and they responded in this way:

DISCUSSION

We should at this point like to consider the general question of whether all verbal information is stored in the same system or whether, as we have assumed here, there are two independent mnemonic processes that contribute to retention even over very short intervals. The proponents of a unitary theory of memory, eloquently led by Melton (1963), have argued that recall after a few seconds is affected in very similar ways by the variables that govern recall over much longer intervals; and that therefore the distinction between a short-term memory mechanism, on the one hand, and a longer–term mechanism, on the other, is purely arbitrary. The following facts have been cited in support of this argument:

1. Short-term retention improves, just as does long-term retention, when the material to be recalled is repeated before a test of retention, or when it is repeated between successive tests (Hebb, 1961; Hellyer, 1962).
2. Retention after a brief delay is subject to proactive interference, as is retention after a long delay (Keppel and Underwood,

1962; Loess, 1964). Why, asks the unitary theorist, should we distinguish between short- and long-term retention if we cannot find any quantitative and experimentally manipulatable differences between them? This question might well be disturbing if one took the position that the two processes have sharply defined non-overlapping temporal boundaries such that items recalled within some critical interval after their initial occurrence must have been retrieved from one system, whereas items recalled beyond this interval must have been retrieved from another. (Such a view would imply, interestingly enough, that an item would have to remain in a short-term storage for some specified number of seconds before passing into longer term storage, if it did so at all.)

But what if we do not require that the two systems be mutually exclusive? Then the probability that an item will be recalled will depend on both the probability that it is still in PM and the probability that it has entered into SM in the interval between its presentation and the start of the interfering sequence (or even during this sequence, if the subject is able to rehearse). All those variables that determine the likelihood of recalling a given item from SM—such as its position in a closely spaced series of tests, or the number of times it has been repeated—will then determine the observed proportion recalled after a brief interval. We believe we have shown, however, that the likelihood of recalling an item from PM depends only upon how far it was from the end of the list, quite independent of whether or not it was also in SM; and we submit that most of the published data on short-term retention actually reflect the properties of both memory systems.

We would like to make one final point: the existence of some rather compelling introspective evidence in favor of two distinct mnemonic systems. PM, as we have defined it here, is best illustrated by a person's ability to recall verbatim the most recent few words in a sentence that he is hearing or speaking, even when he is barely paying attention to what is being said, or to what he is saying. Given that the flow of speech is intelligible, failures in the immediate recall of words we have just heard—errors of either omission, transposition, or substitution—are probably so rare as to be abnormal. Indeed, we believe that it would be impossible to understand or to generate a grammatical utterance if we lacked this rather remarkable mnemonic capacity. In order to recall a sentence verbatim at a later time, however, we usually have to rehearse it while it is still available in PM.

The same effect holds for meaningless arrangements of verbal items. If we present a subject with a random string of words, letters, or digits, and ask him to reproduce them in any order he chooses, he can maximize the number he recalls by "unloading" the last few items immediately. Most subjects in free-recall experiments report that these very late items tend to be lost if they are not recalled immediately, whereas items that came earlier in the list can be retrieved at leisure, if they can be recalled at all. In the colorful terminology of one such subject (Waugh, 1961), the most recent items in a verbal series reside temporarily in a kind of "echo box," from which they can be effortlessly parroted back. When an experienced subject is trying to memorize a list of serial items, moreover, he "fills up" successive echo boxes as the list is read to him and attempts to rehearse the contents of each. He will invariably lose some items if rehearsal is delayed too long or if he attempts to load his echo box with more items than it can hold. We think it very likely that the PM function describes the (variable) capacity of this mechanism. We would remind you in this connection that, within very broad limits, the rate at which someone is speaking does not affect your ability to follow his words —just as differences in the rate at which meaningless lists of digits are presented do not exert any profound effect on the PM function (Pages 100–102).

In the years since 1965 new experiments have been performed, and new knowledge has surfaced. Today, the picture looks somewhat different than it did then, but the effort to learn the older, neat picture will not be wasted. As you will see, the new picture builds heavily on the conceptualization you have just finished reading. Recent work simply provides a better viewpoint.

SUGGESTED READINGS

Studies of visual short-term memory are numerous. A review of much of the work is provided in the article by Dick (1974). Theoretical treatments are provided by Rumelhart's book (in press), Estes (1973, 1974), and Shiffrin and Geisler (1973). Treisman, Russell, and Green (1975) showed that visual short-term memory can maintain information about movement.

The literature on other memory systems is not quite so easy to find. Bliss, Crane, Mansfield, and Townsend (1966) studied the tactile system. Some studies of taste and odor have been performed, but the difficulties of experimentation with those stimuli preclude any firm results so far. Darwin, Turvey, and Crowder (1972), and Massaro (1972, 1975) have looked at auditory short-term memory. These studies are reviewed in Massaro's book (1975), which also provides a good general review. The book edited by Deutsch and Deutsch (1975) on short-term memory is an excellent source.

One line of investigation not included in this chapter is the work initiated by Sternberg on the method of retrieving information held in short-term memory. Sternberg's experiments have revealed some interesting puzzles. A subject is either presented with a list of items to remember or asked to recall a list of items from long-term memory. Then the subject is shown an item and asked to judge as quickly as possible whether that new item was a member of the list. The amount of time that it takes to make the judgment is a linear function of the number of items in the list, regardless of whether the correct answer is yes or no. The results imply that subjects must search their short-term memories in their entirety in order to determine whether an item is in the memory. This appears to be true despite the possibility that the subject may come across the item early in the search. Sternberg argues that the entire list must be scanned anyway. (The argument is that the subject is not aware of finding the item until the search phase has been completed. Then the subject can ask whether anything was found during the search phase and select the appropriate response.) As might be imagined, these experiments have generated a lot of interest. The best review paper is Sternberg (1975).

Reitman (1971) attempted to determine whether information in short-term memory disappears by the passage of time or as a result of inter-ference from other material. The distinction is difficult; the obvious experi-ment is to present material to a person, then wait some period of time and see if the material is still present. If material decays with the passage of time, it should not be present. Obviously, however, subjects simply rehearse the material during the time period, and so the result is mean-ingless unless some method of stopping rehearsal during the retention period can be found. This is not easy to accomplish, for the method of stopping rehearsal cannot itself be thought to interfere with retention of information in short-term memory.[5]

Reitman distracted her subjects from rehearsing by having them listen to a series of sounds, requiring them to detect slight variations in the series as they listened. These experiments appeared to demonstrate that in the absence of rehearsal, when no new interfering material was presented to a person, memory did not decay. The result was repeated by Shiffrin (1973), but a different series of similar experiments, using a different kind of rehearsal-prevention task, cast some suspicion on the results (Watkins, Watkins, Craik, and Mazuryk, 1973). Finally, Reit-man herself repeated her original experiments, this time with a very ex-tensive and exhaustive analysis of what her subjects actually did during the retention interval (Reitman, 1974). Her results are summarized in the

[5] It is at times like this that experimental psychologists wish for mysterious hypnotic powers that would allow them to command their subjects "Here is a word. Now, let your mind go blank and think of nothing until I snap my fingers. Then tell me the word." Alas, such powers do not exist. In the case of hypnotic suggestion, one would have to prove that the subject's mind did indeed go blank and that no rehearsal took place. Even a casual reading of Hilgard's (1975) review of the current status of hyp-nosis indicates that this would be no easy task.

title of her article: "Without Surreptitious Rehearsal, Information in Short-Term Memory Decays."

The mechanism for retention and for loss of information in short-term memory still remains unexplained. Yes, material does get lost from short-term memory unless rehearsed (whether surreptitiously or overtly), but this by itself proves little. There seems to be less loss when there is less interference from memory for other items, which is why the rehearsal can be surreptitious—not very much is needed. The obvious, but as yet unproved, conclusion is that information in short-term memory is lost as a result of both time and interference from other items.

6
Depth of Processing

The preceding chapter provided a straightforward portrayal of the structure of memory. There are three forms of memory: sensory short-term storage (such as visual short-term memory), short-term or primary memory, and long-term or secondary memory. Material is transferred from short- to long-term memory by the process of rehearsal.

This description is too simple. The structure is simply not viable; it provides a convenient outline, but there is much left unsaid. How do the processes of attention and pattern recognition interact with memory? Can rehearsal be the way that new information gets into long-term memory? Yes, to learn a telephone number or a new word in a foreign language, we quite often will rehearse it, repeating it over and over again to ourselves. But rehearsal is a slow, laborious process and not very effective. I hope you have learned something from the other chapters of this book, but certainly not by energetically rehearsing each new concept.

Consider the process of interpreting the world, the process discussed in Chapter 3. We make sense out of sensory information by comparing it with information learned previously, information that must be in long-term storage. The process of pattern recognition requires that information from sensory sources and from long-term memory interact. In order to read, we must decipher the arbitrary symbols on the page into the underlying words and meaning. This could not be done without extensive interaction with permanently stored information. Thus, by the time information gets into short-term memory it must already have been processed by means of information in long-term memory.

CONTROL STRUCTURES

The warnings that the simple stage model of memory was indeed oversimplified came early in the game. Two lines of research were influential. First, there was the emphasis on the flexibility of the human being's use of his own internal processes: the emphasis on *control structures*. Second, it became increasingly obvious that the purposeful activities people engaged in had important effects on how well they remembered things. People who were asked to organize or to make meaningful judgments about material presented to them often were able to recall it later, even though not asked to remember it. Other people given the same material for the same length of time and simply asked to learn it often failed to remember it as well as those who had only organized it. The best way to learn new material seems to be to use it in a meaningful way.

Let us examine these early statements of human flexibility. The importance of control processes was first pointed out by Atkinson and Shiffrin, both then at Stanford University.

Control Processes in Memory*

RICHARD ATKINSON and RICHARD SHIFFRIN

The term *control process* refers to those processes that are not permanent features of memory, but are instead transient phenomena under the control of the subject; their appearance depends on such factors as instructional set, the experimental task, and the past history of the subject.

— — —

CODING PROCESSES AND TRANSFER BETWEEN SHORT- AND LONG-TERM STORE

— — —

Transfer from [short-term store (STS)] to [long-term store (LTS)] may be considered a permanent feature of memory; any information in STS is transferred to LTS to some degree throughout its stay in the short-term store. The important aspect of this transfer, however, is the wide variance in the amount and form of the transferred information that may be induced by control processes. When the subject is concentrating upon rehearsal, the information transferred would be in a relatively weak state and easily subject to interference. On the other hand, the subject may divert his effort from rehearsal to various coding operations which will increase the strength of the

* R. Shiffrin and R. Atkinson. Human memory: A proposed system and its control processes. The Psychology of Learning and Motivation. K. W. Spence and J. T. Spence (Eds.). Vol. 2. New York: Academic Press, 1968. Pages 106; 115–116. Copyright © 1968 by Academic Press, Inc. With permission of authors and publisher.

stored information. In answer to the question of what is a coding process, we can most generally state that a coding process is a select alteration and/or addition to the information in the short-term store as the result of a search of the long-term store. This change may take a number of forms, often using strong preexisting associations already in long-term store. A number of these coding possibilities will be considered later.

Experiments may be roughly classified in terms of the control operations the subject will be led to use. Concept formation problems or tasks where there is a clear solution will lead the subject to strategy selection and hypothesis-testing procedures (Restle, 1964). Experiments which do not involve problem solving, where there are a large number of easily coded items, and where there is a long period between presentation and test, will prompt the subject to expend his efforts on long-term coding operations. Finally, experiments in which memory is required, but long-term memory is not efficacious, will lead the subject to adopt rehearsal strategies that maintain the information the limited period needed for the task.

We can contrast two different aspects of a person's information processing structures: fixed structures and flexible structures. Fixed structures are specific neurological entities. The sensory systems, complete with their sense organs, specialized analyzing mechanisms, and sensory information storage systems, are fixed structures. Short-term and long-term memory systems are fixed structures. The ability to rehearse is a fixed structure, for the mechanisms of rehearsal and their effect are permanent, fixed properties of the human organism. The ability to use these fixed structures in variable ways comes about through the flexible structures.

The flexible structures are control processes—the rules and strategies that a person may wish to use. The control of rehearsal is an example of a variable, flexible control process that a person can choose to use in a variety of ways. Thus, the decision of when, what, and how to rehearse can change from moment to moment, depending on the guidance and interpretation from control processes. When one actually rehearses, one must use the fixed structures of the rehearsal and memory mechanisms. Atkinson and Shiffrin contrasted fixed and flexible structures by an analogy between psychological mechanisms and the operations of modern computers. The memory system, they pointed out, can be categorized along two major dimensions.

One categorization distinguishes permanent, structural features of the system from control processes that can be readily modified or reprogrammed at the will of the subject. Because we feel that this distinction helps clarify a number of results, we will take time to elaborate it at the outset. The permanent features of memory, which will be referred to as the memory structure, include both the physical system and the built-in processes that are unvarying and fixed from one situation to another. Control processes, on the other hand, are selected, constructed, and used at the option of the subject and may vary dramatically from one task to another even though superficially the tasks may appear very similar. The use of a particular control process in a given situation will depend upon such factors as the nature of the instructions, the meaningfulness of the material, and the individual subject's history.

A computer analogy might help illustrate the distinction between memory structure and control processes. If the memory system is viewed as a computer under the direction of a programmer at a remote console, then both the computer hardware and those programs built into the system that cannot be modified by the programmer are analogous to our structural features; those programs and instruction sequences which the programmer can write at his console and which determine the operation of the computer, are analogous to our control processes. In the sense that the computer's method of processing a given batch of data depends on the operating program, so the way a stimulus input is processed depends on the particular control processes the subject brings into play. The structural components include the basic memory stores; examples of control processes are coding procedures, rehearsal operations, and search strategies (Page 90).

ORGANIZATION AND MEMORY

The retrieval of material from a large-capacity system such as our long-term or secondary memory must be quite a different process from that of retrieval from a small-capacity storage system, such as primary memory. With any large memory, a random search of the contents becomes impractical. In fact, the knowledge that the information sought is stored in the memory is, by itself, useless. The necessity of an organizational scheme is easily illustrated by the problem faced by a large library. If a book is misplaced on the library shelves, it might as well be lost. It does not matter at all that the book is actually within the library; if it is not in its proper place, it will not be found by any ordinary search. So it is with human memory: even if the information of interest is there, it is useless unless it can be reached. How do we search our memory for a fact we know is there? The problem is to get to the proper associates of the target; once there, the rest flows naturally.

When we deal with verbal material, associations are readily available through the semantic structure of the items. We have already read, however, that our ability to learn verbal material after one presentation seems to be limited to a few words by the principles of the magical number 7. Is it possible to organize verbal material in such a way as to overcome this limitation?

A number of studies of memory have emphasized the role of organization in the learning of verbal material. These studies appear to provide us with a link between the limitations of primary memory and the large capacity of secondary memory through the mechanism of proper and efficient organization. The basic idea arises from Miller's realization that although we seem able to learn no more than seven (plus or minus two) things at any one time, each of these things can be rich in structure and meaning.

A general principle seems to be emerging: people group and categorize the objects they intend to learn. When we look for evidence of this principle, we find it everywhere. Telephone numbers are subdivided into smaller sequences. The names of the months are divided into the four seasons. Poetry is easier to learn than prose. Children naturally form sing-song rhythms of lists they wish to remember. For example, consider how the alphabet is learned. To a child the alphabet is a long, rather arbitrary, string of items. Children go through seemingly endless hours of recitation while they get all the letters together, but they do it in a nice, orderly fashion. They use a rhyme that divides the 26 letters into 3 chunks, each chunk having 2 elements, each element having 2 units, and each unit having 1 to 4 letters. Thus: [(ab—cd) (ef—g)] [(hi—jk) (lmno—p)] [(qrs—tuv) (w—xyz)]. What better example of all the principles we have just enumerated: there is rhythm; there is rhyme; no single chunk is large enough to strain the capacity of primary memory. Do you doubt that you learned the alphabet in this way; do you claim that you know the letters as one whole, smoothly organized unit? Then say the alphabet backward and see if the places you stumble don't match up with the boundaries between the groups you once used.

Grouping, categorization, clustering: these principles have all been demonstrated in the experimental laboratory. Experimental subjects form groups of the items they are trying to learn. Bousfield (1953), Bousfield and Cohen (1955), and Bousfield and Sedgewick (1944) noted clustering in the words recalled by their subjects. Tulving (1962, 1964) examined the response strategies used by subjects learning lists of unrelated words. He found that subjects organized the words and that once formed, these organizations tend to stick throughout the rest of the experiment. That is, once a subject puts together some of the words on the list he is trying to learn, he tends always to recall them together, regardless of the way that the words are scrambled up by the experimenter. Moreover, learning of new words builds on the previously acquired structures.

One must always be wary of comparisons of human psychology with any man-made device, most especially with computers. The human mind is not a computer, and the differences between the two far outweigh the similarities. But both the mind and artificial devices such as computers process information. The demands of basic considerations cause all information-processing structures to have a number of principles in common. Some comparisons between mind and machine are valid. The point made by Atkinson and Shiffrin about the distinction between structural features and control processes is one of these—the distinction is fundamental.

It seems inescapable that the human memory system is organized in such a way that information is arranged in meaningful, useful structural units. That this must be so seems obvious, for the massive quantities of information that each of us has acquired over a lifetime must be organized sensibly if any of it is to be found again. Moreover, the organization seems to put related things together, so that when searching for one thing in memory, we are forced to retrieve all sorts of related material along the way. To remember what you ate for dinner two days ago, you will be forced to remember where and with whom you ate. The organization does not guarantee that we can recover information from memory, of course. Many things cannot be retrieved. Thus, what we ate exactly 23 days ago is unlikely to be retrievable, unless there was something special about that date. Here the problem is that what was eaten on a given day gets lost in the middle of the tens of thousands of times we have eaten. The problem is to distinguish the one event of interest from the many that took place. Other things can be unretrievable for other reasons. Thus, things that happened many years ago are difficult to recover, although with patience and perserverance (months of trying, sometimes), it is remarkable what tiny details of the past may be remembered.

How and when does the meaningful organization take place? Presumably, when new information has arrived at our sensory systems, it cannot be organized and placed properly within memory until it is understood and interpreted. These steps will take time. Short-term memory provides a valuable stage in the processing of information. It can serve as a temporary holding place for newly arrived information. The information in short-term memory will already be recognized as representing some meaningful structure, but it will not yet be organized into new structures.

REHEARSAL

Among the most noticeable activities that a person performs on information in short-term memory in attempting to learn new material is rehearsal. When it is words, names, or numbers that are being learned, then rehearsal appears to be a simple repetition of the items—silently, mentally. No sounds need be produced, no actual movements of the speech organs need be involved. Nonetheless, the subjective impression is that of a silent, internal speech, saying the items over and over again.

There have been numerous studies of rehearsal. Rundus and Atkinson (1970) and Rundus (1971) had their subjects rehearse audibly, and so were able to do a direct comparison of the number of rehearsals and the later ability to retrieve the items from memory. This technique is quite useful, and variations on it might prove to be informative in examining the differences between the various modes of rehearsal.

Maintenance and Elaboration

It seems clear that subjects can and do perform different operations when they are rehearsing. Craik and Watkins (1973) characterized the two operations by the phrases "maintenance rehearsal" and "elaborative operations." That these two operations are quite different from one another has been amply demonstrated several times (for example, Craik and Watkins, 1973, and Woodward, Bjork, and Jongeward, 1973). The operations are so distinct that Bjork reported that it was easy to instruct subjects to switch between the two forms at will (Bjork, personal communication; see Bjork, 1975). Thus, the maintenance rehearsal is described as a "telephone strategy," one like the operations performed to keep a new telephone number in mind from the time one gets it until it can be dialed on the telephone. This, of course, is simply repetitive rehearsal, and subjects have no problem doing it. In fact, many believe this is the proper method to learn things. The elaborative process is described as a "meaningful connections strategy." Subjects are instructed "to form associations, sentences, images, and so forth."

In an experiment performed by Bjork and Jongeward (1975), subjects had to learn six word sequences for a 20-second retention interval using one or the other rehearsal technique. (They were told which rehearsal strategy to use.) When memory for the items was tested immediately after the retention interval, both types of rehearsal proved to be quite effective, with maintenance rehearsal slightly superior to elaborative mechanisms. To the surprise of the subjects, memory for all the items was tested at the end of the entire experiment. Trials on which elaborative processes had been used showed a clear superiority to those on which only maintenance rehearsal was used. Bjork (1975) concluded that maintenance rehearsal is better as an operation for temporarily holding information following its presentation, but it is clearly inferior to elaborative processes in terms of facilitating long-term performance. Each type of rehearsal has its virtues and deficits. Bjork argued that the two are complementary, each helping out the other, and summarized (using the terms "primary" and "secondary" rehearsal in place of maintenance and elaboration):

The Interaction of Primary and Secondary Rehearsal*

ROBERT A. BJORK

To some extent, primary and secondary rehearsal can be viewed as having a symbiotic relationship. On the one hand, even if one's goal is long-term storage [LTS] of the items being rehearsed, primary rehearsal provides the basis for subsequent secondary rehearsal. Since secondary rehearsal is relatively inefficient as a maintenance operation, interspersed periods of primary rehearsal are necessary to keep the current contents of [short-term storage (STS)] available for additional secondary processing. Primary rehearsal is "primary" in the sense that it is a kind of re-presentation scheme by means of which a faithful copy of items is kept available in STS over the short term, either to be reported in that form or to be transferred in modified form to LTS. Secondary rehearsal, on the other hand, can . . . facilitate primary rehearsal by chunking separate items in STS and can, to some extent, remove the need for additional primary rehearsal by storing an adequate representation of the items in LTS.

LEVELS OF PROCESSING

The flexible nature of the control processes of memory, coupled with studies of the differing effectiveness of different types of rehearsal strategies, provides us with a natural place to reexamine our ideas about the nature of memory. This time we will be guided by our thoughts about the importance of the proper organization of information if stored material is ever to be found again. We can view the studies of short-term memory as studies of the status of information while in the transitional stages between its receipt and initial interpretation and its final structuring into the long-term memory system. We view studies of rehearsal as studies of the process of organization.

Material retrieved from memory soon after presentation has characteristics quite different from those of material retrieved later on. Yet close examination of the differences does not yield any sharp dividing point. There is a difference in emphasis, but not of form.

Craik and Lockhart at the University of Toronto suggested that what really matters is the kind of processing the material has received. Shallow, cursory processing leads to the phenomena we associate with short-term storage. Thorough, deep processing leads to memory characteristics attributed to long-term memory. Craik and Lockhart's position

* R. A. Bjork. Short-term storage: The ordered output of a central processor. Cognitive Theory. F. Restle, R. M. Shiffrin, N. J. Castellan. H. R. Lindeman, and D. B. Pisoni (Eds.). Vol. 1. Hillside, N.J.: Lawrence Erlbaum Associates, 1975. Pages 162–163. Copyright © 1975 by Lawrence Erlbaum Associates. Reprinted by permission.

has had a major influence on memory research, and the selection reviews the properties of different memory systems.

Levels of Processing: A Framework for Memory Research*

FERGUS I. M. CRAIK and ROBERT LOCKHART

MULTISTORE MODELS

The Case in Favor

When man is viewed as a processor of information (Miller, 1956; Broadbent, 1958), it seems necessary to postulate holding mechanisms or memory stores at various points in the system. For example, on the basis of his dichotic listening studies, Broadbent (1958) proposed that information must be held transiently before entering the limited-capacity processing channel. Items could be held over the short term by recycling them, after perception, through the same transient storage system. From there, information could be transferred into and retained in a more permanent long-term store.

— — —

It is now widely accepted that memory can be classified into three levels of storage: sensory stores, short-term memory (STM) and long-term memory (LTM). Since there has been some ambiguity in the usage of terms in this area, we shall follow the convention of using STM and LTM to refer to experimental situations, and the terms "short-term store" (STS) and "long-term store" (LTS) to refer to the two relevant storage systems.

— — —

The distinguishing features of the three storage levels are summarized in Table 6.1.

The attractiveness of the "box" approach is not difficult to understand. Such multistore models are apparently specific and concrete; information flows in well-regulated paths between stores whose characteristics have intuitive appeal; their properties may be elicited by experiment and described either behaviorally or mathematically. All that remains, it seems, is to specify the properties of each component more precisely and to work out the transfer functions more accurately.

Despite all these points in their favor, when the evidence for multistore models is examined in greater detail, the stores become less tangible. One warning sign is the progressively greater part played by "control processes" in more recent formulations (for example, Atkinson and Shiffrin, 1971).

— — —

Although we believe that the multistore formulation is unsatisfactory in

* F. I. M. Craik and R. S. Lockhart. Levels of processing: A framework for memory research. Journal of Verbal Learning and Verbal Behavior. 1972, 11, 671–676. Copyright © 1972 by Academic Press, Inc. Reprinted by permission.

TABLE 6.1. Commonly Accepted Differences Between the Three Stages of Verbal Memory

Feature	Sensory registers	Short-term store	Long-term store
Entry of information	Preattentive	Requires attention	Rehearsal
Maintenance of information	Not possible	Continued attention Rehearsal	Repetition Organization
Format of information	Literal copy of input	Phonemic Probably visual Possibly semantic	Largely semantic Some auditory and visual
Capacity	Large	Small	No known limit
Information loss	Decay	Displacement Possibly decay	Possibly no loss Loss of accessibility or discriminability by interference
Trace duration	¼-2 seconds	Up to 30 seconds	Minutes to years
Retrieval	Readout	Probably automatic Items in consciousness Temporal/phonemic cues	Retrieval cues Possibly search process

terms of its capacity, coding, and forgetting characteristics, obviously there are some basic findings which any model must accommodate. It seems certain that stimuli are encoded in different ways within the memory system. A word may be encoded at various times in terms of its visual, phonemic, or semantic features, its verbal associates, or an image. Differently encoded representations apparently persist for different lengths of time. The phenomenon of limited capacity at some points in the system seems real enough and, thus, should also be taken into consideration. Finally, the roles of perceptual, attentional, and rehearsal processes should also be noted.

One way of coping with the kinds of inconsistencies we have described ever, we think it is more useful to focus on the encoding operations themselves and to consider the proposal that rates of forgetting are a function of the type and depth of encoding. This view is developed in the next section.

Many theorists now agree that perception involves the rapid analysis of a number of levels or stages (Selfridge and Neisser, 1960; Treisman, 1964; Sutherland, 1968). Preliminary stages are concerned with the analysis of such physical or sensory features as lines, angles, brightness, pitch, and loudness, while later stages are more concerned with matching input against stored abstractions from past learning; that is, later stages are concerned with pattern recognition and the extraction of meaning. This conception of a series or hierarchy of processing stages is often referred to as "depth of processing," where greater "depth" implies a greater degree of semantic or cognitive analysis. After the stimulus has been recognized, it may undergo further processing by enrichment or elaboration. For example, after a word is recognized, it may trigger associations, images, or stories on the basis of the subject's past experience with the word. Such "elaboration coding" (Tulving and Madigan, 1970) is not restricted to verbal material. We would argue that similar levels of processing exist in the perceptual analysis of sounds, sights, smells, and so on. Analysis proceeds through a series of sensory stages to levels associated with matching or pattern recognition and finally to semantic-associative stages of stimulus enrichment.

One of the results of this perceptual analysis is the memory trace. Such features of the trace as its coding characteristics and its persistence thus arise essentially as byproducts of perceptual processing (Morton, 1970). Specifically, we suggest that trace persistence is a function of depth of analysis, with deeper levels of analysis associated with more elaborate, longer lasting, and stronger traces. Since the organism is normally concerned only with the extraction of meaning from the stimuli, it is advantageous to store the products of such deep analyses, but there is usually no need to store the products of preliminary analyses. It is perfectly possible to draw a box around early analyses and call it sensory memory and a box around intermediate analyses called short-term memory, but that procedure both oversimplifies matters and evades the more significant issues.

— — —

Highly familiar, meaningful stimuli are compatible, by definition, with existing cognitive structures. Such stimuli (for example, pictures and sentences) will be processed to a deep level more rapidly than less meaningful stimuli and will be well-retained. Thus, speed of analysis does not necessarily predict retention. Retention is a function of depth, and various factors, such as the amount of attention devoted to a stimulus, its compatibility with the analyzing structures, and the processing time available, will determine the depth to which it is processed.

Thus, we prefer to think of memory tied to levels of perceptual processing. Although these levels may be grouped into stages (sensory analyses, pattern recognition, and stimulus elaboration, for example) processing levels may be more usefully envisaged as a continuum of analysis. Thus, memory, too, is viewed as a continuum from the transient products of sensory analyses to the highly durable products of semantic-associative operations. However, superimposed on this basic memory system there is a second way in which stimuli can be retained—by recirculating information at one level of processing. In our view, such descriptions as "continued attention to certain aspects of the stimulus," "keeping the items in consciousness," "holding the items in the rehearsal buffer," and "retention of the items in primary memory" all refer to the same concept of maintaining information at one level of processing. To preserve some measure of continuity with existing terminology, we will use the term primary memory (PM) to refer to this operation, although it should be noted that our usage is more restricted than the usual one.

We endorse Moray's (1967) notion of a limited-capacity central processor which may be deployed in a number of different ways. If this processing capacity is used to maintain information at one level, the phenomena of short-term memory will appear. The processor itself is neutral with regard to coding characteristics: The observed PM code will depend on the processing modality within which the processor is operating. Further, while limited capacity is a function of the processor itself, the number of items held will depend upon the level at which the processor is operating. At deeper levels the subject can make greater use of learned rules and past knowledge; thus, material can be more efficiently handled and more can be retained. There is apparently great variability in the ease with which information at different levels can be maintained in PM. Some types of information (for example, phonemic features of words) are particularly easy to maintain while the maintenance of others (such as early visual analyses—the "icon") is apparently impossible.

The essential feature of PM retention is that aspects of the material are still being processed or attended to. Our notion of PM is, thus, synonymous with that of James (1890) in that PM items are still in consciousness. When attention is diverted from the item, information will be lost at the rate appropriate to its level of processing—slower rates for deeper levels. While PM retention is, thus, equivalent to continued processing, this type of processing merely prolongs an item's high accessibility without leading to formation of a more permanent memory trace. This Type I processing, that is, repetition of analyses which have already been carried out, may be contrasted with Type II processing which involves deeper analysis of the stimulus. Only this second type of rehearsal should lead to improved memory performance.

These excerpts complete the summary of the evidence. Craik and Lockhart emphasize three major points. First, they point out that the amount of processing that an item has received is more important than whether we speak of it as being in a short-term or long-term memory system. Second, they propose that the characteristics of the memory for that item depend on how much processing it has received. Third, they emphasize the two different rehearsal processes. One type of rehearsal (Type I) serves no function except that of maintaining a memory image; the other (Type II) actively organizes the material and increases the chances of retrieval at a later time.

Depth of processing is a useful concept. It has one necessary component of any good scientific formulation: it feels right. We still do not know precisely what is meant or exactly how it fits with our previous notions, but there can be no question that Craik and Lockhart have described an important issue. Let us now return to the final excerpts from their paper:

> . . . [Assume] that a flexible central processor can be deployed to one of several levels in one of several encoding dimensions, and that this central processor can only deal with a limited number of items at a given time. That is, items are kept in consciousness or in primary memory by continuing to rehearse them at a fixed level of processing. The nature of the items will depend upon the encoding dimension and the level within that dimension. At deeper levels the subject can make more use of learned cognitive structures so that the item will become more complex and semantic. The depth at which primary memory operates will depend both upon the usefulness to the subject of continuing to process at that level and also upon the amenability of the material to deeper processing. Thus, if the subject's task is merely to reproduce a few words seconds after hearing them, he need not hold them at a level deeper than phonemic analysis. If the words form a meaningful sentence, however, they are compatible with deeper learned structures and larger units may be dealt with. It seems that primary memory deals at any level with units or "chunks" rather than with information (see Kintsch, 1970, pp. 175–181). That is, we rehearse a sound, a letter, a word, an idea, or an image in the same way that we perceive objects and not constellations of attributes.
>
> As pointed out earlier, a common distinction between memory stores is their different coding characteristics; STS is said to be predominantly acoustic (or articulatory) while LTS is largely semantic. According to the present argument, acoustic errors will predominate only insofar as analysis has not proceeded to a semantic level. There are at least three sources of the failure of processing to reach this level; the nature of the material, limited available processing capacity, and task demands. Much of the data on acoustic confusions in short-term memory is based on material such as letters and digits which have relatively little semantic content. The nature of this material itself tends to constrain processing to a structural level of analysis and it should be no surprise, therefore, that errors of a structural nature result. Such errors can also occur with meaningful material if processing capacity is diverted to an irrelevant task (Eagle and Ortoff, 1967).

— — —

CONCLUDING COMMENTS

— — —

Our approach does not constitute a theory of memory. Rather, it provides a conceptual framework—a set of orienting attitudes—within which memory research might proceed. While multistore models have played a useful role, we suggest that they are often taken too literally and that more fruitful questions are generated by the present formulation. Our position is obviously speculative and far from complete. We have looked at memory purely from the input or encoding end; no attempt has been made to specify either how items are differentiated from one another, are grouped together and organized, or how they are retrieved from the system. While our position does not imply any specific view of these processes, it does provide an appropriate framework within which they can be understood (Pages 679–682).

Craik and Lockhart's formulation of memory offers a new approach, one that complements the views we have already discussed. Consider the issues: the evidence for different memory systems, the importance of control processes in memory, and a new formulation of different types of rehearsal strategies. Incoming information is kept in a temporary state of memory—short-term or primary memory. This is a holding state, whose function is to provide time for further depth of processing to take place. Unless further processing does occur, the information will not leave any long-lasting trace. Material can be maintained in this holding state by simply repeating it, reviving the psychological representation of the information. This is what we earlier discussed as maintenance rehearsal and what Craik and Lockhart have called Type I rehearsal. To ensure that information can be recalled later requires that relationships be found between the newly arrived information and what a person already knows. Forming these relationships constitutes the processing we earlier discussed as elaborative rehearsal and which is called Type II rehearsal by Craik and Lockhart.

The different types of rehearsal have different functions; each is superior for some things, inferior for others. Thus, the actions required to organize new material—elaborative processes—seem destructive in terms of the ability to maintain as much as possible of just-presented material. It is easy to see why this might be so: To do elaborative encoding requires that new associations and new structures be formed between the newly presented material and information currently stored in long-term storage. This may well require temporarily adding extra material to short-term memory, and certainly it will mean increasing the demand on one's processing resources. In the terminology of the chapters on attention, elaborative processing is a resource-limited operation. In a similar fashion, maintenance rehearsal minimizes the extra burden on short-term memory or on processing resources, but at the same time it fails to construct the new structures in long-term memory that will be so important for future recall. Thus, if you want to recall material later on, use elaborative processing. If you simply need to hold material temporarily, use maintenance rehearsal (see the discussion by Bjork and McClure, in press).

One area of research related to studies of rehearsal is concerned with "directed forgetting." Here, subjects are asked to learn material, but then told that some particular items that they have studied will not be tested at a later time—they should "forget" these items and concentrate on the others. Studies of directed forgetting (sometimes now called "updating of memory") provide an interesting area of research, for they provide another tool to explore the possible methods of encoding information. Moreover, because one simply cannot arbitrarily decide to forget something, the real issue is determining how to distinguish those items that are no longer of interest from those that are. Thus, directed forgetting studies get at some fundamental issues of organization of material within memory. Lest the question of directed forgetting seem frivolous, note that it is a basic aspect of our daily use of memory. We simply do not need to retain all that we experience. It is useful to notice the traffic patterns, the sights along one's travels, or the sights and sounds of the day, but certainly it would be an unbearable burden to retain all of them. For some people, the very nature of their job requires them to retain material for a brief time and then forget it as much as possible. A telephone operator would have great trouble if numbers that were from the previous user were confused with numbers for the current caller. Waiters and clerks must retain information long enough to perform the customer's request, but then not get one order confused with the next. Even in adding a column of digits, we need to remember the current digit and sum and forget the previous ones. All of these tasks require efficient updating of memory; all require a means of discriminating the current set of material from previous sets. (See the Suggested Readings section of this chapter.)

All these issues point to the need to know more about the nature of memory before we can reach some final understanding. We must certainly learn more about the nature of the storage and organization of information in long-term memory. When a person learns something new, how is it stored? How is it later retrieved? Human memory must contain millions—billions—of items. How does one ever find the appropriate item at the appropriate time? In the answer to this question will lie the answer to the nature of memory. Elaborative rehearsal strategies presumably guide the storage process in such a way as to make later retrieval easier. What is done at the time of learning probably is a critical determinant of what will later be retrievable. Thompson and Tulving (1970) suggested that memory retrieval is entirely determined by what happens at storage. They argued that no cue, however strongly associated with the item to be remembered, can be effective unless the to-be-remembered item is specifically encoded with respect to that cue at the time of storage.

In the next two chapters we examine what is known about the nature of long-term memory. A convenient place to start, one that adds to our knowledge and provides some interesting examples, is the study of mnemonics: the memory skills people have practiced through the ages as a means for improving memory. These mnemonic skills can be considered to be expansions of the elaborative mechanisms that we have briefly examined in this chapter as a method of rehearsal. In Chapter 8, we examine what is known about the organization and representation of information within long-term memory. In both chapters, it is useful to remember the lessons of this one—that organization of information is a critical component of human memory; successful retrieval depends heavily on an appropriate organization. The levels of processing reflect the level of organization applied to information.

SUGGESTED READINGS

Most of the critical issues for the material presented in this chapter have been covered by the excerpts cited in the chapter. Although there have been large numbers of studies in recent years on the issues covered here, there is not yet any good comprehensive summary of results.

Craik and Lockhart's arguments about the nature of the memory system have had considerable influence. Experimental psychologists are thoroughly investigating the notion of levels of processing as an indicator of how well information is retained in memory. An amazing variety of tests is being reported, demonstrating the results of asking people to perform all sorts of manipulations on the material presented to them. Interestingly, these investigations show that one of the least effective ways to get someone to remember something is to ask them to remember it. Evidently, most people have very little awareness of how they should go about learning new information, and therefore the various manipulations required by the memory experiments are usually more effective than whatever feeble attempts the subjects muster by themselves. (More on how to learn is presented in the next chapter.)

Perhaps the best summary of all this activity is by Postman (1975), whose paper reviews the verbal learning literature and cites and discusses large numbers of studies on many different aspects of memory. It is a caustic critique of the field, and a valuable one. The book edited by Restle, Shiffrin, Castellan, Lindeman, and Pisoni (1975) contains position statements by several of the major investigators of short-term memory, including most of those cited in this chapter. The book of papers edited by Cofer (1976) discusses a number of the issues of this chapter, including some of the more recent views of the role of short-term memory and depth of processing.

Work on directed forgetting can be best approached by starting with the review chapters by Bjork (1972) and Epstein (1972) and then proceeding to the paper by Reitman, Malin, Bjork, and Higman (1973) and the paper by Geiselman (1975). Studies on different types of rehearsal can be approached first through the review by Postman (mentioned above), then through such papers as Bjork and McClure (1974), Bjork (1975), and papers in the levels of processing area, such as Craik and Lockhart (1972), Craik and Watkins (1973), and Craik and Tulving (1975).

One critically important aspect of memory storage is the organization of the material that is to be retained. In earlier years, a good deal of the research on memory was concentrated on the study of organizational factors. That research succeeded admirably, as Postman remarks in his summary of research:

> The ultimate sign of the success of a theoretical idea is that it comes to be taken for granted as part of the current body of knowledge in a discipline. This is what has happened to the concept of organization in recall, although some investigators still seem to find it useful to document it anew.
>
> **(Postman, 1975, Page 323)**

For reviews of this literature, see Bower (1972b) and Mandler (1967a, 1967b).

7
Mnemonics

Throughout the centuries humans have been concerned with the practical art of memory. Everyone knows that normally it is difficult to memorize things. Yet a few people have always known special techniques that made the task possible with apparent ease. In the past, psychologists tended to ignore these techniques because they were thought to be mere tricks and sophistry—the practitioners exhibited themselves as stage entertainers or advertised themselves and their methods in unrespectable classified advertisements. But the techniques work. In fact, we ought to examine procedures that simplify the job of memorizing with great care. Not only might they be useful in our lives, but the secrets of those who practice the art of memory ought to shed some light on the organization and operation of the mechanisms involved in memory. Certainly, the things one must do in order to learn material easily bear some relationship to the way that information processes operate.

In this chapter we examine some of the popular systems for improving one's memory. First, we question the common notion that memory is simply a skill that improves with practice. Then, we move to the study of the principles underlying techniques for efficient memorization. Some of these principles come from the literature of experimental psychology, but most come from the popular proponents of various memory systems. Finally, we conclude by examining what is known about the plans and organization of memory and by speculating on the nature of the psychological principles that lie behind the operations of the popular memory systems.

The study of methods for improving memory has long been popular, for a good memory can serve its owner well in many activities. Who among us has not wished for better ability to retain important material? Through the years a number of systems have been developed for the purpose of improving memory. The details of the systems are not always known, for often their designer has kept them secret, hoping to gain either an advantage over his competitors or wealth from his students. But a study of most public systems (and guesses about the techniques used by practitioners of secret systems) indicates that they all have similar bases: they teach the user to pay attention and to learn how to organize.

Through their experiments, psychologists have unearthed a number of principles underlying the retention of material. One of the first results of these studies was a negative finding: the debunking of the notion that memory is a skill in the sense that weightlifting is. It used to be thought (and indeed, by some people, still is) that if one wants a good memory (or good muscles) one simply practices memorization (or lifting weights). The most positive stand against this idea seems to have been taken by William James who spent five pages of his textbook denouncing the notion that exercises in memory strengthen the capacity to memorize. Indeed, James was so moved by the force of his own arguments that he did, what was for him, a very unusual thing: he did an experiment. He laboriously trained himself daily in the learning of poetry "by heart." For 8 consecutive days he learned 158 lines of Victor Hugo's *Satyr*. Then he spent 38 days learning the entire first book of *Paradise Lost*. All this effort, James thought, should have tremendously improved his memory. But when he went back to Victor Hugo, he found that an additional 158 lines took him, if anything, longer to learn than the first set of 158 lines. Apparently no good had resulted from his efforts. Not trusting these results, James set out to test a whole series of surprisingly docile friends who spent many weeks learning many lines of poetry and found, on the whole, no improvement in their ability to learn material after all their labor.

Studies of the effect of performance in one task on learning or performance in another task are called studies in transfer. Thus, James's experiments on memory training can be considered experiments on transfer of memory skill. Although James was correct in his conclusion that practice alone does not improve one's ability to memorize, he was a bit premature in concluding that it is all wasted effort. It turns out that it is possible to learn techniques to improve considerably the skills of memory. But practice is useless unless the rules are known. For example, it helps considerably to form rhymes and to form images and associations among the items to be learned. It helps also to relax and have confidence in one's own ability to memorize.

In 1927, Woodrow repeated James's experiment, only with more care. He wanted to see what improvement in memorization would come about after practice in "proper methods of memorizing." He found that a group of students who simply practiced memorizing lists for several hours did no better than a control group of students who did not practice. This verified the conclusion reached by James. But a group of students who were instructed in proper techniques of memorizing did much better after the same amount of study. Thus, in memory, as in most things, sheer blind practice is of little or no use; informed learning of a set of rules and techniques does prove useful.

An Anecdote

An interesting way to start our examination of mnemonic techniques is with an anecdote offered by the psychologists George Miller, Eugene Galanter, and Karl Pribram in their book *Plans and the Structure of Behavior.* The authors argued that the human organism consists of a hierarchical organization of flexible decision units and introduced an important new basic concept, the Plan, which they defined as "any hierarchical process in the organism that can control the order in which sequence of operations is to be performed." A Plan is, for an organism, essentially the same as a program is for a computer. The way that Plans enter into the process of remembering is illustrated in these excerpts from Chapter 10.

PLANS FOR REMEMBERING＊

GEORGE MILLER, EUGENE GALANTER, and KARL PRIBRAM

The usual approach to the study of memorization is to ask how the material is engraved on the nervous system, how the connections between the parts of it become learned, or imprinted, or strengthened, or conditioned. The usual answers have to do with the amount of practice, with the beneficent consequences of success, with the facilitating or inhibiting effects arising from similarity among parts of the materials or between these materials and others, with the meaningfulness or other sources of transfer of previous learning, and so on. No one who knew the experimental data would question that all these factors are important in determining how fast and how well a person will be able to commit a particular string of symbols to memory. The reason for returning to this well-cultivated plot and trying to crowd in another crop is that an important aspect of the memorizing process seems to have been largely ignored.

— — —

A memorizer's task in the psychological laboratory is to learn how to produce a particular sequence of noises that he would never make ordinarily,

＊ *George Miller, Eugene Galanter, and Karl Pribram.* Plans and the Structure of Behavior. *New York: Holt, Rinehart and Winston, 1960. Pages 125, 128–129, 134–136. Copyright © 1960 by Holt, Rinehart and Winston. Reprinted by permission.*

that have no significance, and that will be of no use to him later. Rote serial memorization is a complicated, tricky thing to learn to do, and when it is mastered it represents a rather special skill. The argument here is that such a skill could not run itself off successfully unless it were guided in its execution by a Plan of the sort we have been discussing. What the subject is telling us when he reports all the wild and improbable connections he had to use is the way in which he developed a Plan to control his performance during the test period.

Now, it would be extremely easy at this point for us to become confused between two different kinds of Plans that are involved in rote memorization. On the one hand, the subject is attempting to construct a Plan that will, when executed, generate the nonsense syllables in the correct order. But at the same time he must adopt a Plan to guide his memorizing, he must choose a strategy for constructing the Plan for recall. There are a variety of ways open to the subject for memorizing. One is to translate the nonsense syllables into words, then to organize the words into sentences and/or images, even, if necessary, to organize the sentences and images into a story if the length of the list demands such higher-order planning. Another Plan the person can use is sheer drill without any translation, perhaps aided by rhythmic grouping, until the list rolls out as the letters of the alphabet do. Or he can play tricks with imagery—imagining each syllable at a different location in the room, then simply looking there and "reading" it when it is needed, etc. There are a variety of such strategies for learning, and they should be investigated. But it is the impression of the present authors that the average person, when confronted with a list of nonsense syllables for the first time, will do something similar to the performance described above.

Unless a person has some kind of Plan for learning, nothing happens. Subjects have read nonsense syllables hundreds of times and learned almost nothing about them if they were not aware that they would later be tested for recall. In order to get the list memorized, a subject must have that mysterious something called an "intent to learn." Given the intention, the act follows by a steady, slow heave of the will.

— — —

The antagonistic attitude of experimental psychologists toward mnemonic devices is even more violent than their attitude toward their subject's word associations; mnemonic devices are immoral tricks suitable only for evil gypsies and stage magicians. As a result of this attitude almost nothing is known by psychologists about the remarkable feats of memory that are so easily performed when you have a Plan ready in advance. Anecdotes do not contribute to science, of course, but they sometimes facilitate communication—so we shall lapse momentarily into a thoroughly unscientific vein.

One evening we were entertaining a visiting colleague, a social psychologist of broad interests, and our discussion turned to Plans. "But exactly what is a Plan?" he asked. "How can you say that *memorizing* depends on Plans?"

"We'll show you," we replied. "Here is a Plan that you can use for memorizing. Remember first that:

> one is a bun,
> two is a shoe,
> three is a tree,
> four is a door,
> five is a hive,
> six are sticks,
> seven is heaven,
> eight is a gate,
> nine is a line, and
> ten is a hen."

"You know, even though it is only ten-thirty here, my watch says one-thirty. I'm really tired, and I'm sure I'll ruin your experiment."

"Don't worry, we have no real stake in it." We tightened our grip on his lapel. "Just relax and remember the rhyme. Now you have part of the Plan. The second part works like this: when we tell you a word, you must form a ludicrous or bizarre association with the first word in your list, and so on with the ten words we recite to you."

"Really, you know, it'll never work. I'm awfully tired," he replied.

"Have no fear," we answered, "just remember the rhyme and then form the association. Here are the words:

1. ashtray
2. firewood
3. picture
4. cigarette
5. table
6. matchbook
7. glass
8. lamp
9. shoe
10. phonograph."

The words were read one at a time, and after reading the word, we waited until he announced that he had the association. It took about five seconds on the average to form the connection. After the seventh word he said that he was sure the first six were already forgotten. But we persevered.

After one trial through the list, we waited a minute or two so that he could collect himself and ask any questions that came to mind. Then we said, "What is number eight?"

He stared blankly, and then a smile crossed his face, "I'll be damned," he said. "It's 'lamp.'"

"And what number is cigarette?"

He laughed outright now, and then gave the correct answer.

"And there is no strain," he said, "absolutely no sweat."

We proceeded to demonstrate that he could in fact name every word correctly, and then asked, "Do you think that memorizing consists of piling up increments of response strength that accumulate as the words are repeated?" The question was lost in his amazement.

Call them what you will—plans, tricks, mnemonics—it is clear that they aid memory. Let us examine some of these tricks in more detail and see what we can make of them. To do so, we leave experimental psychology and go to the advertisements in magazines, to second-hand book stores, and to other, similar, sources of literature. There are hundreds of books on methods for improving one's memory. They differ mainly in the skill with which they are written and the dogmatism with which their "secrets" are presented. But, though it is easy to sneer at their style, it is not wise to deny their content.

MNEMONIC TECHNIQUES

A comparison of the many techniques for improving memory offered by the various proponents shows that everyone's system seems to have much in common with everyone else's. In fact, the prevalence of common features makes us suspect that there might really be something to the methods, although a search through the literature of memory systems is something like a search through the literature of the alchemists for the recipe for gunpowder. The alchemist tells us that the secret is the powdered frog's tongue (gathered by the light of the full moon). But if we look carefully, we can also discover some charcoal, sulfur, and saltpeter. Let us see if we can do the same with mnemonic techniques. All mnemonic devices try to relate the material to be learned to some previously learned organizational scheme. There are many ways that this relation can be established in principle, but, in practice, there is heavy reliance on but a few standard techniques.

Rhymes

Metrical mnemonics are popular, for they let us connect items that otherwise seem wholly unrelated into a rythmic pattern. Rhymes are particularly good at establishing order relations, for when it is well constructed, any mistake in the order of recall of the items destroys the rhyme. Thus we find rhyme used when the difficulty in memorization centers around the difficulty of learning the proper ordering.

I before e
except after c

or

Thirty days hath September,
April, June, and November

Obviously, in these examples it is not difficult to learn the two letters *i* and *e* or the fact that of the 12 months, one has 28 days, some 30, and some 31. The difficulty comes in remembering the order and exact association among the items. The rhymes establish a rule of organization that is easy to learn and apply. In a sense, rhymes (like most mnemonic devices) serve their purpose too well: one who relies on rhymes finds it difficult to remember one particular thing (say, how many days hath October?) without recalling the rhyme in its entirety.

Method of Loci

One peculiar method, but a surprisingly powerful one, is to imagine that the various items to be learned are located in different physical locations (loci). Recall is accomplished by visualizing each location and, thereby, discovering the object. "Thus, if it were desired to fix in the memory the date of the invention of printing (1436), an imaginary book, or some other symbol of printing, would be placed in the thirty-sixth quadrate or memory-place of the fourth room of the first house of the historic district of the town" (Mitchell, 1910).

The history of the method of loci is presented by the English historian Frances A. Yates in *The Art of Memory*. The use of mnemonic techniques has played an important role in the development of philosophy and architecture from the time of the Greek civilization to Elizabethan England. Although the method has a long history, it seems to have been presented best in its original form, first as an anecdote about the Greek poet Simonides and then as a formal system in the very first textbooks. The basic method of loci is described by Yates in the opening pages of *The Art of Memory*.

THE GREEK ART OF MEMORY*

FRANCES A. YATES

At a banquet given by a nobleman of Thessaly named Scopas, the poet Simonides of Ceos chanted a lyric poem in honour of his host but including a

* *Frances A. Yates.* The Art of Memory. *Chicago: University of Chicago Press, 1966. Pages 1–3, 6–10. Reprinted with permission of The University of Chicago Press and Routledge and Kegan Paul Ltd.* *Copyright © 1966 by Frances A. Yates. All rights reserved.*

passage in praise of Castor and Pollux. Scopas meanly told the poet that he would only pay him half the sum agreed upon for the panegyric and that he must obtain the balance from the twin gods to whom he had devoted half the poem. A little later, a message was brought in to Simonides that two young men were waiting outside who wished to see him. He rose from the banquet and went out but could find no one. During his absence the roof of the banqueting hall fell in, crushing Scopas and all the guests to death beneath the ruins; the corpses were so mangled that the relatives who came to take them away for burial were unable to identify them. But Simonides remembered the places at which they had been sitting at the table and was therefore able to indicate to the relatives which were their dead. The invisible callers, Castor and Pollux, had handsomely paid for their share in the panegyric by drawing Simonides away from the banquet just before the crash. And this experience suggested to the poet the principles of the art of memory of which he is said to have been the inventor. Noting that it was through his memory of the places at which the guests had been sitting that he had been able to identify the bodies, he realised that orderly arrangement is essential for good memory.

> He inferred that persons desiring to train this faculty (of memory) must select places and form mental images of the things they wish to remember and store those images in the places, so that the order of the places will preserve the order of the things, and the images of the things will denote the things themselves, and we shall employ the places and images respectively as a wax writing-tablet and the letters written on it.[1]

The vivid story of how Simonides invented the art of memory is told by Cicero in his *De oratore* when he is discussing memory as one of the five parts of rhetoric; the story introduces a brief description of the mnemonic of *places* and *images* (*loci* and *imagines*) which was used by the Roman rhetors. Two other descriptions of the classical mnemonic, besides the one given by Cicero, have come down to us, both also in treatises on rhetoric when memory as a part of rhetoric is being discussed; one is in the anonymous *Ad C. Herennium libri IV*; the other is in Quintilian's *Institutio oratoria*.[2]

The first basic fact which the student of the history of the classical art of memory must remember is that the art belonged to rhetoric as a technique

[1] Cicero. *De oratore. II,* lxxxvi. Pages 351–4. (See Cicero, 1942.)

[2] The translations used here come from the Loeb edition of the classics, in particular, *Rhetorica ad Herennium* (1954), Cicero (1942), and Quintilianus (1921). Yates sometimes modified the translations "in the direction of literalness, particularly in repeating the actual terminology of the mnemonic rather than in using periphrases of the terms." (Yates, 1966, p. 1.)

by which the orator could improve his memory, which would enable him to deliver long speeches from memory with unfailing accuracy. And it was as a part of the art of rhetoric that the art of memory travelled down through the European tradition in which it was never forgotten, or not forgotten until comparatively modern times, that those infallible guides in all human activities, the ancients, had laid down rules and precepts for improving the memory.

It is not difficult to get hold of the general principles of the mnemonic. The first step was to imprint on the memory a series of *loci* or places. The commonest, though not the only, type of mnemonic place system used was the architectural type. The clearest description of the process is that given by Quintilian.[3] In order to form a series of places in memory, he says, a building is to be remembered, as spacious and varied a one as possible, the forecourt, the living room, bedrooms, and parlours, not omitting statues and other ornaments with which the rooms are decorated. The images by which the speech is to be remembered—as an example of these Quintilian says one may use an anchor or a weapon—are then placed in imagination on the places which have been memorised in the building. This done, as soon as the memory of the facts requires to be revived, all these places are visited in turn and the various deposits demanded of their custodians. We have to think of the ancient orator as moving in imagination through his memory building *whilst* he is making his speech, drawing from the memorised places the images he has placed on them. The method ensures that the points are remembered in the right order, since the order is fixed by the sequence of places in the building.

— — —

In what follows I attempt to give the content of the memory section of *Ad Herennium,* emulating the brisk style of the author, but with pauses for reflection about what he is telling us.

The artificial memory is established from places and images *(Constat igitur artificiosa memoria ex locis et imaginibus),* the stock definition to be forever repeated down the ages. A *locus* is a place easily grasped by the memory, such as a house, an intercolumnar space, a corner, an arch, or the like. Images are forms, marks or simulacra *(formae, notae, simulacra)* of what we wish to remember. For instance if we wish to recall the genus of a horse, of a lion, of an eagle, we must place their images on definite *loci.*

The art of memory is like an inner writing. Those who know the letters of the alphabet can write down what is dictated to them and read out what they have written. Likewise those who have learned mnemonics can set in places what they have heard and deliver it from memory. "For the places are very much like wax tablets or papyrus, the images like the letters, the ar-

---

[3] Quintilianus. *Institutio Oratoria. XI,* ii. Pages 17–22.

rangement and disposition of the images like the script, and the delivery is like the reading."

If we wish to remember much material we must equip ourselves with a large number of places. It is essential that the places should form a series and must be remembered in their order, so that we can start from any *locus* in the series and move either backwards or forwards from it. If we should see a number of our acquaintances standing in a row, it would not make any difference to us whether we should tell their names beginning with the person standing at the head of the line or at the foot or in the middle. So with memory *loci*. "If these have been arranged in order, the result will be that, reminded by the images, we can repeat orally what we have committed to the *loci*, proceeding in either direction from any *locus* we please."

The formation of the *loci* is of the greatest importance, for the same set of *loci* can be used again and again for remembering different material. The images which we have placed on them for remembering one set of things fade and are effaced when we make no further use of them. But the *loci* remain in the memory and can be used again by placing another set of images for another set of material. The *loci* are like the wax tablets which remain when what is written on them has been effaced and are ready to be written on again.

In order to make sure that we do not err in remembering the order of the *loci* it is useful to give each fifth *locus* some distinguishing mark. We may for example mark the fifth *locus* with a golden hand, and place in the tenth the image of some acquaintance whose name is Decimus. We can then go on to station other marks on each succeeding fifth *locus*.

It is better to form one's memory *loci* in a deserted and solitary place for crowds of passing people tend to weaken the impressions. Therefore the student intent on acquiring a sharp and well-defined set of *loci* will choose an unfrequented building in which to memorise places.

Memory *loci* should not be too much like one another, for instance too many intercolumnar spaces are not good, for their resemblance to one another will be confusing. They should be of moderate size, not too large for this renders the images placed on them vague, and not too small for then an arrangement of images will be overcrowded. They must not be too brightly lighted for then the images placed on them will glitter and dazzle; nor must they be too dark or the shadows will obscure the images. The intervals between the *loci* should be of moderate extent, perhaps about thirty feet, "for like the external eye, so the inner eye of thought is less powerful when you have moved the object of sight too near or too far away."

A person with a relatively large experience can easily equip himself with as many suitable *loci* as he pleases, and even a person who thinks that he does not possess enough sufficiently good *loci* can remedy this. "For thought can embrace any region whatsoever and in it and at will construct the setting of some locus." (That is to say, mnemonics can use what were afterwards called "fictitious places," in contrast to the "real places" of the ordinary method.)

Pausing for reflection at the end of rules for places I would say that what strikes me most about them is the astonishing visual precision which they imply. In a classically trained memory the space between the *loci* can be measured, the lighting of the *loci* is allowed for. And the rules summon up a vision of a forgotten social habit. Who is that man moving slowly in the lonely building, stopping at intervals with an intent face? He is a rhetoric student forming a set of memory *loci*.

"Enough has been said of places," continues the author of *Ad Herennium,* "now we turn to the theory of images." Rules for images now begin, the first of which is that there are two kinds of images, one for "things" (*res*), the other for "words" (*verba*). That is to say "memory for things" makes images to remind of an argument, a notion, or a "thing"; but "memory for words" has to find images to remind of every single word.

I interrupt the concise author here for a moment in order to remind the reader that for the rhetoric student "things" and "words" would have an absolutely precise meaning in relation to the five parts of the rhetoric. Those five parts are defined by Cicero as follows:

> *Invention is the excogitation of true things* (res), *or things similar to truth to render one's cause plausible; disposition is the arrangement in order of the things thus discovered; elocution is the accommodation of suitable words to the invented (things); memory is the firm perception in the soul of things and words; pronunciation is the moderating of the voice and body to suit the dignity of the things and words.*[4]

"Things" are thus the subject matter of the speech; "words" are the language in which that subject matter is clothed. Are you aiming at an artificial memory to remind you only of the order of the notions, arguments, "things" of your speech? Or do you aim at memorising every single word in it in the right order? The first kind of artificial memory is *memoria rerum*; the second kind is *memoria verborum*. The ideal, as defined by Cicero in the above passage, would be to have a "firm perception in the soul" of both things and words. But "memory for words" is much harder than "memory for things"; the weaker brethren among the author of *Ad Herennium*'s rhetoric students evidently rather jibbed at memorising an image for every single word, and even Cicero himself, as we shall see later, allowed that "memory for things" was enough.

To return to the rules for images. We have already been given the rules

---

[4] Cicero. *De inventione.* I, vii, 9. (See Cicero, 1949.) Translation made more literal in reproducing *res* and *verba*.

for places, what kind of places to choose for memorising. What are the rules about what kind of images to choose for memorising on the places? We now come to one of the most curious and surprising passages in the treatise, namely the psychological reasons which the author gives for the choice of mnemonic images. Why is it, he asks, that some images are so strong and sharp and so suitable for awakening memory, whilst others are so weak and feeble that they hardly stimulate memory at all? We must enquire into this so as to know which images to avoid and which to seek.

> Now nature herself teaches us what we should do. When we see in every day life things that are petty, ordinary, and banal, we generally fail to remember them, because the mind is not being stirred by anything novel or marvellous. But if we see or hear something exceptionally base, dishonourable, unusual, great, unbelievable, or ridiculous, that we are likely to remember for a long time. Accordingly, things immediate to our eye or ear we commonly forget; incidents of our childhood we often remember best. Nor could this be so for any other reason than that ordinary things easily slip from the memory while the striking and the novel stay longer in the mind. A sunrise, the sun's course, a sunset are marvellous to no one because they occur daily. But solar eclipses are a source of wonder because they occur seldom, and indeed are more marvellous than lunar eclipses, because these are more frequent. Thus nature shows that she is not aroused by the common ordinary event, but is moved by a new or striking occurrence. Let art, then, imitate nature, find what she desires, and follow as she directs. For in invention nature is never last, education never first; rather the beginnings of things arise from natural talent, and the ends are reached by discipline.
>
> We ought, then, to set up images of a kind that can adhere longest in memory. And we shall do so if we establish similitudes as striking as possible; if we set up images that are not many or vague but active (imagines agentes); if we assign to them exceptional beauty or singular ugliness; if we ornament some of them, as with crowns or purple cloaks, so that the similitude may be more distinct to us; or if we somehow disfigure them, as by introducing one stained with blood or soiled with mud or smeared with red paint, so that its form is more striking, or by assigning certain comic effects to our images, for that, too, will ensure our remembering them more readily. The things we easily remember when they are real we likewise remember without difficulty when they are

> *figments. But this will be essential—again and again to run
> over rapidly in the mind all the original places in order to
> refresh the images.*[5]

Our author has clearly got hold of the idea of helping memory by arousing emotional affects through these striking and unusual images, beautiful or hideous, comic or obscene. And it is clear that he is thinking of human images, of human figures wearing crowns or purple cloaks, bloodstained or smeared with paint, of human figures dramatically engaged in some activity—doing something. We feel that we have moved into an extraordinary world as we run over his places with the rhetoric student, imagining on the places such very peculiar images. Quintilian's anchor and weapon as memory images, though much less exciting, are easier to understand than the weirdly populated memory to which the author of *Ad Herennium* introduces us.

It is easy to see why the method of loci helps one to learn the order of events when the path to be followed in looking for the stored items is a logical or familiar one. The principle is similar to that used in rhyming: the external structure of the mnemonic device enforces a unique ordering. But, it is not at all clear why placing objects in imaginary locations should make it any easier to remember the objects themselves. This is exactly the psychological problem raised by the introduction of mnemonics. It is one thing to say that these tricks are simply clever utilizations of well-known psychological processes. It is another thing to illustrate how those psychological processes are actually used. It is interesting to note, however, that the rules of *Ad Herennium* emphasized a number of techniques well established by today's experimental psychologists: for one, rehearse (". . . run over rapidly in the mind . . ."); for another, unique and isolated items are remembered best.

Analytic Substitutions

A favorite technique for learning long lists of items or numbers is to change numbers into sounds, sounds into words, and words into sentences. Credit for this system seems to lie with Stanislaus Mink von Wenussheim (otherwise known as Winckelmann), who developed a scheme for representing numbers by consonants in 1648. Winckelmann's scheme evidently is the basis for almost every subsequent memory system, although few people give him credit. One elaboration of this method

---

[5] *Ad Herennium. III,* xxii.

that gained favor (and also resentment and lawsuits) in London and Washington in the 1890s was that of Loisette.[6]

Loisette proposed three basic ways by which the user of his system might choose to relate arbitrary items to one another:

1. *Inclusion:* Different items may overlap in meaning or ideas or sounds.
2. *Exclusion:* One word may exclude the other or both words may relate to one and the same thing, but occupy opposite positions in regard to it.
3. *Concurrence:* Impressions or ideas may accidentally or casually appear together.

Loisette's system involves forming relations among all the items to be learned by various (and sometimes strained) applications of these three basic principles.

Numbers are more difficult to learn than words, so Loisette suggests a special technique for them, namely his "own" (slight) modification of the Winckelmann scheme. In the excerpt from Loisette, note that the substitution of numbers to letters is to be used only by those pupils who failed to learn numbers by a more basic application of the three rules of memory.

Analytic Substitutions*

PROFESSOR A. LOISETTE

ANOTHER METHOD FOR REMEMBERING DATES AND FIGURES

This lesson in figures is given for the benefit of those who have not yet mastered Numeric Thinking. The pupil will appreciate its practical value the moment he masters the key to it.

---

* A. Loisette. Assimilative Memory or How to Attend and Never Forget. *New York: Funk and Wagnalls Co., 1896. Pages 66–67, 74–76.*

[6] Although the *Encyclopaedia Britannica* (see Mitchell, 1910) credits the German Winckelmann with the invention of the number-consonant alphabet in 1648, the idea evidently was first originated in the modern form by the French mathematician Pietro Herigon in 1634. (Personal communication from M. N. Young.) For a comprehensive discussion of the history and techniques of mnemonics see the articles (starting with *Mnemotecnia*) in the *Enciclopedia Universal Ilustrada, Europeo-Americana* (Madrid: Espasa-Calpe, S.A. Vol. 35. Pages 1148–1159). Also see *Herigon, Pietro* and *Winkelmann, Johann Justus* in Young (1961).

In the discussions that follow I use excerpts from Loisette to illustrate the number-consonant system primarily because, of the books available to me, his presentation was the most enjoyable.

This is given in the next few pages, and it will be found to be easy of comprehension and interesting to a surprising degree.

The whole thing is in a nutshell. Numbers, as such, are abstractions and hard to be remembered. To make them hard to forget, we translate them into words or phrases. These are easily remembered and they always instantly *give back* the figures they stand for.

We represent the figures 1, 2, 3, 4, 5, 6, 7, 8, 9, and 0, by certain *consonants*; and then, as the vowels [a, e, i, o, u, and y, together with w] have *no numerical* value assigned to them, we turn dates or any numbers into translating *words,* which will always tell us precisely the figures the words stand for.

As this simple process enables us to remember any dates or numbers with *absolute certainty,* the pupil will be pleased to know that he can learn *how it is done* by only *one thoughtful* perusal.

The questions at the bottom of each page constitute an invaluable aid to test the accuracy of his knowledge and the correctness of his inferences.

The nought and the nine digits are *represented* by the following *consonants* when they are *sounded* or *pronounced*; viz., 0 (nought) by *s, z,* or c^{soft} as in *cease,* 1 by *t, th,* or *d,* 2 by *n,* 3 by *m,* 4 by *r,* 5 by *l,* 6 by *sh, j, ch,* or g^{soft} as in the first g of *George,* 7 g^{hard} as in *gorge, k, c^{hard}* as in *cane, q,* or *ng,* 8 by *f* or *v,* and 9 by *b* or *p.*

Ample practice in translating the sounded consonants of words into figures, or of figures into the sounded consonants of words will now be given. If the reader can *remember* the foregoing consonant equivalents of figures in connection with the tabulated Figure Alphabet (Table 7.1), he can at once

TABLE 7.1. Tabulated Figure Alphabet

0	1	2	3	4	5	6	7	8	9
S	t	n	m	r	l	sh	g^{hard}	f	b
	th					j	k	v	p
Z	d						c^{hard}		
						ch			
C^{soft}						g^{soft}	q		
							ng		

1. Is it possible to exaggerate the importance of this lesson? 2. Will the pupil appreciate its practical value? 3. Where is this key given? 4. Are numbers hard to remember? 5. How do we make them hard to forget? 6. By what are the figures represented? 7. What letters have no numerical value assigned to them? 8. What do the questions at the bottom of each page constitute?

pass on through the book. If not, he must carefully study the intervening pages with painstaking—for when once learned, no further difficulty can arise.

The tabulated Figure Alphabet of this lesson expresses the consonant values of the nought and nine digits in perpendicular columns, as under nought (0) are placed s, z, and c^{soft}; under nine are placed b and p; under six are placed sh, j, ch, and g^{soft}, etc. Only those who possess first-rate natural memories can learn the equivalents of the sounded consonants in figures from this table. But when learned in this way, the pupil requires much practice in translating words into figures and figures into words. Even this exceptional pupil had better carefully study the ensuing examples.

The first thing to be done is to learn *which* consonants are used to stand for and represent the nought (0) and 1, 2, 3, 4, 5, 6, 7, 8, and 9. Let the student remember that we use vowels to make words with, but we do not give the vowels [a, e, i, o, u], or w, or y, *any number value whatever.*

WE REPRESENT THE NOUGHT OR CYPHER [0] BY THE CONSONANTS S, Z, OR C^{soft} [as in *cease*].

The figure value of *sew*, therefore equals or is represented by a cipher [0]. $S=0$, and the vowel e and the consonant w have *no figure value.* Cannot the student understand at once that *say*=0, *see*=0, *ease*=0, *is*=0, and *zoe* =0, and *seize*=00, *size*=00, *sauce*=00?

The following is another way of fixing in mind this first rule.

If the capital letter S were cut into two parts, and the bottom half attached to the top half, it would make a nought (0). So *it is easy to remember that S represents* 0. C^{soft} as in *cease* has the same sound as S, and should therefore stand for the same figure, viz., 0; and Z is a cognate of S—that is, it is *made by the same organs of speech in the same position* as when making S, only it is an undertone, and S is a whispered letter. Besides Z should represent 0 because it begins the word *zero*—C^{soft} should also stand for 0 for the additional reason that C^{soft} begins the word *cipher. In translating a word into figures we always turn S, Z, or C^{soft} into nought* (0); *in turning figures into words we always translate a nought* (0) *into S, Z, or C^{soft}.*

1 IS REPRESENTED BY THE CONSONANT T, TH, or D.

Toy=1. As t stands for 1, and o and y are vowels, and have no figure value, the numerical value of *toy must* be 1.

Thee=1, *thou*=1, *day*=1, *dew*=1, *this*=10, *thus*=10, *does*=10, *ties* =10. *toes*=10, *deed*=11, *doth*=11, *to-day*=11, *tattoo*=11, *tut*=11, *toad*= 11, *tied*=11, *sat*=01, *said*=01, *seat*=01, *days*=10, *toys*=10, *these*=10, *those*=10.

t stands for 1, because it is made with *one* downward stroke. h has no figure value except when it is united with s or c in sh or ch, and therefore th

1. In translating a word into figures, what do we always do? 2. By what letters is the figure 1 represented? 3. Why does t stand for 1? 4. When does the letter h have a figure value? 5. By what is 2 represented? 6. Why? 7. How do we represent 3? 8. Why? 9. By what consonant is 4 represented? 10. Why?

must represent 1, and *d*, being the cognate of *t*, it is represented by 1. Hence we translate *t, th,* and *d* by the figure 1, and when we want to represent 1, by letters, we translate it into *t, th,* or *d*.

— — —

If the pupil has mastered the Figure Alphabet he will proceed with the greatest satisfaction and profit. If he has not mastered it, let him carefully review the foregoing pages of this chapter, and then he can advance with the assurance of meeting no difficulties.

HOW TO FIND WORDS WITH WHICH TO TRANSLATE DATES AND NUMBERS

It is a simple and easy process; knowing exactly what consonants are used to represent each of the numbers, you simply write at the side of the numbers to be turned into words the consonants which stand for them; and using any vowels you please, you find out by experimenting what words can translate the figures. Suppose you wish to find out what words will translate the date of the settlement of Jamestown, Va., 1607. You place the figures under each other as below, and then you place at the right hand of each figure the consonants which translate it.

$1 = t, th, d.$
$6 = sh, j, ch, g^{soft}$ (as in *gem*).
$0 = s, z, c^{soft}$ (as in *cease*).
$7 = g^{hard}, k, c^{hard}, q,$ and *ng*.

By experimenting you soon find the following phrases will represent 1607; as "a *Dutch song*," "*dash a sack*," "*to wash a sock*," "*the choosing*," "*the chasing*," "*touches a key*," etc.

Try the date of the adoption of the Constitution of the United States, 1787. Writing down the numbers as before, you place *t, th, d,* opposite 1; $g^{hard}, k, c^{hard}, q, ng,$ opposite 7; *f* and *v*, opposite 8; $g^{hard}, k, c^{hard}, q,$ and *ng*, opposite 7; and then you soon find translating words, as follows: "*to give a key*," "*the giving*," *the quaffing*," "*the coughing*," etc.

In all cases you must carefully comply with the rules and explanations heretofore given. A little practice will enable you to dispense with writing

---

1. What would be your method of procedure? 2. What must be done in all cases? 3. What will a little practice enable you to do? 4. What must be done to secure accuracy at first? 5. Deal with an original date in the way indicated here. 6. In dealing with the date of the foundation of Yale College, would the phrase "taxes due" express 1701? 7. If not, why? 8. Can you translate into a word or phrase the date of your own birth? 9. Translate into words or phrases the birth and death dates of some of the historic characters which you admire most. 10. Keep a record of these words or phrases for future examination.

down the figures and the consonants which represent them; but at first pains must be taken in the above way to secure accuracy.

Try 1636, the date of the founding of Harvard College: You obtain *"dash a midge," "the chum age," "teach much," "to show my joy,"* etc.

The founding of Yale College in 1701 gives: *"took a seat," "the cost," "the quest," "the cast," "a tax due,"* or *"took a city,"* etc.

Sometimes the first consonants only of words are used. Comenius, Educational Reformer (things before words, pictured illustrations, etc.) and Moravian Bishop, was born 1592: or (1) *Th*ings (5) We*l*l (9) *P*ictured (2) *N*ow. He died 1671; or A (1) *T*eaching (6) *Ch*urchman (7) *G*ave (1) Ou*t*.

Loisette goes on and on, but the technique is clear. Obviously, for all the complicated rules, Loisette's (or, more properly, Winckelmann's) scheme is identical in principle to the "one is a bun, two is a shoe, . . ." scheme illustrated by Miller, Galanter, and Pribram. These systems do seem to work, although at the cost of a large initial investment by the user in the time and effort required to learn the system in the first place. For example, the author of *How to Improve Your Memory* says this about the number-consonant system:

> If *you learn the system and practice it constantly, you acquire facility in translation and in interpreting your translations. You might decide whether you consider the system worth learning and using by selecting a few numbers that you wish to remember—such as your social security number, the number of your bank account, and a telephone number or two—and (1) seeing whether you can translate them into words or phrases, then (2) deciding whether you could remember the translations more easily than the numbers.*
>
> *As for appointments, it would probably be better to enter your appointment for April 16 at 4:00 on your calendar than to keep it on your mind to "ride ashore."*
>
> *The translation device is useful for the performance of memory stunts with numbers. But the average person will probably consider it more of a curiosity than a helpful device.*
>
> **(Weinland, 1957, Page 107)**

This particular book, by James D. Weinland, a retired professor of business psychology, describes the principles of most mnemonic systems without dogmatism and with an attempt to connect each method with the findings of experimental psychology. More important, Weinland provides us with statements about the limitations of each technique, something seldom found in popular writing.

What is it about mnemonic systems that improves our ability to memorize? All the systems seem to share common emphasis on organization. Evidently one just cannot go about memorizing things as they happen. One has to organize the material, group it into meaningful structures, and tuck it away in memory according to a formal, orderly plan. If the material does not lend itself to visualization and associations as it stands, it must be transformed by the use of key words or analytic substitutions until images can be used.

The emphasis on the structure of stored material, whether it be imposed by rhythmic techniques, formally learned memory loci, or unique vivid imagery, indicates that the difficulty in memorizing material has more to do with retrieval than with storage itself. If storage of information were the bottleneck, one would hardly wish to use a mnemonic device that increased the amount of information to be stored. Yet every technique we have examined appears to do just that. Nowhere in the literature can we find a system that tries to condense and simplify the material; every system enriches and adds to the information. The implication is that organization plays an important role in retrieval.

If you doubt that mnemonic techniques really do work, here is a very simple demonstration experiment performed by Gordon Bower and Michal Clark of Stanford University. They were somewhat skeptical of the wild claims made by proponents of mnemonic techniques, so they performed the following basic experiment, reprinted almost in its entirety from the journal ("subjects" is designated "Ss"):

Narrative Stories*

GORDON H. BOWER and MICHAL C. CLARK

A technique recommended by mnemonists (e.g., Young & Gibson, 1962) for learning serial lists is the "chaining" method, whereby S is enjoined to construct a narrative story around the critical words to be remembered. The critical words are to be woven into the story in the order they are to be recalled, and these words should be emphasized in some manner, e.g., by vocal stress, pausing, or by making them the main actors or objects in the narrative. The prescriptions permit a wide latitude in constructive details (e.g., the number of critical words per sentence) depending upon the ease of organizing the particular list of words to be learned. A common additional prescription is that S should try to visualize the scenes he is constructing for linking the successive words.

— — —

* G. B. Bower and M. C. Clark. Narrative stories as mediators for serial learning. Psychonomic Science. 1969, 14, 181–182. Copyright © 1969 by Psychonomic Society, Inc. Reprinted by permission.

. . . our initial study with the chaining technique was done simply to see whether it "worked" efficiently in circumstances for which it plausibly might be efficient. These circumstances were (a) self-paced exposure to the complete serial list, (b) the critical recall units were content words (nouns), and (c) S had a large number of lists to learn and remember, so that massive interference and forgetting would normally be expected for control Ss not using the narrative chaining technique.

METHOD

Each S studied and recalled 12 successive serial lists consisting of 10 concrete nouns chosen to be apparently unrelated. All Ss were run individually; they first received general instructions for the serial learning task. The Narrative Ss were then briefly instructed on the mnemonic technique, as follows: "A good way to learn a list of items is to make up a story relating the items to one another. Specifically, start with the first item and put it in a setting which will allow other items to be added to it. Then, add the other items to the story in the same order as the items appear. Make each story meaningful to yourself. Then, when you are asked to recall the items, you can simply go through your story and pull out the proper items in their correct order."

The Narrative S was handed the first list of 10 words and told to make up his story. He did not have to say his story aloud, and he could take as long as he needed. When S was finished, he handed the list back to E (who recorded the time taken by S), and then S immediately recalled the serial list just studied. Then the second through twelfth lists were gone through in the same way. For each Narrative S, a yoked Control S was run who received the 12 lists in the same order, each for a study-time equal to that taken by the Narrative S. The Control S was told simply to study and learn each serial list, and he also did an immediate recall of each list just after he had studied it. After the twelfth list had been studied and immediately recalled, S was asked to recall the first list again, then the second list, and all subsequent lists. The cue for recall of a list was the first word in that list; S was asked to recall the remaining nine words of that list in their correct order.

The Ss were 24 undergraduates fulfilling a service requirement for their introductory psychology course. Alternate Ss were assigned to be in the Narrative versus yoked Control condition. Each pair of Ss received the 12 lists in a different order within the day.

RESULTS

The times taken by the Narrative Ss to construct their story varied from 40 sec to 199 sec with a grand mean of 104 sec. Fifty-seven percent had times between 1 and 2 min. These times grew shorter over the first four lists, as though Ss were becoming more proficient at concocting their stories.

Neither group experienced any difficulty in the immediate recall test that followed study of a list. Median percentages recalled were 99.9% and 99.1% for the Narrative and Control Ss, respectively. However, the differential learning and/or forgetting for the Narrative Ss showed up strongly in their later recall, when S tried to recall all 12 lists. The median percentages of words recalled in their correct list and correct absolute position are shown in Fig. 7.1 for the two groups for the 12 lists. There is a tremendous difference, with the Narrative Ss recalling six to seven times more than their yoked Controls. There was no overlap in recall scores of the two groups on any list; the average of the median scores was 93% for the Narrative Ss versus 13% for their yoked Controls.

The picture is much the same if one scores recall leniently, counting a word correct regardless of the order or intended list in which it was recalled. For Control Ss, the list words have simply become unavailable, whereas this has been prevented in some way by the narrative-story constructions.

There are small effects due to list order apparent in Fig. 7.1, an improvement over early lists for Narrative Ss, and a slight serial-position curve for Control Ss. These are ancillary findings of no interest here.

We next examined the relationship between study-time on a list and later recall of that list. First, for each S, recall of the six lists with his longer study times was compared to recall of the six lists with his shorter study times. In this within-S comparison, there was no suggestion of a short versus long difference in recall for either the Narrative or Control Ss. This may have been because variation of an S's study times was relatively small. Second, over the 12 Ss by 12 lists in each condition, the 144 cases were divided at the median study time, and average recall scores computed for the shorter versus longer times. For the Narrative Ss, average recall for the lists with the shorter study times was 88% versus 92% for the lists with the longer study times. For the

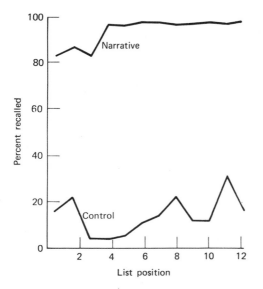

Fig. 7.1. Median percentages recalled over the 12 lists.

TABLE 7.2. Sample Stories

A LUMBERJACK DARTed out of a forest, SKATEd around a HEDGE past a COLONY of DUCKs. He tripped on some FURNITURE, tearing his STOCKING while hastening toward the PILLOW where his MISTRESS lay.

A VEGETABLE can be a useful INSTRUMENT for a COLLEGE student. A carrot can be a NAIL for your FENCE or BASIN. But a MERCHANT of the QUEEN would SCALE that fence and feed the carrot to a GOAT.

One night at DINNER I had the NERVE to bring my TEACHER. There had been a FLOOD that day, and the rain BARREL was sure to RATTLE. There was, however, a VESSEL in the HARBOR carrying this ARTIST to my CASTLE.

Control Ss, average recall was 12% for the shorter-time and 41% for the longer-time lists; these differ significantly, indicating that Control Ss yoked with fast Narrative Ss recalled less than those yoked with slow Narrative Ss.

These comparisons reveal that recall of Control Ss was affected by study time, while that of Narrative Ss was not. However, this effect of study time on Control Ss is still far from accounting for the main effect of the narrative elaboration. (Incidentally, Control Ss always felt that they had more than enough time to learn each list—until the final recall tests.)

Stories were taken from a few Narrative Ss after their final recall; a sample of these are shown in Table 7.2 with the 10 critical words capitalized. These have a certain "stream of consciousness" sense and unity about them, and they are not bad solutions to the task of connecting 10 unrelated nouns in a specified order.

DISCUSSION

We think the effect in this experiment is *probably* due to thematic organization. The person generates meaningful sentences to relate successive words, and he tries to relate successive sentences of his generated text around some central theme or action imagery. The sentences and themes from successive lists are different and probably are kept distinct from one another in memory. The first-word cue prompts recall of the theme, and from that the person appears to *reconstruct* the sentences and pull out the critical words. The reconstruction appears to be hierarchical, from theme to sentences to critical words. We would presume that this thematic organization affects learning and that it also reduces interference between the many lists S is learning. Further studies of this effect could yield more useful information by recording Ss total verbal behavior ("thinking aloud") at study and at recall.

A remarkable aspect of the performance of Narrative Ss is that they rarely intruded nonlist words in their recall (less than 0.5 per S). One might first suppose that this discrimination between critical versus context words was based on form class, since all critical words were concrete nouns. But a glance at the sample stories in Table 7.2 shows (a) some context words are nouns, and (b) some critical words are used as verbs or adjectives in the stories. The basis for this high level discrimination between critical and context words added by S remains somewhat of a mystery.

MNEMONIC PRINCIPLES

Mnemonic methods are powerful. If anyone had any doubts, the data presented by Bower and Clark are certainly convincing. Notice that there seems to be a suspicion of similarity between the *elaborative-processes* method of rehearsing discussed in the previous chapter and mnemonic methods of this chapter. Notice, too, that most people simply don't know how to learn things. First, the techniques described in this chapter are not particularly obvious, at least not to most people. Second, we noted in the previous chapter that when people were asked to learn the material given to them they did not remember it as well as those who were asked to do things with it, even if the latter group were not told they had to learn it. Third, in Bower and Clark's experiment, the control subjects who were trying hard to learn the words thought they were doing so— "Control subjects always felt that they had more than enough time to learn each list—until the final recall tests."

Simply stating the connection between rehearsal strategies and mnemonics does not explain anything, of course. Of the mnemonic techniques, several different kinds of principles can be deduced. Among them are:

> the use of mental images
> the use of spatial location
> the use of rhymes
> the use of organization
> attention to the critical items

Some of these principles seem obvious. Thus, rhymes help, in part, by simply reducing the number of different possible items that can be involved (nicely demonstrated by Bower and Bolton, 1969). Attention to the material is quite an obvious issue, for without appropriate attention, the other strategies simply do not get a chance. It seems perfectly obvious that one must attend to something in order to remember it, yet it is surprising how many people fail to attend.

Most people claim they have difficulty remembering people's names. At a party or meeting, they might be introduced to numerous new people and fail to remember most of the names. Yet, when introduced, they barely attend to the name. A few simple rules turn out to be very effective. If you wish to be better at remembering names, listen to the name of the person you are meeting. Say it again, aloud, right away and then again, after a delay of a minute or so. Forcing yourself to repeat the name does wonders. If you do not remember the name you must ask again what it is. If this is done at the time of the introduction, it is not embarassing to ask; on the contrary, it is often regarded as a compliment. The simple techniques of making sure the name was heard in the first place, and then repeating it during the conversation, ensure that there is immediate attention to the problem of learning the name. Repeating the name after a delay of a minute or so increases the chance of longer-term retention. It all helps. Thinking of associations to the name or the appearance of the person ensures deeper processing, and these techniques help best of all. Almost any book on "how to remember" will provide numerous techniques one can use.

Imagery, spatial position, and organization are powerful mnemonic tools. Imagery and spatial organization are important, and we will have more to say about them in the next chapter. Organization seems to help by providing structure to the material that is to be learned. Moreover, the structure of organization used in long-term memory encoding seems to be determined in part by the limitations of short-term memory. That is, if material is maintained in short-term memory while it is organized, then the material is apt to be clustered in groups of items, each group about the size that can be held comfortably in short-term memory.

The power of mnemonic systems may be the result of a very simple principle: they reduce long, unrelated strings of material into short, related lists. Mnemonic systems provide us with the rules and techniques for shortening the sequence that is to be learned and finding meaning, even where there appears to be none.

A common objection to mnemonic systems is that they increase the amount of material that is to be learned. This is certainly true, in a limited sense. All systems make the users learn rhymes or associations or images in addition to the basic material that they are really interested in retaining, but these additions may actually amount to a decrease in the amount of actual material that must be learned. The span of human memory is limited by the number of meaningful items presented to it, not by physical variables such as the number of words or images. Thus, a mnemonic technique may actually decrease the number of meaningful units in the material to be learned. Formally, a sequence of four digits is shorter than an image of those four digits arranged in a meaningful pattern. But when we try to learn the digits, we need to learn four things; when we try to learn the image, only one thing need be learned, the pattern.

We can illustrate the points by looking at specific examples provided by our readings. The key word system, illustrated by the transformation rule that "one is a bun, two is a shoe, . . ." is a good example of a technique that can only lengthen the sequence to be remembered. The rule transforms sequences of digits into sequences of words, but with an exact one-to-one equivalence of one for the other. Thus, any improvement in memory performance that results from this rule must come about from the added meaning that the words provide, not from a reduction in the number of items to be learned.

The number-consonant system (of Winckelmann, illustrated by the excerpt from Loisette) is a more powerful mnemonic device than the key word system because it manages both to add meaning to a sequence of digits and simultaneously to shorten the actual number of items that need be learned. For example, in his paper on the magical number 7 (Chapter 5), Miller discussed an experiment by Sidney Smith on a method of encoding a string of items into a shorter string. Smith had his subjects learn sequences of binary numbers by encoding each group of three binary digits into one octal number. In this way they could almost triple the number of binary digits they could retain. The number-consonant scheme uses a similar principle to reduce the number of elements that must be retained, but then goes one important step further: it adds meaning to the string.

Consider how one would go about learning the sequence of binary digits: 001100001001100001101010001111111100000. This is more than our memory span can encompass. We can use Smith's trick and encode them into octal digits: 1411415217740 (pages 92–94). This is a much shorter sequence, but it is still too long to be learned easily. But now, if we apply the number-consonant transformation, we get *trttrtlntkkrs.* After a moment's thought we realize that we can change those letters into the equivalent sequence of *trd drt ln tng grs.* This consonant sequence leads us to the word-picture of a *tired dirty lion eating grass.* Thus, we have reduced 39 binary numbers to 13 octal ones, 13 octal numbers to 5 words, and finally, 5 words to one picture. This mnemonic system is powerful (for the practiced user) because it tremendously reduces the amount of material we need to learn. The system costs effort, however, first in the hours of practice it takes to learn the rules, and then in the effort it takes to apply them. This example of mnemonic techniques somewhat destroys their charm, but it should also illustrate their power.

Summing up, it appears that the organization important for efficient learning is of two forms. One corresponds to the organization that is used in human storage itself. The other corresponds to the organization of the material to be learned: chunking and categorization. If we had to state rules for efficient memorization, they might look something like these:

1. *Small basic units.* The material to be learned must be divisible into small, self-contained sections, with no more than four or five individual items in any section.
2. *Internal organization.* The sections must be organized so that the various parts fit together in a logical, self-ordering structure.

3. *External organization.* Some relationship must be established between the material to be learned and material already learned, so that one fits neatly within the other.
4. *Depth of processing.* Any mental activity performed on the material, such as forming images or putting it into mental settings or stories, increases the depth of processing, thereby automatically helping to form the relevant connections that improve retrievability.

The various memory systems we have examined provide systematic techniques for taking arbitrary material and forming it into organizations that obey these four rules. The known properties of human memory suggest reasons for these principles. To summarize these reasons briefly, the requirement that material be categorized into small groups seems to result from the limited capacity of short-term memory. The requirement for a logical ordering of sections (categories or chunks) is imposed by the extreme difficulty of learning order relationships. The requirement for rich associations to previously learned material seems to be a requirement of the retrieval process, for the well-learned associations provide the starting place for the search of memory when recall is desired.

We are now able to create a general maxim for those who wish to improve their memory. If you wish to learn something, rather than plunge blindly ahead reciting the material endlessly, it would be best to first summarize briefly its overall meaning and structure; second, to decide how it relates to what you already know; finally, to divide the material into a small set of logical subdivisions.

By following these procedures, one automatically uses a number of psychological principles known to improve learning. The procedure forces full attention to be applied to the material; it forces partial learning of the whole and partial learning by parts; it provides components of sufficiently small size to be learned as one "chunk"; and it provides structure, both to relate the individual chunks to one another and to integrate the whole with what has been learned previously. Finally, these techniques all correspond nicely to those that increase the "depth of processing" of the material, thereby forming the final link between studies performed in the experimental laboratory (and discussed in the previous chapter) and the methods of the mnemonist.

SUGGESTED READINGS

Despite some attention to mnemonic devices in recent years, surprisingly little is known about the actual techniques. Two delightful books that might be consulted by the interested reader are Luria's *The Mind of a Mnemonist* (1968), and Crovitz's *Galton's Walk* (1970). For almost thirty years, Luria worked with a famous Soviet mnemonist (identified in the book only as S), who had unique memory skills, including an in-ability to forget. S creates a fascinating case history for psychology. Crovitz wrote a rare and wonderful book. Of course, the book is anything but sensible—it is chaotic, rambling, abrupt, surrealistic. But these are the reasons why it is both a delight and of value. The author tells us of the workings of real and imaged visions, of real and reconstructed memory, and, most important of all, of thinking, intelligence, and creativity.

Serious scientific studies of mnemonics have been performed. Paivio (1971) reviews quite a number in his book. Bower's (1970a) article in the *American Scientist* is perhaps the best introduction, however, and his article on the pegword system is also recommended (Bower, 1970b). (Bower has perhaps done more studies than anyone else on these topics: Bower and Bolton, 1969; Bower, 1972; Bower and Reitman, 1972.) If you wish to learn mnemonic techniques for yourself, the best-selling book by Lorayne and Lucas (1974), *The Memory Book*, or the book by Young and Gibson (1962) provide excellent introductions. The keyword technique has been applied to foreign language vocabulary learning, with apparently very high success (Atkinson and Raugh, 1975; Raugh and Atkinson, 1975).

Finally, there have been some studies of individuals who possess unusual memories. Luria's study of S has already been mentioned. Hunt and Love (1972) studied a person whom they called *VP*. Another form of memory is that known as a "photographic memory" or, in psychology, as eidetic imagery. There is quite a bit of literature on this phenomenon, and it is discussed in the Suggested Reading section of Chapter 8.

8
The Representation of Knowledge

WORDS AND IMAGES

. . . and now we enter the magical world of mental images. . . .
Step right up for bizarre wonderful sights. First, Professor Brooks
showing how the mind works its ways differently for verbal and spa-
tial material. Others will astound, compound, and confound. Come,
enter the wonderful world of mentalism. . . .

The questions we tackle in this chapter revolve about one issue:
how is information stored in human memory? In remembering a novel,
do we remember the visual appearance or the sounds of the words, or
some abstraction of the meaning, or perhaps a mental image of the
things described by that book? When we remember some event that we
have experienced, do we do so by a mental image of that event, complete with the images of the sights, sounds, feelings, smells? Questions
like these get at the heart of the problem of mental processing. If we
knew how information was represented in the mind, we would have overcome one of the major stumbling blocks to our understanding. Not only
do we not know, we are still stumbling over the appropriate ways to ask
the questions.

Let us start with a demonstration. As promised, we bring you Brooks
and his marvelous mentalisms. Here is the problem:

Spatial and Verbal Components of the Act of Recall*

LEE R. BROOKS

When a person is asked to describe from memory a diagram such as a map or floor plan, he is likely to say that he generated a mental representation of the diagram and then derived his description from that. Even in the absence of vivid mental imagery, there is a clear impression that some underlying visual or spatial process is involved in this type of performance. In contrast, the process involved in recalling a specific sentence seems to have more to do with speech than with vision or spatial movements. If there is a visualized component in sentence recall, it appears to be less crucial than in the recall of spatial relationships.

This paper will present performance data to support the subjectively plausible notion that verbal and spatial information are handled in distinct, modality-specific manners. These data are obtained from experiments which induce conflict between overt responding and the act of recall. Subjects are asked to recall memorized material (sentences or line diagrams) and to simultaneously signal information about that material. If making signals in one modality (for example, speaking) uniquely disrupts recall of one of these types of material, then it will be assumed that the recall of that material is accomplished in a modality-specific manner. If a different modality of response (for example, pointing to a sequence of symbols) provides the strongest conflict when the recall material is changed, then this type of material will be assumed to be specific to a different modality.

The best way to appreciate the experiments that Brooks performed is to do them yourself. Four simple experiments are presented, organized into two groups of two experiments each. Please do all four. They are easy to do, and the results are usually quite impressive.

Sentences and Saying

Learn this sentence:

Rivers from the hills bring fresh water to the cities.

Now, close your eyes. As quickly as possible, and without looking at the sentence, go through the sentence mentally (without looking at it again), word by word. If a word is a noun, say "yes" (aloud). If the word is not a noun, say "no." Remember, do it as quickly as possible, from memory of the sentence. This task is considered to be difficult by most

* L. R. Brooks. *Spatial and verbal components of the act of recall.* Canadian Journal of Psychology. *1968, 22, 349–350. Copyright © 1968 by the Canadian Psychological Assn. Reprinted by permission.*

who try it. Saying the words "yes" and "no" aloud interferes with the process of going through the sentence.

Sentences and Pointing

Now, try the task again, but with a new sentence and with a slight difference in procedure. This time, as you go through the sentence mentally (but with your eyes open), simply point at the letters in Fig. 8.1. Point to a *Y* if the word is a noun, point to an *N* if it is not. Use a different letter each time, moving your hand down the figure as you go through the sentence. (This is to force you to look at the letters.) Here is the sentence:

A bird in the hand is not in the bush.

The pointing task is much easier for most people than the naming-aloud task. Does this mean that it is harder to say a response than to point to one? No. To demonstrate that, Brooks used another pair of tasks.

Diagrams and Saying

Figure 8.2 shows a block outline of the letter *F*. Go through the figure, starting at the point marked by the star and in the direction shown by the arrow. Each time you come to an outside corner, say the word "yes." Each time you come to an inside corner, say the word "no."

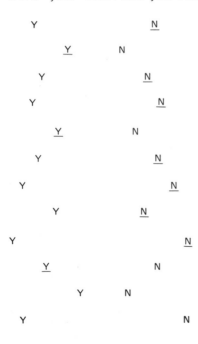

Fig. 8.1. A sample output sheet for the pointing condition of the first experiment. The underlined letters are those one would point to in categorizing the sentence "a bird in the hand is not in the bush." The letters are staggered to force close visual monitoring of pointing.

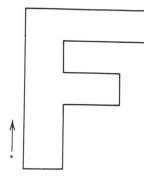

Fig. 8.2. Examples of block letters showing starting point (star) and direction (arrow) in which to follow the outline.

Thus, for Fig. 8.2, you should say: "Yes, yes, yes, no, no, yes, yes, no, yes."

Now, for the real task: learn Fig. 8.3. Do the task, saying the words "yes" and "no" aloud whenever appropriate. Do *not* look at Fig. 8.3. Do the task from your memory of the figure.

Diagrams and Pointing

Finally, here is the last task. Learn Fig. 8.4. This time, do the same task as you did with Fig. 8.3, but this time make your answers by pointing to the *Ys and Ns* of Fig. 8.1, just as you did in the second experiment (*Sentences and Pointing*). Make sure you move down the column of *Ys* and *Ns* as you point. As before, this is to force you to look at them.

The Results

When Brooks did these experiments, there were striking differences in the amount of time it took subjects to do each of the tasks. In the four conditions just described, we have two different types of materials— sentences and diagrams—and two different types of responses—saying

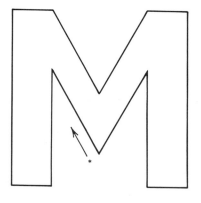

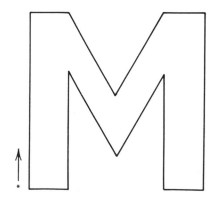

and pointing. Brooks measured the average number of seconds it took to complete each condition:

	Saying	Pointing	Difference
Sentences	13.8	9.8	+ 4.0 seconds
Diagrams	11.3	28.2	− 16.9 seconds

Compare the differences in times. When people were given sentences, it took 4.0 seconds *longer* to do the task by saying the answers than by pointing. When people were given diagrams, the results were dramatically reversed: It took 16.9 seconds *less* time to do the task by saying the answers than by pointing.[1] As Brooks reports:

> *Both major predictions, then, were strongly confimed; vocal output was slowest for categorizing the sentences, and pointing (visually monitored) output was slowest for categorizing the diagrams. The subjects reported that they "could say the sentences to themselves" while tapping or pointing, but not while saying "yes" or "no." The diagrams could be "pictured" while the subjects were tapping or saying "yes" or "no," but not while trying to point. These conflicts reportedly had the effect of making it easier to lose track of where one was in the sentences or the diagrams.*
>
> **(Brooks, 1968, Page 354)**

The results seem plain: the mental operations involved in maintaining the words of the sentence and examining the grammatical class of the words seems incompatible with generating a spoken response, but not with generating a pointing response. Similarly, the mental operations involved in holding a representation of a diagram and making judgments about its parts seem incompatible with a pointing response, but not a verbal one. The incompatibilities must result from interaction of the processes of maintaining the mental representations and selecting and doing the responses. Thus, there is clear evidence for different types of encoding for the two different tasks.

These experiments have been extended, both by Brooks and by other experimenters. For example, a team of workers at the University of Stirling in Scotland demonstrated that a concurrent spatial task can interfere with memory processing of spatial information, and memory processing can interfere with spatial tasks. These experimenters (Bad-

---

[1] Brooks actually had three different types of responses, rather than just the two illustrated here. In one other condition, his subjects were asked to tap (on the table) with the left hand for nouns (or one type of corner) and with the right hand for nonnouns (and the other type of corner). In addition, the task with the diagram was to make a slightly different judgment about the type of corner than described here. None of these changes are important for the present purposes.

deley, Grant, Wight, and Thomson, 1975) examined what happened with performance on a spatial task, a *pursuit rotor,* when it was combined with some of Brooks' tasks. A pursuit rotor has a target that moves around on a variable-speed phonograph turnable. The subject attempts to keep a hand-held stylus on the moving target, and the amount of time that he manages to do this is measured. When subjects had to classify the corners on one of Brooks' diagrams by saying the words "yes" and "no" aloud, performance on the pursuit rotor deteriorated. Yet classifying the words of sentences by saying "yes" and "no" aloud did not affect the pursuit performance. With a different set of tasks (also taken from the work of Brooks), when subjects were instructed not to let performance on the pursuit task suffer, then performance on a spatial mental task deteriorated while doing the pursuit task, but performance on a verbal mental task did not.

The pursuit task is one that requires visual spatial perception. The corner classification task also requires spatial information, whereas the sentence classification task does not. When the corner classification task is done at the same time as a pursuit task, one (or both) of the tasks must suffer. But the sentence classification task does not interfere with the pursuit rotor task. (Note that the sentence classification task interferes with itself. The spoken responses interfere with memory for the sentence, as we saw in the report of Brooks' experiments. But this interference does not carry over to the spatial, pursuit rotor task.)

The evidence seems to be overwhelming. The mental representation of spatial information is in the same form as the information arriving from a spatial task. Thus, if one tries to do a spatial task using information from memory while at the same time doing a spatial task in the world, the two different things interfere with one another. Similarly, verbal information from memory must at some point be in the same form as verbal information coming in through the sensory system. Finally, verbal information and spatial information do not conflict with one another, so they must be represented differently. Baddeley, Grant, Wight, and Thomson described the practical implications:

> *Anyone who has tried to steer a car along a winding road while listening to a football game on the radio will probably have experienced some conflict between the steering and the task of visualizing the play. . . . Listening to a sports commentary is thus probably not the safest way of whiling away a long drive.*
>
> **(Baddeley, et al., 1975, Pages 207, 210)**

VISUAL IMAGES

If more evidence is needed that we process information in memory by means that seem analogous to our processing of real visual scenes, it exists in large quantities. Thus, Moyer (1973) asked people to judge which of two animal names represented the larger one:

Which is larger, a frog or a wolf?

The time it took to make the judgment was a function of the difference in size between the two animals; the larger the size difference, the faster the judgment. It is as if you did the task by looking at the two animals and comparing their sizes. If so, this is a mental looking. Paivio (1975) extended this result in an interesting series of experiments. He showed that he could manipulate the size comparison of two objects by presenting discrepant information. He did this by presenting the two objects that were to be compared as pictures rather than printed names. Sometimes, the apparent sizes of the objects shown in the pictures were the opposite of the actual size relationships. Thus, the subject might be shown the two objects of Fig. 8.5 and asked to determine which was actually the larger one.

Subjects were quicker to respond correctly when the two objects had appropriate size relationships (as in the top part of Fig. 8.5) and

Fig. 8.5. Examples of congruent (top of figure) and incongruent (bottom of figure) physical-size–memory-size relations between pictures. (From A. Pavio Perceptual comparisons through the mind's eye. *Memory and Cognition*, 1975, *3*, 635–647. ©1975 by the Psychonomic Society Inc. Reprinted by permission.

slower when the relationships were discrepant (as in the bottom part). Again, the conclusion is that visually presented and mentally retrieved information is in similar format and therefore can conflict.

Kosslyn (1973) demonstrated another interesting comparison between scanning a mental image and a real image. Think of a tall building, perhaps the Leaning Tower of Pisa in Italy. Focus your attention on the bottom of the structure. Is there a window in the door? Now try another question. Again focusing on the bottom, does the building have a flag on top? Kosslyn showed that the farther the location of the place being tested from the point at which the subject was focusing attention, the longer the time taken to answer the question. (Kosslyn had his subjects make judgments about previously memorized drawings, so there was no problem in judging their answers.) Kosslyn suggests the following interpretation of his results:

Scanning Visual Images*

STEVEN M. KOSSLYN

The results clearly indicated that people can selectively retrieve information from preset spatial locations in a generative image. Furthermore, retrieval of items from an image is a function of actual physical distance from the point of initial focus. One way to look at this result would be to think of an internal representation analogous to the actual picture where S merely fixates on one part, and then scans over the representation if the queried feature is not at the point of focus. Another way of interpreting this finding, which is consistent with some S's introspections, is to think of S having an image of only the part he is immediately "looking" at. When the query comes on, he then retrieves the remainder of the image from memory. In the first case, the image is like a billboard that is all lit up at night and one merely stares at a selected portion of it. In the second case, the billboard is dark except for a portion that is under the immediate spotlight of attention. Both notions involve S's retrieving perceptual features from memory which are organized in terms of spatial relations. In the first case, images are conceived of as inherently integral—the parts are inextricably part of the whole. In the second case, images themselves may be retrieved piecemeal.

Finally, a number of experimenters have asked people to manipulate their mental images. Shepard and Metzler (1971) and Cooper (1975) performed numerous variations on the theme of presenting people with two drawings, asking them to determine whether one is simply a rotated version of the other. They found that the amount of time it takes to make

* S. M. Kosslyn. Scanning visual images: Some structural implications. Perception and Psychophysics, 1973, 14, 93. Copyright © 1973 by Psychonomic Society, Inc. Reprinted by permission.

the comparison depends on how much rotation is involved. More important, the time is linear with the rotation, suggesting that the subjects perform a mental rotation of one image in order to match it to the other. The speed of the mental rotation is not affected by the complexity of the item, but it is affected by how many spatial dimensions it has. It takes about ⅜ second to rotate a two-dimensional object halfway around (180 degrees) and about three seconds to rotate a three-dimensional object the same amount (see Fig. 8.6).

The list of experiments demonstrating the properties of images can

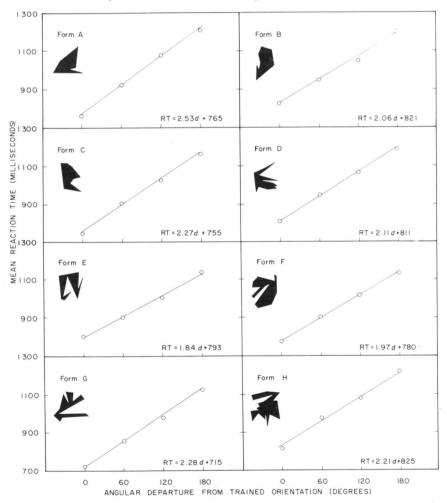

Fig. 8.6. Mean reaction time (*RT*) as a function of angular departure of the test form from the trained orientation, plotted separately for each of the eight forms used in the first experiment. Equations for the best-fitting straight lines are shown. (From L. A. Cooper. Mental rotation of random two-dimensional shapes. *Cognitive Psychology*, 1975, 7, 27. Copyright © 1975 by Academic Press, Inc. Reprinted by permission.)

go on and on. The point seems clear that a number of people have experiences of manipulating images mentally. Images have been reported for all the sensory modalities, but reports of visual, auditory, and kinesthetic (muscle movement) images are most dominant. The reports from people differ, however. Some people claim to have very vivid, dominant mental images, others deny ever having experienced them at all. But experiments such as those just reported seem to require some sort of internal representation closely related to the sensory modality of the material. Whether one wishes to call these experiences images or not seems irrelevant. People do have and do make use of mental representations that mirror some of the properties of the original perception.

The experiments by Brooks indicate that certain types of mental processing can be interfered with by ongoing operations. The hampering of one's memory for the words of a sentence when required to say whether each word is a noun or not, but not when required to indicate the same judgment by a pointing motion, strongly implies that both the memory for the sentence and the generation of the verbal responses compete for the same mechanisms. Similarly, the diagram-judging tasks argue for competition with some spatial or visual mechanism.

Recall our discussions about pattern recognition. There we saw that pattern recognition, and perception in general, required the interaction of conceptually driven processing with data driven processing. That is, the sensory evidence had to be interpreted by means of the information permanently stored within memory. In recognizing an incoming sensory experience, at some point along the processing, the information arriving through the sensory organs has to be in the same form as the information presented by the long-term memory representations. This information must therefore be different for different sensory systems. The information must be specific for the modality. If information from long-term memory must reflect the special characteristics of the sensory system in which the information is being analyzed, then clearly there must be modality-specific information stored within the human memory system.

The experiments by Brooks indicate that there are specialized processing mechanisms for each modality of sensory information. This by itself is not much of a surprise. After all, the ears, eyes, mouth, nose (and so on) represent obvious, highly visible, specialized processing mechanisms. But Brooks's experiments tell us something about how far the difference in specialization is maintained. Thus, all along the way toward holding the words of a sentence or the shape of a diagram temporarily in memory there is specialization. Experiments such as those we discussed on mental scanning and mental rotation indicate that when we manipulate the information held temporarily in memory, the manipulations act as if we were operating on an image in the world. The amount of time it takes to go from one form or one part of a mental image to another form or another part depends on how far apart those two are from each other. There is an analogy between the operations we perform mentally and the operations we actually perform in the world.

THE REPRESENTATION OF INFORMATION IN LONG-TERM MEMORY

The mental representations of information about the world mirror some of the properties of the world. When a representation has this property, we call it an *analogical* representation; it is an analog of the perceptual experience. Another basic representational format has interested psychologists studying memory: *propositional* representation. A propositional system encodes information in terms of interpreted, abstracted statements of the perceptual events. Propositions categorize the objects. The sentences of language, for example, are propositional in nature, and indeed there is a close relationship between work on language analysis and the studies of propositional representation in memory. But proponents of the propositional representation do not restrict their claims to the study of language. They believe that all knowledge could be represented in this form.[2]

The basic problem is this. We wish to understand how information is stored in human memory. All the work on perceptual and pattern recognition processes emphasizes the interpretative, constructive nature of perception, and because the information about the world that gets into a person's memory must have first passed through the perceptual system, the information must also reflect this interpretive, constructive nature.

The representation of knowledge is a fundamental, difficult issue. There is probably no single answer to the question of how knowledge is stored. Moreover, knowledge might be stored in a form different from the form in which it is used. All the experiments on mental imagery were studies of the use of the knowledge, not about how it was stored. Operations performed on the mental representations held in short-term memory seem to be analogous to operations in the world. Moreover, these representations are specific to the modality they present. But these demonstrations do not say much about what the permanent representations might be like.

A number of recent theories of long-term memory in psychology have been concerned with the problem of representation. Perhaps the most popular representational format being studied is that of a *semantic*

---

[2] Note that philosophers have a much more restrictive view of propositional representation than is used here. To most schools of philosophy, a proposition must have a truth value that reflects its veracity as a statement about the world. Thus, philosophers will appear to be using the same language as psychologists, but in fact will be talking about completely different issues.

network, a graphic representation of the network of interrelations among propositions about actions, events, and concepts. The next section of this chapter looks at the literature on the semantic network. We start by examining the major argument for propositional representation, presented by a group of researchers at the University of California, San Diego, known as the LNR Research Group (after the initials of the group's founders—Peter Lindsay, Donald Norman, and David Rumelhart). Their semantic network representation is called an "active structural network."

On Propositional Representation*

DONALD A. NORMAN, DAVID E. RUMELHART, and THE LNR RESEARCH GROUP

A critical issue in the research reported in this book is the format for the representation. The representational format we have adopted suggests that humans retain knowledge in the form of specific statements about the conceptual information present in the information that is stored. The alternative view is that information—most especially perceptual information—is retained as an image that is somehow analogous to the original experience. Many people believe that they have mental images of scenes that they have experienced. This is particularly true in visual and auditory perception. Many people claim to "see" or to "hear" in their mind an accurate, detailed image of past experiences; many can call up from memory the "sounds" of the voices of their acquaintances or "music" that they have experienced. Similar statements are made about all of the senses.

Are these images compatible with the representation of the active structural network? The issues that are involved in this question are complex. There is no easy resolution. Yet, it is our impression that the two apparently differing points of view are, in reality, not quite so different. To separate out all the issues is not easy, and any attempt to do so is bound to raise numerous new issues. It is important to discuss these problems, however, for they are critical to the understanding of much work in contemporary cognitive psychology and artificial intelligence.

To start with the most elementary level at which the problem is often stated, there are two extreme forms of representation:

> A propositional system in which concepts are expressed as statements about the conceptual relationships among the items in the proposition.
> An analogical representation, in which an accurate image of the original scene is maintained.

* *D. A. Norman, D. E. Rumelhart and the LNR Research Group.* Explorations in Cognition. *San Francisco: Freeman, 1975. Pages 16–20. Copyright © 1975 by W. H. Freeman, Inc. Reprinted by permission.*

Thus, if we had piles of blocks on a table, a propositional system might encode the information by such statements as

> Block A is above block B.

> Block A is to the right of block C.

and so on. An analogical representation would be like a photograph—an accurate pictorial image of the table and blocks.

This comparison is not really very accurate. It provides a caricature of both alternatives. In considering a representational format, one must ask about the desired properties of that representation. In part, one wishes to have a representation that allows an easy transaction of operations that need to be performed, whereas operations that are not necessary may be hard to do. With the human memory system, there are a number of different operations that will be required. Sometimes a person needs to perform perceptual tasks, to perform pattern recognition, or to manipulate objects mentally (see Shepard and Metzler, 1971). At times, a person needs to know conceptual relationships.

Humans are flexible in their use of information. They can read upside-down print (although not easily, unless they practice). They can perform mental manipulations of sensory information, and they can recognize sights, sounds, touch, taste, and smells, including visual and tactile texture and auditory timbre. All of this implies the encoding of some sort of direct sensory information. Similarly, they can answer questions about the information that has been stored in ways that imply the storage of conceptual information. We suspect that people are capable of using different forms of representation of the information stored within their memory, and that they are capable of either retrieving an appropriate form or of transforming the information stored into whatever format is most appropriate for answering the questions put to them.[3]

In considering these issues, it is important to note what it means to have a good mental image of something. As soon as a person realizes that mental images—even analog ones—are not the same as photographic reproductions of the original sensory experience, then the door is open for a merger of the two supposedly conflicting ideas about representation. To have a good mental image implies that the mental phenomenon is somehow analogous to the original perception. The mental image is reasonably complete and continuous (to all apparent purposes), and the operations that can be performed upon that image are homomorphic with the operations that can be performed upon perceptions.

The fact that a person "perceives images" when recalling perceptual

---

[3] These issues have been discussed at length in the literature on psychology and artificial intelligence. The critical discussion for us, which has formed the basis for this section, is summarized in Bobrow (1975).

experiences from memory does not mean that information is stored within memory in that way. It only implies that they are processed as images. Thus, on could very well store information within the memory system in one format, and then, when occasion demands, use that information to regenerate the image of which one then becomes aware (see Bower, 1972a). The regenerated image could be a reasonably complete analogy to the original perception of the real world, with all the properties that people ascribe to their images. The regenerated image is likely to contain errors, of course, and the errors will be conceptual ones that reflect the underlying propositional base from which they were constructed. It is the existence of gross conceptual errors in what appears to be a highly detailed accurate memory image that lends support to this suggestion.

There is an alternative explanation of mental images. All that the introspective arguments tell us is that the form of the information reconstituted from memory as an "image" is similar to that of the form of the original perception. But of what form is the original perception?

We know the perceptual information undergoes considerable transformation as it is processed by the sensory nervous system. Physiological mechanisms pull apart the components of the arriving signals and perform intricate types of frequency, temporal, and spatial transforms on the signals. Feature detectors pull out significant parts of the wave forms. And then context, meaning, and past experience play a large role in the interpretation of the information, evidently in the very initial stages of perception and pattern recognition. Items in focal attention stand out as *figure,* with all else perceived as *ground.* Relationships among the various parts of the perceptual field become a fundamental part of what we call the perception of the sensory world. Suppose, for the sake of argument, that the perceptual system that analyzes the arriving sensory signals produces as the result of its operations a conceptual, propositional representation. If so, then the first stage of conscious awareness of the world is already in the form of propositions. Thus we "see" the objects in front of us as books or as pieces of paper, not as gradations of light energy that arrive at the retina: The natural perception of the world is in terms of meaningful patterns.

If this be so, then when we re-create an image from memory, the propositions that we are able to recall are in a form similar to those that we originally perceived. Hence, the claim that we "see" or "hear" a facsimile of the original perception.

There is more to the argument. The major other points concern the need to get access to information that is stored within memory, and to get that access, one must retrieve the individual components of experiences. A detailed argument about the problem of retrieval is provided by Pylyshyn (1973) in his review article and critique of the concept of mental imagery. In fact, Pylyshyn states this particular point so well that it seems best simply to present the argument from his paper.

We take our quotation from the section where Pylyshyn is discussing the commonly held view that people store accurate images of the world and then, when the occasion arises, recall those images and examine them. Thus, this view of things holds that a person is able to re-experience some aspects of the original and, in that re-examination of the image, discover the information that is being sought. This view, says Pylyshyn, runs into difficulty because

> . . . *we can retrieve information about a whole scene or any part of it by addressing aspects of the* perceptually interpreted content *of the scene. Even if we confine ourselves to the retrieval of phenomenal images, we can argue that the content of such images must be already interpreted—in spite of the fact that we seem to be "perceiving" them as we would novel stimuli. This must be so because retrieval of such images is clearly hierarchical to an unlimited degree of detail and in the widest range of aspects. Thus, for example, I might image a certain sequence of events at a party as I recall what happened at a certain time. But I might also image someone's facial expression or the jewel in their ring or the aroma of some particular item of food without first calling up the entire scene. Such perceptual attributes must therefore be available as interpreted integral units in my representation of the whole scene. Not only can such recollections be of fine detail but they can also be of rather abstract qualities, such as whether some people were angry. Furthermore, when there are parts missing from one's recollections, these are never arbitrary pieces of a visual scene. We do not, for example, recall a scene with some arbitrary segment missing like a torn photograph. What is missing is invariably some integral perceptual attribute or relation, for example, colors, patterns, events, or spatial relations (we might, for example, recall who was at the party without recalling exactly where they were standing). When our recollections are vague, it is always in the sense that certain perceptual qualities or attributes are absent or uncertain— not that there are geometrically definable pieces of a picture missing. All of the above suggest that one's representation of a scene must contain already differentiated and interpreted perceptual aspects. In other words, the representation is far from being raw and, so to speak, in need of "perceptual" interpretation. The argument is not simply that retrieval of images would involve a bewildering cross-classification system while retrieval in other forms of representation would not. The point is that because retrieval must be able to ad-*

dress perceptually interpreted content, the network of cross-classified relations must have interpreted objects (i.e., concepts) at its nodes. . . .

We may assume, then, that the representation differs from any conceivable picture-like entity at least by virtue of containing only as much information as can be described by a finite number of propositions. Furthermore, this reduction is not reasonably accounted for by a simple physical reduction such as that of limited resolution. What type of representation meets such requirements? A number of alternative forms of representations are discussed in a subsequent section. For the present, it suffices to point out that any representation having the properties mentioned above is much closer to being a description of the scene than a picture of it. *A description is propositional, it contains a finite amount of information, it may contain abstract as well as concrete aspects and, especially relevant to the present discussion, it contains terms (symbols for objects, attributes, and relations) which are the* results of—not inputs to—*perceptual processes.*[4]

The real issue, it would seem to us, is that the representational format of information that is stored within the human memory system must be one well suited to the kinds of operations that are performed upon it. Arguments about the mode of representation are often really arguments about the type of relations that get encoded. How good is the mapping between the perceptual units and the memory units, between the perceptual operations and the ones of cognitive deduction? How dense or complete is the information that is encoded? Does it include all the information in which one might conceivably later be interested, or does it include only a selected subset of those relationships that were noted at the time of the initial encoding? In the former case, with a rich, dense body of information, retrieval of a particular item might be difficult. In the latter case, with selective encoding, retrieval of information that was not specifically encoded either may be impossible or may require a long chain of deductions.

We believe that the human cognitive system is capable of flexibility in the way it represents the information that it uses. Propositional representation would appear to be well suited for permanent storage of the meaning and interpretation of the events that a person experiences. At times, analogical representations would appear to be better suited for the operations that

[4] From Z. W. Pylyshyn. What the mind's eye tells the mind's brain: A critique of mental imagery. *Psychological Bulletin,* 1973, *80,* 10–11. Copyright © 1973 by American Psychological Association. Reprinted with permission of author and publisher.

one wishes to perform upon mental structures. But because the fundamental differences between the two forms of representation are not clear, and because it appears to be possible to transform one form of representation into the other, we do not feel that this apparently basic issue is, in reality, a fundamental one about mental representation.

SEMANTIC NETWORKS

In March 1971, Endel Tulving and Wayne Donaldson organized a conference on the organizational processes of memory. The conference was held at the top floor of the "Cathedral of Learning," a tall, imposing building at the University of Pittsburgh. The topic of the meeting was meant to be the organizational properties of human memory, and many of the papers indeed reflected that theme. But as the participants sat in the conference room, viewing Pittsburgh through the glass, it became clear that a new area of psychological investigation was beginning. Suddenly, a whole new problem was being discussed by psychologists: the attempt to state in formal terms the representation of knowledge in memory. The conference, and the publication of its proceedings the next year (Tulving and Donaldson, 1972), marked an important new direction in psychological theorizing.

The impact of that conference (or rather, of the book that resulted from the conference) says more about the workings of science than of the originality of the ideas presented there. The fundamental approaches to the study of semantic memory had already been set out prior to the conference. Perhaps the most important works were the book by Reitman six years earlier, (1965) and the doctoral dissertation by Quillian five years earlier (1966, 1968). Quillian's work attracted little attention until the series of experimental studies performed by Collins and Quillian, most especially their paper in 1969. Reitman's book (1965) contained many of the ideas considered new and important today, but it, too, attracted little attention. Quillian and Reitman were simply too far ahead of the field.

Although psychology wasn't ready to accept the work on semantic networks at the time of the conference, the stage for this work had been set in the fields of computer science and artificial intelligence, partly due to the work of Newell and Simon on information-processing models at the Carnegie Institute of Technology (now the Carnegie-Mellon University); both Quillian and Reitman did their work at Carnegie. Some of this early work on human memory structures is reported in the books of papers by Feigenbaum and Feldman (1963: *Computers and Thought*); Minsky (1963: *Semantic Information Processing)*; and Schank and Colby (1973: *Computer Models of Thought and Language)*. The work reported in these books was just starting to attract interest among psychologists at the time of the Pittsburgh conference. Thus, the conference was well timed to provide impetus to the field, and the publication of the book by Tulving and Donaldson constituted the first serious encroachment of the study of memory representation into the mainstream of psychological research.

Perhaps the best way to understand what the work is about is to jump right in. Two books on these issues describe two of the related, but differing approaches. One, by Anderson and Bower (then both at Stanford University), the other by the LNR Research Group. We have already seen a bit of the LNR argument, and we return to it later. We follow Anderson and Bower's description of their work just far enough into the technicalities to get a feel for the representation. (The term HAM stands for their model of human associative memory.)

Human Associative Memory*

JOHN R. ANDERSON and GORDON H. BOWER

We found that memory could no longer be conceived as a haphazard jumble of associations that blindly record contiguities between elements of experience. Rather, memory now had to be viewed as a highly structured system designed to record facts about the world and to utilize that knowledge in guiding a variety of performances. We were forced to postulate entities existing in memory which have no one-to-one correspondence with external stimuli or responses.

— — —

It also became necessary to postulate the existence in the mind of highly complex parsing and inferential systems which function to interface the memory component with the external world. Furthermore, we were forced to postulate the existence of innately specified ideas in the form of semantic primitives and relations. We will therefore be proposing and arguing for a radical shift from the associationist conceptions that have heretofore dominated theorizing on human memory.

— — —

To put it plainly, the purpose of long-term memory is to record facts about various things, events, and states of the world. We have chosen the subject-predicate construction as the principle structure for recording such facts in HAM. In HAM we predicate of some subject S that it has a certain

* J. R. Anderson and G. H. Bower. Human Associative Memory. Washington, D.C.: Winston, 1973. Pages 2–3, 156–157. Copyright © 1973 by V. H. Winston & Sons. Reprinted by permission.

property *P*. Consider the four example sentences in Fig. 8.7*a* and their representations in HAM. In each case, a particular node (called the *fact* node) sprouts two links or arcs, one arc, labeled *S*, pointing to the subject node, and a second arc, labeled *P*, pointing to the predicate node. The fact node represents the idea of the fact being asserted. James Mill would have called it a *duplex* idea, formed from the complex ideas of the subject and of the predicate. It is an idea that has some of the same functional properties as the subordinate ideas to which it points. For instance, we can predicate properties of such ideas (fact nodes) just as we can predicate of simple ideas like "a balloon." To illustrate, a fact can be said to be false, or probable, or

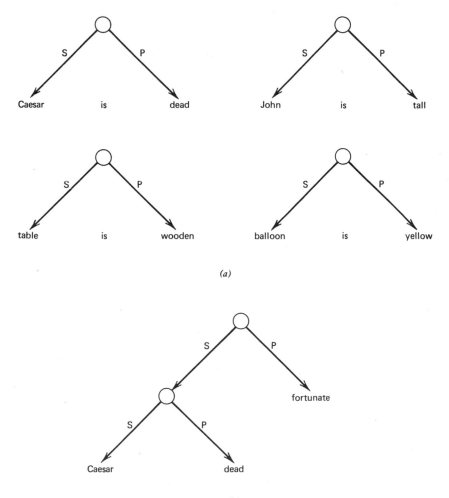

(a)

(b)

Fig. 8.7. (*a*) Examples of how the subject-predicate construction may be used to express simple propositions. (*b*) Example of a predication about a fact node.

amusing, or fortunate, etc. Figure 8.7*b* illustrates how one may predicate a property of a fact, asserting in this case that "It is fortunate that Caesar is dead." This approach permits representation of a number of such predications embedded inside one another to arbitrary depths. For instance, one can encode and represent "It is false that it is believed that it is fortunate that Caesar is dead."

The subject-predicate distinction is an ancient and honorable one which can be traced at least as far back as Aristotle. Roughly speaking, it permits one to introduce a topic (the subject) and then to make some comment about it (the predicate). It is often observed that predication is the principle function of language.

In this excerpt from the work of Anderson and Bower, we can begin to see the format taken by these models of memory. First, they are propositional in nature, representing information in terms of statements. Second, they can be depicted graphically as a set of nodes (points) and relations (arrows) which interconnect the nodes. The work actually is much richer than has been depicted here, but it is difficult to go any deeper without going all the way.

The LNR approach is related, but different, as shown in a further excerpt:

The Representation of Information in Memory*

D. A. NORMAN, D. E. RUMELHART, and THE LNR RESEARCH GROUP

The goal is to represent the conceptual relationships that we believe exist within human memory in a precise and formal manner. The representation must be flexible enough to encompass a wide range of human capabilities. It must not be restricted to a single domain or to a single activity. Thus, it must be able to handle the concepts expressed in natural language, but it should not be restricted to linguistic information. Sensory, experiential, emotional, and cognitive aspects of information must all be present. We would like a homogeneous representational format, so that information can be used in similar manner by all mental processes regardless of its initial source or eventual use. The representation should also be useful in suggesting possible experimental tests.

— — —

THE ACTIVE STRUCTURAL NETWORK

Our approach can be illustrated by considering the analysis of two sentences:

* D. A. Norman, D. E. Rumelhart and the LNR Research Group, 1975, op. cit. Pages 8–12.

Peter put the package on the table.

Because it wasn't level, it slid off.

We want the memory structure to reflect the important underlying propositions. First, there is the existence of the objects that the sentences refer to: Peter, a package, and a table. Next, there are the several events that occurred: Peter was responsible for getting the package on the table; the table was tilted, and as a result, the package slid off it. Figure 8.8 shows how we start the analysis. This figure is a hybrid. It combines a diagrammatic sketch of the information that is to be conveyed with an introduction to the representation of that information.

The basic system that we use for representing information is that of semantic networks. The structure, formally, is a directed graph, with nodes connected to each other by labeled, directed relations. We have expanded upon the procedures normally used in semantic networks, adding the ability to include active procedural information—programs that say how a particular

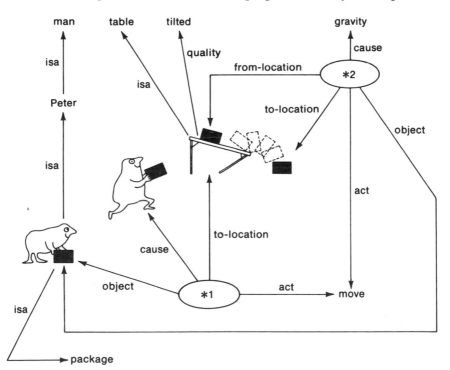

Fig. 8.8. A diagrammatic representation of the active structural network showing the concepts and events that underlie the sentences "Peter put the package on the table" and "Because it wasn't level, it slid off." The two nodes labeled *1 and *2 are instances of the movements involved. The arrows indicate relations. The label on an arrow specifies the type of relation, and the direction of the arrow indicates the direction in which that relation is to be interpreted.

task should be performed. In addition, we have devised a fairly elaborate notational system for incorporating the schemata that we believe underlie human memory into the network representation. For these reasons, we call our structures *active structural networks*. For the moment, consider Fig. 8.8.

The basic conceptual information shown in Fig. 8.8 is that Peter caused the package to move from its earlier location to the top of the table, and that gravity was the causal agent that then acted upon the package, causing it to move from the table top onto the floor. The first movement is represented by a node—the oval numbered *1. The oval is one form of a node, and the labeled arrows that lead from the oval to the concepts (or words) in the figure are called the relations. The relations show how the different nodes and structures in the figure are related to one another. Thus, looking at node *1, we see that it represents an instance of the **act** of **move**. This particular instance of **move** has as its **cause**, Peter (shown diagrammatically), and the **object** being moved is a package (again, shown diagrammatically). The **location** to which the moved object went (the **to-location**) is the table. The second node, the oval labeled *2, is another instance of **move**. Here, the **cause** is gravity, the **object** is the same package, and the movement takes place from a **from-location** (the table top) to a **to-location** (the floor).

The two ovals in Fig. 8.8 represent the two major propositions. The other concepts shown in the figure are also represented within the structural network as nodes, although this diagram does not really show how. The picture of the table is shown to be an instance of a node. The relation **isa** can be read to mean "is an instance of." Thus, the picture of the table is an instance of the concept of table. The drawings of the package and of Peter are instances of the nodes that are named "package" and "Peter."

Clearly, the representation shown in Fig. 8.8 is not yet complete. We need a procedure that allows us to represent not only the basic sentences that are under analysis, but the underlying conceptual structure that they must represent. Figure 8.9 shows how we can expand the first sentence. The top part of the figure represents the basic sentence structure itself: Peter put the package on the table. The bottom part of the figure illustrates the encoding of the underlying conceptual structure.[5]

Expressed in words, Fig. 8.9 conveys the idea that when Peter put a package on the table **iswhen** an **event** (of which Peter was the **agent**) caused the **result** that caused the package to change its location from a place unspecified to a new place, on top of the table.

The action done by Peter to move the package is not known. Hence, it

---

[5] In this figure, and in general throughout the book, we simplify the drawings by omitting the relation **act** between a node and the action of which it is an instance. We then label the node with the name of its action or concept. Thus, in Fig. 8.9, the propositions labeled **put, CAUSE, DO, CHANGE,** and **LOC** (location) are actually instances of the actions defined by those labels.

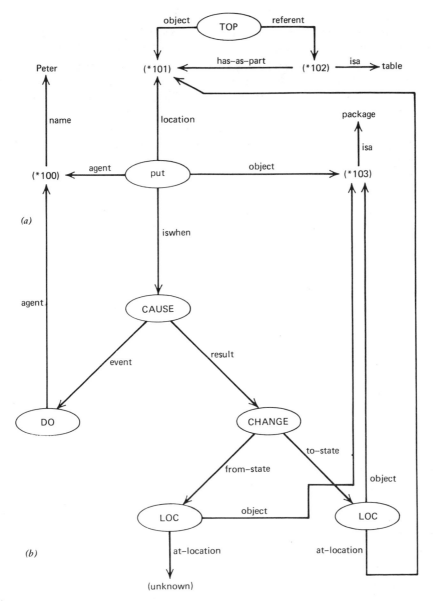

Fig. 8.9. (a) The basic representation of the sentence "Peter put the package on the table." (b) The result after the sentence has been expanded into the underlying conceptual structure.

is specified by the dummy action named **DO** in the figure. The node labeled **CAUSE** shows that the event indicated by **DO** had the result of causing a change, the node represented by **CHANGE**. This change was from a state represented by the **LOC** node on the left (which specifies only that the package had some unknown location) to a state represented by the **LOC** node on the right (which specifies that the package is at a location given by node ***101**).[6] This node ***101** represents a physical object that is the top part of the object represented by node ***102** and, thus, the top part of the table.

The representation for the second sentence should show that when the package slid, it changed location from a position on the table to a position at the edge of the table, where the first position was higher than the second. Moreover, the movement was caused by the force of gravity. The package was in contact with the table during the movement, and afterward, it had traveled beyond the edge of the table where, no longer being supported, it fell to a new supporting surface. This is not the place to continue with a detailed analysis. The point is that the representational system must be able to show the underlying conceptualizations of any information that is to be stored. A large set of conceptual frameworks or schemata is required to organize and interpret the information. Moreover, this conceptual knowledge will often need to use widely based, general world knowledge.

In this excerpt we see the emphasis is on representing the conceptual structures present in memory. Another major issue that has been investigated is the relationships of word meanings to one another. It is clear that different words form close relationships with one another. Thus, verbs of movement (go, move, travel, ride, drive, sail, walk, run, sprint, . . .) are clearly related, as are verbs of possession (have, give, take, transfer, buy, sell, . . .). Similarly, nouns form classes of related concepts, as do other words. These relationships need not be restricted to language, of course, and our concepts for nonlinguistic concepts and experiences are also related to one another. One major relationship among items is a hierarchical arrangement by the classes into which they fall.

In that early conference at Pittsburgh, Collins and Quillian spent considerable time discussing what might be meant by a hierarchical organization. Here is part of what they said.

---

[6] The numbers preceded by asterisks (as in ***103**, pronounced "star 103") are arbitrary names assigned to the nodes for convenience in referring to them. The numbers have no other significance.

How to Make a Language User*

ALLAN M. COLLINS and M. ROSS QUILLIAN

THE HIERARCHICAL ORGANIZATION OF CONCEPTS

Among the semantic properties of concepts, there are several special property relations that are commonly found. They are special because they permit certain kinds of inferences to be made. A frequently used kind is the *superset* or superordinate relation. All properties of a superset (e.g., people can see) also hold for the instances of that superset (e.g., Aristotle) unless otherwise indicated (e.g., Helen Keller could not see). In many cases, the superset is the most accessible property of a concept, though not always (e.g., it is probably not the most accessible property of a nose that it is an appendage or a body organ). In contrast, the subsets of a concept are not easily accessible properties in general (e.g., when thinking about cows, a person is not likely to consider the fact that one kind is a Guernsey). This asymmetry between supersets and subsets probably stems, at least in part, from the asymmetry in inference, since properties of a subset do not usually hold for a concept.

There is often more than one superset of a concept; in many cases, there is a frequently used superset and one or more lesser supersets within the frequently used superset. A hawk is a bird, but it is also a bird-of-prey; a dog is an animal, but it is also a mammal, and within that group a canine; Paraguay is a country, but it is also a Latin American country, a South American country, an underdeveloped country, and a military dictatorship.[7] Occasionally, there are other supersets that do not lie within the frequently used superset (e.g., a canary is a bird, but also is commonly a pet). There are clearly large differences in accessibility between these different supersets.

* A. M. Collins and M. R. Quillian. How to make a language user. Organization of Memory. E. Tulving and W. Donaldson (Eds.). New York: Academic Press, 1972. Pages 319–322. Copyright © 1972 by Academic Press, Inc. Reprinted by permission.

[7] This raises the problem of whether all properties should be stored as supersets, since this makes inferences easier. It is easier to retrieve the properties of military dictatorships (e.g., they imprison dissidents) for Paraguay, if Paraguay is stored as a military dictatorship rather than as having a military dictator. Similarly, it would be easier to retrieve properties of hot objects (e.g., they burn hands) for an oven rack, if oven rack is stored as a hot object rather than as being hot. We don't know where to draw the line in setting up supersets, but it seems a bit much to have supersets such as hot objects or objects on Gorky Street. More likely, a person infers that oven racks will burn hands by analogy with the fact that irons (or whatever object he has learned about) burn hands. In the same sense though, canine and marsupial may not generally be supersets either, except to zoologists. If asked whether marsupials hop, people who know kangaroos are marsupials will probably answer "yes," but they must get the property from kangaroos and not from marsupials. That is to say, the property is inferred from an example just as with the iron.

Superset is a transitive relation so that concepts form chains where each concept has a more general concept as its superset. For instance, a hawk is a bird and a bird is an animal, so that indirectly animal is a superset of hawk. It is also possible to find superset chains among verbs. For example: to sprint→ to run→ to go→ to do; to speed→ to drive→ to go→ to do. A rather long superset chain is: mallard→ duck→ bird→ animal→ living thing→ object. (If this is the longest such chain, it puts mallard squarely at the bottom of memory.) Generally though, these chains do not seem to be more than about three or four steps long, so that semantic memory must be rather shallow on the whole.

Supersets are frequently used in the formation of questions like those in Table 8.1. For example, if a teacher wants to quiz a student about information he should have learned, then, the teacher will usually formulate the kinds of questions shown in Table 8.1. The first two groups show that appropriate questions can be phrased in terms of the superset of the concept sought for both verbs (group 1) and nouns (group 2). By trying to formulate questions of this sort, it is possible to determine the superset(s) of a concept. The last group of examples in Table 8.1 show that the distinction between who, what, where, and when rests on high-level supersets (in parentheses). We think people use superset chains to reach these high-level supersets every time they formulate these kinds of questions.

As alternatives to the structure described, at least two other kinds of structures might be proposed. One possibility is that all the supersets of which a concept is a member are stored directly with the concept. The five supersets listed above for mallard would all be direct supersets of mallard,

TABLE 8.1. Examples of Superset Use in Formulating Questions

Information	Question about the Information
He *sped* to the hospital.	How did he *drive* to the hospital?
He *drove* to work.	How did he *go* to work?
He *went* to the movie.	What did he *do*?
He killed a *mallard.*	What kind of *duck* did he kill?
She liked *ducks.*	What kind of *birds* did she like?
He saw a *doctor* he knew (*person*).	*Whom* did he see?
He saw a *camel* (*animal*).	*What* did he see?
He put it on the *desk* (*thing*).	On *what* did he put it?
He went to a *football game* (*event* or *activity*).	*What* did he go to?
He saw it in the *sky* (*place*).	*Where* did he see it?
He saw it in *September* (*time*).	*When* did he see it?

just as canine, mammal, and animal are, according to our suggestion, direct supersets of dog. The other possible extreme is that the memory is rigidly hierarchical such that each higher-level superset can only be reached indirectly via a lower-level superset. For example, dog would have animal as an indirect superset via some chain like: dog→ canine→ mammal→ animal. Either of these alteratives is much tidier than the proposed structure.

The latter of these alternatives can be ruled out, we think. Reaction time data (Collins and Quillian, 1971) indicate that it takes longer to decide that mammals, such as dog, are mammals, than to decide they are animals. This cannot be due to a difficulty in retrieving the concept "mammal" from the word "mammal" as compared with "animal," because the category name was given in advance and a series of trials used the same category. This is opposite the finding that it takes longer to decide birds such as hawk are animals than to decide they are birds. The finding about mammals and animals is not possible if a person decides a dog is an animal via a path through mammal.

On the other hand, the first alternative hypothesis, namely that all the supersets are stored directly with the concept, is not ruled out by the above experiment. The fact that it takes longer to decide a hawk is an animal than to decide it's a bird agrees with our earlier suggestion that deciding a hawk is an animal involves the path through bird. But on the first alternative hypothesis, animal might merely be a less accessible superset stored with each bird name. Against this possibility, we would point out that if a person is told what a mallard is, he only is told that it is a duck. It is very unlikely he would be told directly it is an animal, a living thing, or an object. When he learns a mallard is a duck, he may possibly infer from his previous knowledge that it must also belong to the higher level categories and store that information directly with mallard. However, all the evidence to date (Collins and Quillian, 1969, 1970), though not conclusive, indicates that the inference is made each time it is needed.

Work on representational issues has taken a number of different forms in psychology. Much of it has been concerned with examining the details of the representation and with trying to establish the principles for applying it to a wider variety of knowledge domains. Other work has concentrated on examining the hierarchical nature of the representation. Thus, the first interpretations of the statements by Collins and Quillian led researchers to test strict hierarchies, to see whether a dog was stored as a mammal, and a mammal as an animal, and an animal as an animate being, and so on. As early as the Tulving and Donaldson conference in 1971, Collins and Quillian denied that view, but it still was attractive enough for many people to pursue actively. Here is their refutation of that view, a statement continuing from the previous excerpt from Collins and Quillian (Pages 322–323):

SEMANTIC ORGANIZATION AND INFERENCE

One possible misinterpretation of the last section is that mammal is stored as a superset directly with most mammals. In our view, it is not likely that many animals would have a pointer to mammal other than odd cases such as whale, bat, maybe kangaroo, and a few of the most obvious examples, such as dog. We think this is so because people learn when they are children that beavers and seals are animals, but it is rare that they learn that a beaver or a seal is a mammal. Furthermore, while canine may be stored as a superset of dog, it probably is not for wolf, though wolves are canines. There are various kinds of information that can be used to decide whether a wolf is a canine or a beaver is a mammal, so such facts need not be stored directly. We will discuss how people make such decisions in a later section, but one kind of information that people may use depends on the *similarity* relation. Like the superset relation, this has implications for the structure of memory.

At this point one can see the general thrust of the work. First, there is some representational system for diagramming the way that units of knowledge are interrelated within human memory. Then, there are various strategies for showing how information in sentences or information extracted from the world by perceptual processes might be represented within these representational systems. Finally, there are statements about how the various informational structures are used. Above all the representational issues, there are considerations about the processes operating on the memory structures. Thus, in their paper at the Pittsburgh conference, the LNR Research Group identified several different aspects:

*A Process Model**

D. E. RUMELHART, P. H. LINDSAY, and D. A. NORMAN

Consider two basic aspects of the problem. The first is the structure of the data base, the way by which information is represented in the LTM. The second is the nature of the processes which operate upon the data base. There need be no formal distinction between that information which is a part of the data base and which is a process operating upon the data base. One very important aspect of our process model of memory is that processes are stored in the data base. They may be retrieved and used like any other information, or they may be activated and thereby perform their processing operations upon other data. Finally, we propose that there is an *interpretive process* which operates on information contained within the data base, retrieving

* D. E. Rumelhart, P. H. Lindsay and D. A. Norman. A process model for long-term memory. Organization of Memory. E. Tulving and W. Donaldson (Eds.). New York: Academic Press, 1972. Pages 198–199. Copyright © 1972 by Academic Press, Inc. Reprinted by permission.

information when necessary and activating (or interpreting) the processes when that is necessary.

To see how these concepts interact, consider the following query:

> Query: In the house in which you lived three houses ago, how many windows were there on the north side?

Most people claim to solve this problem by visualizing the house they now live in, then moving back to each previous house until they arrive at the proper goal. Then they determine in which direction north was with respect to the house, visualize the north wall and mentally traverse the house in a systematic fashion, counting the windows as they proceed. In this retrieval we see several factors operating. First is the determination of a *process* for reaching the solution. Second is the factual information in the *data base* concerning the detailed structure of the house. Third is the *enactment* of the processes in order to complete the task set by the query.

FEATURES AND PROTOTYPES

If a hierarchical organization is not present, and if concepts are indeed related to one another, then how are they stored? Moreover, how are they formed? What causes people to categorize the objects in the world the way that they do? A number of workers have examined the nature of the interrelationships among concepts and have argued that they are organized around "good examples" or "prototypes" of the general concept. Thus, a person's notion of an animal may be derived by judging how well a particular example fits a general, abstract prototype of an animal. Rosch (1973a, 1973b) and Rips, Shoben, and Smith (1973) have argued that to most people, the prototypical animal is something like a horse or dog. Things that look like wolves and dogs are readily judged to be animals, whereas things that do not (fishes, spiders, sea sponges) are not so readily identified. It takes a person longer to decide that a dog is a mammal than that it is an animal, clearly indicating that the organizational structures of these concepts do not simply line up dog, mammal, and animal in a simple chain of supersets. To most people, a robin or sparrow is a bird, but other animals, such as ostriches, are less directly thought to be birds. "Well," someone might say, "technically speaking I suppose that an ostrich is a bird, but it really isn't my idea of one." The word "technically" is what the linguist George Lakoff (1972) has called a *hedge*.

People use hedges to indicate a less than positive belief in a concept. Is a butterfly a bird? Well, loosely speaking, it is. The hedge "loosely speaking" allows the speaker to state what is in fact a false statement, but without uttering a falsehood. (These examples come from Smith, Shoben, and Rips, 1974.) The problem for our understanding of memory is to determine how concepts such as moths, chickens, and sparrows can be represented in memory so that they differ in how well they represent the concept of birds. Smith, Shoben and Rips (1974) suggest that this is done by storing with each concept, lists of *defining features* and *characteristic features*. Defining features are those that are necessary for a particular categorization—for example, that a sparrow has wings and is a biped. Characteristic features are those that are associated with the concept, but need not necessarily hold. Thus, a sparrow's characteristic features might include such things as "perching in trees" and "not a domestic animal." Then, whether or not a concept fits a category is determined by how well the features of that concept match the defining and characteristic features of the category.

The work of Rips, Shoben, and Smith points out a major problem in many contemporary models of memory representation. In general, things that are typical instances of the categories to which they belong are readily and easily judged to be members of that category. Things that are not so typical are not so readily judged. Thus, the amount of time it takes most people to decide that a robin or a sparrow is a bird is considerably less than the amount of time it takes to make the same decision of an ostrich, or even a chicken. Any model of memory that simply has lists or networks that interrelate the different members of a category with the name of the category simply cannot explain these results. There seem to be only two possible routes one can take in attempting to understand how the results come about. Let us examine these possibilities with the specific case of judging whether a sparrow or an ostrich is a bird.

One route is to suggest that the comparison is made by looking at one's representation of a bird, then comparing the features of birds with the features of sparrows and of ostriches. If there is a general, prototypical representation for birds, one would expect "typical" instances such as sparrow to be very close, and therefore match readily. Atypical instances such as ostriches should not match well at all, so for most of us there is some difficulty in making the judgment. For similar reasons, we would tend to believe that bats were birds. Indeed, animals such as butterflies would be more birdlike than some birds. This is the approach taken by Smith, Shoben, and Rips (1974). They believe that one makes judgments by seeing how far away the item to be judged is from the characteristics of the general concept.

The other possible route to explain the observations is to assume that the semantic network does not have a simple, uniform structure. Some of the interconnections between items may be less accessible than others; some may be harder to follow than others. Most of us have encountered sparrows frequently, and the judgment that they are birds is also frequent. Ostriches are not in the normal daily experience of most of us, so information about ostriches is simply less accessible than information about other things. This is the approach taken by Collins and Loftus (1975).

Both routes have their virtues and their deficits. It is likely that people have direct evidence about the class of objects. Most people know that ostriches are birds, that bats are mammals, and that whales and porpoises are also mammals, not fishes. Even if they do not know these things, they can easily be taught by such simple procedures as telling them. Moreover, the ability for people to use information about animals in general to predict attributes or behavior of particular animals argues for direct information about the classification of items, the type of information given by semantic-network hierarchical representations. But if people do know that bats and porpoises are mammals, why do they sometimes make mistakes, why does it take so long to make judgments about these types of instances? This type of behavior argues for the type of representation and comparison operation postulated by Smith, Shoben, and Rips.

Whenever there is a problem such as this, one suspects that the answer lies in some amalgamation of all the ideas. This case is no exception. It would seem likely that the semantic-network representation contains a good deal of the information people do have and use. But it seems equally likely that the type of processing that compares features and that is easier when the two concepts being compared are very similar is a reasonable description of processing mechanisms used by humans. Thus, there is an argument for a particular form of representation on the one hand, and for a particular processing strategy on the other. It is too early to tell, but one suspects that future research will show that the comparison mode of processing advocated by Smith, Shoben, and Rips is applied to representations of knowledge of the sort advocated by semantic-network theorists—not all the time, perhaps, but in cases such as those studied in the experiments now in the literature.

EPISODIC AND SEMANTIC MEMORY

Different studies of semantic memory emphasize different things. Some studies examine definitional structures: how one encodes information such as the concepts of birds and animals or the definitions of words. Other studies are more concerned with how one recalls events and experiences. At the Pittsburgh conference, Tulving argued that these two different emphases are important, and that they mark two different aspects of memory. Tulving calls these two aspects semantic and episodic memory:

*Episodic versus Semantic Memory**

ENDEL TULVING

Episodic memory receives and stores information about temporally dated episodes or events, and temporal-spatial relations among these events. A per-

* E. Tulving. Episodic and semantic memory. Organization of Memory. E. Tulving and W. Donaldson (Eds.). New York: Academic Press, 1972. Pages 385–387. Copyright © 1972 by Academic Press, Inc. Reprinted by permission.

ceptual event can be stored in the episodic system solely in terms of its perceptible properties or attributes, and it is always stored in terms of its autobiographical reference to the already existing contents of the episodic memory store.

—   —   —

Semantic memory is the memory necessary for the use of language. It is a mental thesaurus, organized knowledge a person possesses about words and other verbal symbols, their meaning and referents, about relations among them, and about rules, formulas, and algorithms for the manipulation of these symbols, concepts, and relations. Semantic memory does not register perceptible properties of inputs, but rather cognitive referents of input signals. The semantic system permits the retrieval of information that was not directly stored in it, and retrieval of information from the system leaves its contents unchanged, although any act of retrieval constitutes an input into episodic memory. The semantic system is probably much less susceptible to involuntary transformation and loss of information than the episodic system. Finally, the semantic system may be quite independent of the episodic system in recording and maintaining information since identical storage consequences may be brought about by a great variety of input signals.

—   —   —

The following memory claims are based on mnemonic information stored in episodic memory: (a) I remember seeing a flash of light a short while ago, followed by a loud sound a few seconds later; (b) Last year, while on my summer vacation, I met a retired sea captain who knew more jokes than any other person I have ever met; (c) I remember that I have an appointment with a student at 9:30 tomorrow morning; (d) One of the words I am sure I saw in the first list I studied was LEGEND; (e) I know the word that was paired with DAX in this list was FRIGID.

Each of these statements refers to a personal experience that is remembered in its temporal-spatial relation to other such experiences. The remembered episodes—whether they be as amorphous as "meeting a retired sea captain" or as precisely circumscribed as "seeing a flash of light"—have no necessary extra-episodic reference of any kind. They are autobiographical events, describable in terms of their perceptible dimensions or attributes and in terms of their temporal-spatial relations to other such events.

Now, consider some illustrations of the nature of information handled by the semantic memory system: (a) I remember that the chemical formula for common table salt is NaCl; (b) I know that summers are usually quite hot in Katmandu; (c) I know that the name of the month that follows June is July, if we consider them in the order in which they occur in the calendar, or March, if we consider them in alphabetical order; (d) I know that uncertainty of an event having five equiprobable outcomes is 2.322 bits; (e) I think that the association between the words TABLE and CHAIR is stronger than that between the words TABLE and NOSE.

Although some of these statements refer to the speaker's "knowledge" rather than his "remembering," all of them can be regarded as memory statements in that their content clearly depends upon information entered into the semantic memory at some earlier time. Unlike episodic memory claims, these statements do not refer to personally experienced unique episodes. Rather, content words in these statements represent linguistic translations of information retrieved about general concepts and their interrelations.

The differences between semantic and episodic information are interesting, but controversial. At least one researcher has argued vehemently (although privately) against the concept, stating that all information in memory is encoded reasonably uniformly, so that it makes no sense to attempt to classify it according to such notions as semantic or episodic. Moreover, inasmuch as a classification can be made, all memory is episodic, at least in its inception.

In general, it would appear that concepts that are encountered frequently, especially when encountered in a variety of different settings, all take on aspects that Tulving would call *semantic*. Thus, my memory of my university campus and of the paths I must traverse to get from one building to another seems to have the characteristics of a semantic memory. I know the relationships among the buildings, and in making use of this information, no episodes about past use seem to be required. Similarly, I use the words of the language fluently, without considering when I previously encountered those words.

Other information would seem to be episodic. Thus, my memory for the University of Toronto campus in Canada, where Tulving resides, cannot be separated from my memory of my last visit to Toronto. Trying to recall how one goes to the Psychology Department automatically recreates the last visit there—the snow, the heavy traffic, the various people I met, and the restaurants at which I ate.

But the distinction between the memories of these two university campuses isn't really all that strong. Certainly, repeated exposure to the Toronto campus would cause information about it to become more semantic in quality, more like the memory for the meaning of a word. But this may reflect the ease of memory retrieval for the different aspects of the memory for a campus, not anything as fundamental as a difference in memory storage. Presumably, all information in a semantic memory must derive from information that has been experienced. Thus, although there are differences in our memories that correspond to the distinction between episodic and semantic memory, we must use the distinction with care. As Tulving himself pointed out, the distinction is a useful guideline for the analysis of different aspects of the memory system; it need not reflect a real difference in memory systems.

SOME PROPERTIES OF REPRESENTATIONS

What is meant by a representation? Basically, we mean the manner by which a human retains information about the world. For example, when we see or hear an event, how do we retain that event? Do we maintain something like a photograph or a sound recording? Do we remember only verbal statements about the nature of the event?

It seems clear that we do none of these. Our memory for visual scenes is simply not as accurate or complete as a photographic image, and our memory for sounds is nothing like a recording. But neither are our memories as crude and unsophisticated as a verbalization of the scenes we experience. Moreover, there is good reason for the form of our memory. A photograph or exact recording of events would be relatively useless. It would be so precise and accurate that we might not recognize new repetitions of the same event if they differed even slightly from the original. We could not easily pull out different parts of events. Human memory must be flexible. It must be possible to recognize the scenes we experience in new surroundings. We need to be able to relate one thing to another, to form analogies and metaphors. At the same time, the memories must be rich enough and detailed enough to be able to provide us with information about a variety of questions later on, long after the event occurred.

Memory must be organized according to some fundamental principles, probably according to the contents of the information that is stored. In this chapter we have briefly examined several different formats for a representational scheme. One talked of images, the other of propositions. Some propositions were interconnected by labeled links that pointed from one source of information to another. Some memory structures were composed of lists of relevant features, and access among the different concepts was performed by seeking structures with similar feature lists. All of these systems have virtues, all have deficits. When we ask which might best describe the properties of human memory, we find that each representational scheme both succeeds and fails in some respect.

Figure 8.10 shows a drawing of a table with three objects on it. The drawing itself is a representation of the real-life objects. As a representation, it has certain stylized aspects to it. Still, it is a representation that we would call *analogical,* for it attempts to mirror all aspects of the actual visual experience. Inasmuch as Fig. 8.10 does not succeed, it is only a partial representation of the scene.

When we examine different forms of representing the scene shown in Fig. 8.10, we conclude that all possible representations have features that are analogical with respect to at least some properties of the scene. After all, what is a representation? A representation of something stands for that thing. A representation cannot stand for all aspects of a thing, so

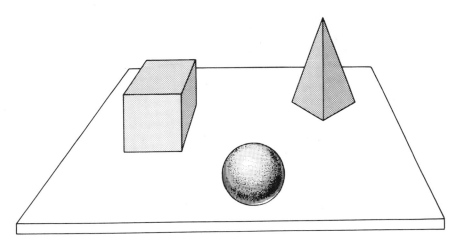

Fig. 8.10. A realistic drawing of a cube, sphere, and pyramid.

it represents only certain aspects. Therefore, the representation must be analogical with respect to those properties. Thus, Fig. 8.10 is analogical with respect to spatial locations, some aspects of shape, and dimensions of the figures. It is not analogical with respect to the color or mass of the figures. Moreover, we cannot tell how many sides the object on the right has: Indeed, it is fundamentally impossible for a representation such as that of Fig. 8.10 to show the properties of the hidden sides of an object.

Consider Fig. 8.11, showing two representations of the same objects shown in Fig. 8.10. These are maps, *not* just top views of that figure. A view from above the table of Fig. 8.10 would be able to see part of the right side of the cube. Figure 8.11*a* is an abstraction of Fig. 8.10; it is still analogical with respect to spatial location along the table and spatial size of the objects, but it has lost other information.

Question: Is Fig. 8.11*b* a propositional or an analogical representation?

Answer: Both. Figure 8.11*b* is propositional with respect to categorizing the properties of the objects. It is analogical with respect to specifying the spatial locations of the center of the bodies.

Moral: Never speak simply of a representation. Always speak of a *representation of X*. Then speak of the representation of X as being *propositional with respect to some specified properties of X* and also *analogical with respect to some specified properties of X*.

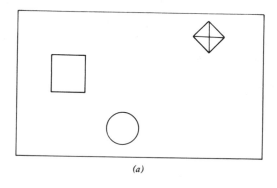

(a)

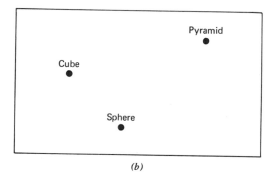

(b)

Fig. 8.11. Two abstract representations of the objects in Fig. 8.10.

Maps

Maps are often thought to be good examples of analogical representation. Do we store maps in the head? This is a favorite question among psychologists. The point that most people overlook, however, is that maps are severe distortions of reality. Moreover, maps contain a large amount of categorical, propositional information. With maps, as with all the other representations, we find that there is a mixture of systems.

Look at the maps shown in Fig. 8.12. The right side (Fig. 8.12b) shows an actual map distributed by students at the University of California, San Diego, to specify where the Psychology Department's students-versus-faculty softball game would be held. The left side (Fig. 8.12a) is taken from the official university map of the same area. In the hand-drawn map there are numerous errors. The scale is incorrect; the two parking lots and the roads leading to them are too regular, with too many right angles. There are gross distortions in the size, shape, and location of the buildings. The shape of the cafeteria is drawn as it is seen from the east side: a T-shaped building. In fact, as the official map shows, the western side of the cafeteria is quite different. Yet it is the western side that is visible from the playing field. Blake Hall is shown in the wrong location and badly distorted in size. The Revelle apartments

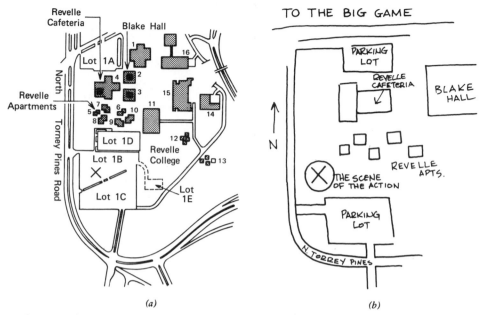

Fig. 8.12. (*a*) A professionally drawn-to-scale map of the Revelle College campus. (*b*) A hand-drawn map of the same area.

(student dormitories) are correct only in spirit; every detail is inaccurate —their number, sizes, shapes, and locations.

Notice that both maps shown in Fig. 8.12 contain a lot of propositional information. The arrow pointing north is a propositional statement, as is the convention used in the official map that north is toward the top. The buildings, roads, and parking lots are shown in outline form, highly contrasted from the surroundings. Neither map looks like a photograph. Both maps use verbal labels to identify the items of interest.

Despite the errors and distortions, despite the discrepancies from reality, both maps are efficient representations. Everyone managed to find the game—the hand-drawn map was easy to follow. Most people were unaware of the errors. All representations are combinations of forms and are analogical with respect to some features, but even maps that might be thought to be purely analogical representations contain highly schematized, propositional information.

Networks and Lists

In Fig. 8.13 we show another representation of the objects on the table in Fig. 8.10. These two representations are of the form that most people would consider to be "pure propositional." Figure 8.13*a* shows the representation commonly called a *semantic network*; Fig. 8.13*b* shows

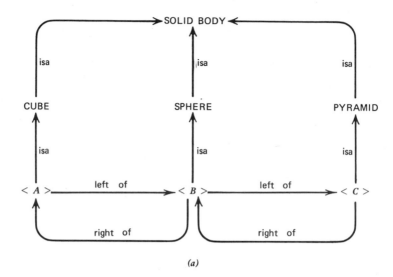

Fig. 8.13. Two more representations of the objects in Fig. 8.10. (*a*) A semantic network. (*b*) A list structure.

A
  isa   CUBE
  left-of   B

B
  isa   SPHERE
  left-of   C
  right-of   A

C
  isa   PYRAMID
  right-of   B

CUBE
  isa   SOLID-BODY

SPHERE
  isa   SOLID-BODY

PYRAMID
  isa   SOLID-BODY

Fig. 8.13(b)

the representation called a *list structure*. Both are exactly equivalent in terms of the information they contain. They do differ, however, in the ease of using the information in the representation. Thus, the semantic network is easier for people to look at and to use. The list structure is closer to how the semantic network would be represented in a computer. Note that both of these representations are analogical with respect to at least one aspect of spatial representation. Look at the objects in Fig. 8.10. If you look from left to right, you first see the cube, then the sphere, then the pyramid. Look at the node marked A in either Fig. 8.13*a* or 8.13*b*. Note that node *A* **isa** cube. Follow the **left-of** relation and you get to the node marked *B*: Node *B* **isa** sphere. Follow the **left-of** relation from *B* and you can get to *C*: *C* **isa** pyramid. Following the **left-of** relations in the propositional representation, you encounter the objects in the same sequence as you get by performing the operation of moving your eyes from left to right in the real world. Different orderings of information result from following other relations or by moving the eyes in different paths.

The representations in Fig. 8.13 do not say anything about size or distance. This information could be added by using other propositions to specify sizes and distances. Figure 8.13 does state directly that the left-most object is a cube, and that a cube is a solid body. To determine this from Fig. 8.10, we must look at the figure, categorize the items we see, and deduce that one of them represents a cube, which we also know to be a solid body.

Representation in Humans

How do people store information? The proper conclusion is that different forms of information are necessary for different purposes. Imagelike information is used for some tasks. Categorization and semantic information seem necessary for other tasks.

Humans have great flexibility in the use of their information. There must be both propositional representation and analogical information intermixed. If images are stored, they must be stored in a meaningful way, grouped and organized by their contents, and accessible by a variety of routes. If several different modes of storage are used in human memory, there must be sufficient interrelationships among the different storage modes to allow access to all modes.

It would appear that people can transform information into the most appropriate form necessary for answering questions. Thus, whatever the storage format of information in memory (and there could be several), when the information is used, it most likely becomes transformed into whatever format is most appropriate.

In an important paper on the nature of representation, the computer scientist Daniel Bobrow has concluded that representations have many different dimensions (Bobrow, 1975). Different representations differ in how well they specify information along the various dimensions. One dimension is the completeness or the continuity of the information. Traditionally, people think of propositional representations as being discrete and not very complete, while analogical representations are considered to be continuous and complete (dense). As the examples we have just discussed show, different representations vary in how complete or continuous they are, and this dimension cuts across the distinction of analogous or propositional formats.

SUGGESTED READINGS

This chapter has examined a broad variety of issues, from mental imagery through the representation of knowledge. Accordingly, there are many sources of information that can be followed.

Mental Imagery

Richardson's book (1969) provides a convenient start. It does not include any of the recent work on experimental studies of imagery, but it does review the earlier work and provides a good discussion of many of the phenomena. Paivio (1971) provided a compilation of literature on verbal learning as it relates to imagery, especially the earlier studies. Paivio believes that the human has two separate storage systems—one for images, one for propositions. His opinion contrasts with the opinions stated in this chapter. Kosslyn (1973, 1975) has completed some interesting papers on the phenomena of mental images. Lea (1975) presented some related experiments and a minor disagreement with Kosslyn. The debate between Pylyshyn (1973) and Paivio (1975) is both fun and enlightening, especially when realizing that although these two psychologists argue with one another in the psychological journals, they both are members of the same department (at the University of Western Ontario, in London, Ontario, Canada).

Photographic Memory

Do people have photographic memories? How about some people? Does anyone? The debate is inconclusive. Eidetic imagery, as the phenomenon is called, was once one of the major areas of study in psychology. Today it is hardly studied, and no one quite knows what to make of it. Haber (1969) and Leask, Haber, and Haber (1969) provided good starts, but Gray and Gummerman (1975) is perhaps the best of the reviews. Perhaps the interested reader should start (and finish?) with it. Perhaps the most dramatic case of eidetic imagery reported in the modern literature is that reported by Stromeyer (1970) and again by Stromeyer and Psotka (1970). The case was also discussed by Gray and Gummerman (1975). These studies report on an unusual memory ability possessed by one woman. The tests appear foolproof. Many psychologists are skeptical, but without any good reason. Unfortunately, the woman is no longer willing to be used as an experimental subject (for very understandable reasons), and despite repeated searches, no other person has yet been found with a similar facility. Anyone seriously interested in eidetic imagery must also read the discussion of the Stromeyer and Psotka experiment by Julesz (1971, Pages 239–246), the person who provided the foolproof test of memory ability. (Julesz's book, by the way, is highly recommended to anyone interested in visual perception, especially stereoscopic perception.) One other person with an unusual sensory memory is the famed Russian mnemonist S, described in the delightful book by Luria (1968). S has remarkable synesthesia, a situation in which the sensory systems interact. Sounds produced a sense of light, color, taste, and touch, and he could remember a person's voice by the visual images it produced. The story is fascinating, and it obviously poses some interesting problems about the representation of information.

Note that an excellent memory for photographs or pictures in general is true for most people. Thus, although most of us do not have photographic memories, we can remember thousands of visual images. When you read a magazine or book, you usually can remember whether or not you have seen the illustrations before, especially if the illustrations are color photographs. This is true even if you originally saw them years previously. A number of people have studied picture memory; see Nickerson (1965), Shepard (1967), and the culmination, Standing's (1973) paper titled *Learning 10,000 Pictures.*

The Representation of Knowledge

A number of papers on representational issues are important. The easiest introduction to semantic networks is provided by chapters 10 and 11 of Lindsay and Norman (1972). Chapters 1, 2, and 11 in the LNR book (Norman, Rumelhart, and the LNR Research Group, 1975) address these issues at a more sophisticated level, as does chapter 7 of Anderson and Bower (1973). Two important papers (both mentioned in the chapter) are those by Bobrow (1975) and Pylyshyn (1973). The *Psychological Review* paper by Collins and Loftus (1975) provides some additional properties of semantic networks, proposing a "spreading activation" theory of processing. The papers by Rips, Shoben, and Smith (1973) and Smith, Shoben, and Rips (1974) suggest a different form of representation, one based on feature spaces. Rosch (1973a, 1973b) has contributed a number of important views on representation that have influenced the discussions in this chapter. In addition, she has two other major papers, Rosch (1975) and Rosch (in press).

There are now a number of major books on the problem of representing information within human memory. The LNR book (Norman, Rumelhart, and the LNR Research Group, 1975) has already been discussed, as has the book by Anderson and Bower (1973). Kintsch's (1974) book is relevant, although it has more emphasis on linguistic analysis. The books by Schank and Colby (1973) and by Bobrow and Collins (1975) emphasize the artificial intelligence aspects of representation. The Bobrow and Collins book does talk about a number of important psychological issues, including the higher-order organizational factors of memory, especially the papers by Bobrow and Norman (1975), Rumelhart (1975), and Schank (1975). Winston's (1975*b)* book has some papers relevant to the representation of visual information (especially by Winston, 1975*a*), and the paper on frames by Minsky (1975) in that book will probably become a major, fundamental contribution to our understanding of memory structures. This paper is a "must" for anyone seriously interested in the problems of the representation of knowledge. [The papers by Kuipers (1975) and Winograd (1975) in the Bobrow and Collins book are follow-ups on Minsky's frames paper.] Some of the more recent work on the representation of knowledge is contained in *The Structure of Human Memory* edited by Cofer (1976). This book goes into the episodic-semantic memory distinction, and also provides several views of higher-order organizational principles—of propositional representation, of schemas, and of scripts. Norman, Gentner, and Stevens (1976) apply some of these notions to problems in education. Nelson Goodman's *Language of Art* (1968) provides an important and readable discussion of some aspects of the philosophical issues of knowledge representation.

9
Practice and Skilled Performance

This chapter is for fun. The main points of the book have been given; the lessons are finished. Now let us examine one set of applications of the principles discussed in the previous chapters: the role of attention and memory in skilled performance. Many of you will find examples other than the ones cited here. Fine—if that happens, the point has been made. The principles stated in this book are real; they apply to all of us. The chapters were not simply sterile lessons in some abstract, theoretical psychology. They govern the way in which we operate in our daily activities.

PERFORMING FROM MEMORY

Today, great accuracy in one's memory is seldom needed. Few people need to memorize speeches, books, or dramatic orations. There is one obvious exception to this statement: stage performers, especially musicians and actors. Professional pianists have developed a tradition of not using a printed score. Thus, a pianist must know about 20 pieces flawlessly (each around 20 minutes in duration), and another 100 well enough to be brought to perfection with some effort. Actors, too, are not expected to read from scripts during a live performance. But the sincere actors seen on television who stare the listener straight in the eye while delivering their lines are probably reading them. Numerous prompting devices are used in television and movies, ranging from simple signs to sophisticated systems that display the script reflected off a half-silvered mirror right along the path of the camera lens. Thus, one reason the actors stare you in the eye is because that is where they must look to see their lines. Motion pictures are usually filmed in short 5- to 10-minute segments so the memory load on the actors is not great. Indeed, actors sometimes learn their lines just prior to playing the scene.

The greatest demands on performers seem to come with professional stage actors and solo musicians. They must face a demanding audience for long periods of time, and scripts or musical scores are simply not permitted. Here the performers face all the problems of memory, attentional demands, and the effects of stress that we have discussed in the book. In a play, with a critical audience, with many different actors involved, and with a lot of props, lights, and scenery that can malfunction, the actor is placed under severe strain. Actors rely heavily on cue lines, and any malfunction may cause the cue to go awry. It is no wonder that actors suffer stagefright, that they sometimes forget their lines, and that prompting is sometimes necessary to remind the actor how the line starts. The folklore of the theatre is rich with stories about actors who have forgotten their lines and of the valient deeds of the supporting actors who must desperately invent new lines and actions until the actors again find their places. Equally demanding is the situation where an actor jumps ahead, saying a line that should not come until much later, sometimes causing another actor to respond to the misplaced cue line. Again, the others onstage must quickly compensate. These performances are the more demanding because the stress of public performance tends to narrow the focus of the activities, reducing the flexibility and often the efficiency of the performer.

PRACTICE, PRACTICE, PRACTICE

One major activity separates the gifted amateur from the professional: practice. Many people are skilled amateur performers or athletes. Many can play a musical instrument well, or do sports, juggling, or magic tricks. But the professionals (or, in the case of sports, the committed amateurs) devote the major portion of their lives to the task, practicing five or more hours a day, every day, for years and years. Moreover, most skilled performers start this extensive practice early in life, certainly by their early teenage years. (Musicians are expected to start around the age of three to five.)

Hour after hour, year after year of practice. Why? There are several reasons. One concerns the need for absolute perfection in memory retrieval. In 20 minutes, a pianist may play some 10,000 notes, each synchronized, each in the correct timing, each exactly the correct one of the 88 notes on the piano. A second reason for so much practice has to do with the need for speed. The skilled sports player must be able to make the correct move rapidly, without exerting effort or time in conscious planning. A pianist playing a Chopin nocturne may be required to play

25 notes each second.[1] In ball sports, there may only be a fraction of a second to make the proper move. A third reason is to avoid the problems of stress. The stress of playing a match or performing in public, the emotional buildup prior to the event, and the emotions generated by one's own performance during the event can cause severe tensions. As we saw in Chapter 4 in our discussions of attention, there is often a marked deterioration of performance in times of stress. Responses fall apart. People in hazardous situations die, even though the actions required to save themselves are relatively simple and have been taught in training courses. With sufficient practice, these responses tend to become "automatic," requiring less resources for their initiation and therefore being less susceptible to disruption in times of stress.

MUSICAL PERFORMANCE

One contemporary composer has said that before a professional musician feels ready to give a solo performance, there must be sufficient training that one can enter the "mindless state." That is, it is necessary to practice so much, to know the entire situation so well, that the actions rattle off effortlessly without conscious awareness. During a public performance, it is essential that if the mind panics or wanders, perhaps burdened with concern about the reaction of the audience, "the fingers will go on in their mindless way, playing their part until finally the mind can come back to the piece." The "mindless" state of performance is what could be called "automatization"—the automatic, unconscious performance of a skill.

Because practice and memory play so important a role in a performer's life, most professional sports players, musicians, and actors have quite a bit of practical knowledge of memory skills. It is instructive to read the articles and books in the professional's literature (every field has its own specialized literature). Even a casual glance at books on how to perform sports reveals extensive discussion of the role of practice, practice that is repeated hour after hour, day after day. Be it table tennis (Leach, 1974), tennis (King, 1970), or even juggling (Carlo, 1974), the story is the same. The professional magician, the mental wizard, the chess player, and even the professional gun fighter in the days of the American "Wild West" all put considerable time into practicing.

An engaging description of the skills needed to perform with the piano is taken from a 1915 journal on music. It starts with a discussion of the necessity for a high degree of learning in order to combat the worries that accompany a public performance, and it then discusses the methods of memorizing music.

[1] F. Chopin, Opus 5, No. 1, Nocturne in F.

Musical Memory in Piano Playing and Piano Study*

EDWIN HUGHES

The moment the pianist plays for other listeners than himself, conscious thought is brought to an uncomfortably sharp focus not felt at all when playing alone, and there come, more likely than not, those awful moments of mental helplessness when everything seems a blank. A slight nervousness, induced by one thing or another, is sufficient to destroy the mental poise of which the player seems so sure when he is by himself. Reflex action can never take the place of conscious knowledge at such moments, which come at times to even the most practised concert pianist. The player can only regain his grip if he is able to say to himself with complete assurance, "I *know* that I know every note."

—   —   —

Piano music may be memorized in three ways: by ear, by visual memory, either of the notes on the printed page or the notes on the keyboard, and by finger memory or reflex action. On one or both of the first two ways are dependent the very useful and important methods of learning the harmonic and formal structure of the composition to be memorized and of being able to *say* the notes, or at least to bring up a very distinct mental picture of them.

—   —   —

When one is perfectly sure of knowing a piece thoroughly after several different methods of memorizing, one can leave the matter of its reproduction more and more to finger memory. Freedom in execution and a concentration of one's attention on the interpretation, so necessary to a beautiful and effective reading of a composition, are in fact only possible when one is able to leave the more mechanical details of reproduction to a very large extent to reflex action. The controlling conscious thought must of course be always present and alert in the background, but the constant thinking of chord and key changes, of figuration patterns and the other technical details of memorizing would mean a hampering of the player's fantasy and feeling, and a taking away of his attention from the finer details of interpretation.

In beginning the study of a new composition one must play it through once or twice to get its meaning as a whole, to become familiar with its character, its form and any striking peculiarities. At this point the work of memorizing should begin, and should be carried on simultaneously with the study of the phrasing, shading, fingering, pedalling and so forth, for these things must all be memorized as well as the mere notes. One may go about the

* E. Hughes. *Musical memory in piano playing and piano study.* The Musical Quarterly. *1915, 1, 592–603.*

memorizing in two ways, either slowly and analytically, proceeding bar by bar or phrase by phrase, or in the more haphazard fashion of merely practising the piece with a view to technical mastery, letting the memorizing come of itself without giving it any special study.

I mention both these ways because I know that both of them seem to work equally well with different individuals. Those who choose the latter method must, if their memorizing is to be successful, possess considerable faculty for learning by heart quickly. And in order to attain surety, they must set aside some time daily for practise away from the instrument, be it during the afternoon walk or a quiet hour with closed eyes in the arm-chair, and must be able to mentally go through the compositions studied with as little hesitation as when seated before the instrument. Every opportunity should in fact be taken for this mental practise, for the pianist who plays in public must live with his pieces constantly. He must *know* them, and not simply *remember* them. They must be a very part of him.

— — —

When one is quite certain of a piece, one must be able to stop anywhere during the course of the composition and to begin again where one left off without the slightest hesitation. To test one's ability in the matter it is an excellent exercise to stop suddenly in the midst of a melodic phrase or a difficult passage, get up from the instrument, walk around the room once and then see if one can take up the thread of the composition again just where it was left off. Or, when studying away from the piano, it is good to try if one can begin at various points during the course of the piece and still keep the continuity of the composition clearly in mind.

When a composition has been completely memorized it is often well in practising to try it over as a test just once, no matter if it is perfectly done or not, leaving it then and coming back to it again later for another single repetition. In public performance remember that there is only *one time*; and therefore, before one airs a piece before an audience, one must be able to get up at three o'clock in the morning, if necessary, and go through it without either fear or trembling for the result. It is good to try to imagine sometimes that there are other listeners in the room besides one's self when playing over memorized compositions. Leschetizky used to recommend calling in anybody for an audience, even the cook, as soon as a piece had been learned by heart. Trying it on the dog is in any case a very beneficial process for the performer, as it shows up any weak spots that may exist: or, if the trial be quite successful, gives him that confidence in himself which is so eminently necessary to successful public performance.

In order to keep a large repertoire in trim there must be a systematic arrangement of practise. Pieces most recently learned will require more frequent repetition, those which have been played for a longer time, less, particularly if they have been through successful appearances on the concert stage.

Compositions learned early in one's pianistic career, especially those studied in the later 'teens and early twenties, seem to enjoy a particularly long lease of memory life—a hint as to the best years of one's life for accumulating a large repertoire.

In these excerpts we see two different things. First is the emphasis on the need to learn a piece well at different levels. There must be memory for the sounds ("by ear"), for the notes ("visual memory"), and for the motor actions of moving the fingers ("by finger memory"). Second, there is emphasis on the need to combat all possible evils that might occur at a performance. One must not be content merely with a good memory; one must have a perfect memory. It must be possible to stop the piece anywhere and then resume it. This is not easy, as anyone who has memorized long passages of text or music will attest. There always seem to be natural starting points, and to start elsewhere is difficult. It must be possible to play the piece while tired and while mentally inefficient ("get up at three o'clock in the morning"). It is important to practice playing before an audience, even if the audience is only a pet dog.

In addition, while continual practice is necessary, some of this practice may be mental. There are rumors of professional musicians who claim to practice almost entirely through thought, devoting several hours each day to the mental performance of their repertoire, sitting in an easy chair, thinking through the music, piece by piece, note by note. If these stories are true, note that mental practice is not an easy shortcut—it is demanding of time and patience.

Finally, after all these techniques, after all the effort and training, the professional still makes errors. As Hughes put it, ". . . some fine day the performer's memory may play him a scurvy trick at a most inopportune moment" (Page 595). The skill of a player, therefore, must also be measured by how well he can extricate himself from an error, as shown by Hughes (1915, Page 603):

The most routined players are not absolutely immune from occasional lapses of memory, even the younger ones. I remember once hearing a very well-known pianist play himself into a maze in the midst of such a lucid composition as the Beethoven G major Rondo. Another concert I remember where the player wandered off into a false key during the Schumann Fantasie. Fortunately he was musician enough to be able to extricate himself very cleverly from the situation. On still another occasion a pianist whom I had always given the credit of possessing a remarkably clear mental grip was playing the Haendel-Brahms Variations. After he had done about two pages of the Fugue-Finale he completely lost himself, but saved the day by calmly beginning the Fugue all over again and going through it this time without the slightest hesitation. A pianist who enjoys in certain countries quite a reputation as a **Bee-thoven** player once became so tangled up during the slow movement of that composer's G major Concerto that both he and the conductor of the orchestra had a most painful few minutes straightening matters out.

CHESS PLAYERS

It is well established in common wisdom that people such as chess masters have exceptional skill at memory. How else can they see so far ahead in the game, appearing to have the whole progress of the game planned out while beginners still struggle to compute the next move? The standard demonstration of a chess master's brilliant memory is to bring him to a covered chess board where the pieces are arranged to represent some point in a game, let him see the board for five seconds, and then watch while he reconstructs all the positions from memory onto another, empty board. When the beginner or even the semiskilled player tries the same task, he can only place a few of the pieces correctly.

This mental feat by the chess master is real, but it does not result from superior memory. To demonstrate this, simply place the same pieces randomly on the board and again only allow the master five seconds in which to examine them. Now, the chess master does as poorly as the novice. In real chess games, pieces are not placed on the board at random. There is a purpose and a plan to all movements. A chess master has studied extensively, and he knows the configurations that can occur. No one could possibly know all the legal board positions, but nonetheless, real board games usually end up with the configurations of pieces in sensible, orderly arrangements. Clumps of pieces either repeat well-known patterns or differ from them in simple ways.

The Dutch psychologist deGroot was the first to study these phenomena extensively. He did the experiments just described, showing that chess masters were no better than regular people at reconstructing random configurations of pieces (deGroot, 1965, 1966). Simon and his colleagues at the Carnegie-Mellon University have conducted numerous studies on the skills of chess masters, and they also agree that the chess master's great superiority results from the large vocabulary of games and of positions that has been learned. In fact, Chase and Simon (1973) showed that the memory superiority appears only for "quiet" moves, configurations of chess pieces that are relatively unchanging, where captures are not in progress. Even positions taken from less than expert games proved to be a problem with the master player studied by Chase and Simon. They describe the phenomenon this way:

> On the hypothesis that memory of positions depends upon recognizing familiar configurations or chunks of pieces, a grandmaster

or master would find it easier to remember positions like those he encounters in his play and study. Our subject, M, when interviewed after the experiment, reported that he was troubled by positions that looked "unreasonable." He also reported difficulty with positions that were not quiet, complaining that he couldn't get the "sense" of the position when it was in the middle of an exchange.

(Chase & Simon, 1973, Page 61)

How much would a person need to learn to perform at this level of skill? In a discussion of chess playing, Newell and Simon (1972, p. 782) computed that the vocabulary of chess configurations would have to be somewhere between 10,000 and 100,000 patterns. This is a large number of patterns, but not unreasonable. A rough estimate of the number of different words a well-educated person knows is somewhere around 50,000. The master or grandmaster at chess needs a vocabulary of chess configurations as large as the vocabulary of language—not an unreasonable goal. It takes people at least 15 years of skill with language—using it continually—to build up that vocabulary. The person who devotes a major portion of his activities for a large number of years to playing chess could therefore also establish such a vocabulary. Now we see why the rest of us do so badly. Our vocabularies of chess (or any other special skill) are likely to be in the hundreds of positions, not the tens of thousands possessed by the serious professional.

WHAT HAPPENS WITH PRACTICE?

Once one understands something, what is there to be learned by more study, or by practice? In another, related vein, why do professors insist on homework? Isn't it sufficient simply to understand the material? If the emphasis on working through homework assignments is correct, and if all that we have said regarding the role of practice is correct, then something else must be happening in the learning of material other than the sheer acquisition of the new memory structures.

The answer to these issues is only partially known today. We have not yet unraveled the processes of memory or of learning sufficiently well to be able to answer all the questions, but some principles can be deduced. Basically, to learn a topic matter well requires two related things. First, the material must be understood thoroughly in all its ramifications, not just in its basic principles. To be efficient, a person must know just how different aspects of the topic are relevant. It isn't enough to know this in principle; the details must have been thought through. Second, to be able to use knowledge in difficult, stressful situations, it must be encoded in such a way as to draw a minimum amount of computing resources. The knowledge must have been automated.

Both these principles are intimately related. To see this, let us consider a particular example: learning how to juggle. Actually, the example will apply to almost any domain. We have used the same principles in such areas as learning how to play the piano, to play tennis, to cook, to program a computer, and to learn the history of the American Civil War.

Juggling

Learning how to juggle three balls at once is a surprisingly simple skill. After a few minutes of lecture and demonstration, most people are well on their way to developing the skill. Only a few memory concepts need to be acquired.

One basic component must be learned: the *toss*. To juggle, take an object (beanbags are good to start with; a solid sponge rubber ball, about the size of a tennis ball, is ideal). Learn the toss. Hold both hands palm up, at waist level, in front of you. Hold one ball in your right hand. Toss the ball from the right hand into the air in front of you so that it passes in an arc about head level and then descends to the left side of the body. Catch it with the left hand. See the path of ball 1 Fig. 9.1*a–d*. This is the *toss from right to left*. Now, learn the *toss from left to right*. This is the same, just reversed. See the path of ball 2 in Fig. 9.1*b–e*.

You now have two concepts, one for each direction of the toss. To learn how to juggle, you simply learn how to synchronize the two tosses: the toss from right to left, and the one from left to right. Now, follow Fig. 9.1 while reading this text. Start with two balls in the right hand and one in the left (Fig. 9.1*a*). Execute a toss from right to left with one of the balls. This is ball 1 (Fig. 9.1*b*). If you do nothing else, ball 1 will eventually get to the left hand, causing two balls to be there. You don't want this to happen, so when ball 1 gets midway in its path, initiate a left-to-right toss with ball 2 in the left hand (Fig. 9.1*c*). That empties the left hand and allows it to catch ball 1 as it comes from the right. But now, the ball of the left-to-right toss, ball 2, soon will arrive at the right hand, causing it to have two balls. To prevent that, when ball 2 is midway in its path, simply initiate a right-to-left toss with the ball now in the right hand, ball 3 (Fig. 9.1*d*). The rest follows automatically. As each ball is midway toward a hand, initiate a toss from that hand.

You now understand how to juggle, right? You understand the schemas—what else is there? Obviously, this description isn't really sufficient. You need to try it, preferably having someone read the instructions to you while you try. The initial attempts will be failures. One reason is that there is too much to keep in mind. By the time you have computed what to do next, it is too late. In addition, having to keep all the tasks synchronized will probably cause them to be badly executed. The tosses will go all over the place. The problem is one of resource allocation. You

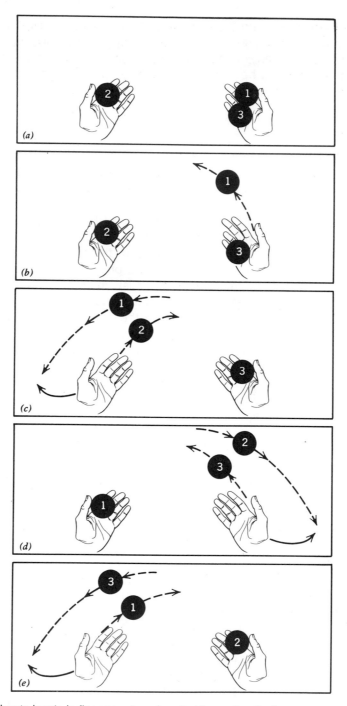

Fig. 9.1. How to juggle in five easy steps (see text for explanation).

need more resources to take care of the tasks than you have available. The solution is automatization. Make the actions so smooth and simple that they are automatic, requiring little or no conscious control.

Bugs

If you actually try to juggle using the sequence descibed here, you will run into numerous problems. Most of the problems come from errors in performance, errors that Seymour Papert and Marvin Minsky at the MIT Artificial Intelligence Laboratories have come to characterize as "bugs" (see Minsky and Papert, 1972; Papert, 1972). In order to learn juggling (or any other body of knowledge, for that matter) you have to learn to "debug" your own errors. Learning to learn is often learning to debug. A number of standard bugs are encountered by learners of juggling, and there are a number of debugging procedures.[2]

One of the standard bugs is that the two tosses are not equally well learned. Usually the toss of ball 2 goes awry. If this happens, back up in the learning sequence. Go back to one ball and practice each toss separately, with emphasis on the weaker direction. Practice to make the tosses more consistent, to minimize movement of the catching hand. How much do you need to practice? Until each toss can be performed properly when combined with the others.

Another bug is that the tosses go forward, each slightly further in front of the body, thereby forcing you to step forward all the way across the room. To stop this, stand in front of a wall. The wall acts as an automatic control of the tossing movement, deterring balls from progressing forward (this debugging technique was devised by Austin. 1974).

Other bugs have to do with horizontal accuracy and vertical height. One has to do with eye movements. It is usual to follow a moving ball with the eyes, but this becomes a bug when two or more balls are in the air at the same time. You must learn to look straight ahead, without moving the eyes. Finally, there are timing bugs. The trick here is to throw the balls high enough to give you time, to initiate tosses when the arriving ball is exactly midway through its arc, to relax. The major secret of correcting bugs lies in discovering them in the first place.

Thus, in learning tasks like juggling, several different things are involved. First, you must learn the basic conceptual memory schemas.[3]

---

[2] Although it is possible to learn to juggle from the instructions given here, anyone who is serious (or just plain curious) is advised to get *The Juggling Book* by Carlo (1974). Carlo describes one major debugging method: the "freeze" (pp. 15–19). His book is interesting as an instructional device, even if you don't want to learn to juggle.

[3] Unfortunately, the word "schema" is clumsy. The singular form is "schema" and the plural is "schemata." In this book I ignore such grammatical niceties and speak of "schema" and "schemas."

Secondly, you must learn to initiate them at the proper time with sufficient accuracy. Third, your performance must be debugged through careful analysis and training methods that will help overcome the problems. It is important that extraneous, irrelevant parts of the task be eliminated, for the more irrelevant and unnecessary things attended to, the larger the drain on resources, After all this, practice and more practice smooths the operations, and makes the transitions between components take place without disruption. With practice, the extraneous, attention-demanding aspects of the task disappear and the body movements become smooth and more regular, thereby simplifying the interactions of all the other components and further reducing demand on resources. With practice and confidence, less mental stress is involved, releasing even more resources.

AUTOMATIZATION THROUGH PARTICULARIZATION

In approaching any task, every person has general memory concepts that help organize the relevant material. Nothing can ever be completely new. All experiences, no matter how wild or novel, are related to other things we have done or heard about. Even things that appear to be in serious violation of our beliefs are related through the violations; we understand them as contradictions of what was previously known. Experiences that are strange have that quality because we relate them to our prior knowledge and find them to be discrepant. Magicians claim that some of their tricks will only work with adults, not with children. "The children don't yet have the correct expectations," one magician reported, "and if they don't have particular expectations, I can't surprise them."

In any body of knowledge there are organized units of knowledge that tie together the central concepts. These units contain information that allows them to be used at appropriate times, perhaps to make decisions or to take actions, perhaps to form relationships with other organized units. Each organized unit of information is a memory schema.

All of us have very general schemas for operating in the world. Consider the juggling task as a specific example. We all have general schemas of throwing and catching. Given any throwable object, we know how to throw it into the air and how to catch it, even if we can't do it well. Any schema that is general enough to be applied to a variety of situations must incorporate very general principles of action. It cannot be restricted by specific rules for specific tasks. This generality has virtues and deficits. A major virtue is that the rules can be applied to almost any situation that arises. The deficits are that the application requires a good deal of reasoning and computation, and therefore a good deal of mental effort or resources. When actually trying to perform the action, applying a general schema to the task may take more resources than are available.

The juggling task provides a good illustration. If you consciously go through all the control sequences necessary to catch and toss the balls, by the time you are ready to act, the ball has long gone by. In most real situations, we simply do not have time to complete an elaborate set of procedures. The procedures have to form a single, automatic unit.

What does it mean to automate a general schema? Let us examine a different simple example: the rules of addition. Suppose we wish to add any two numbers together—let the numbers be called *a* and *b*. We start with a general schema.

> *Schema for adding a to b.*
> Repeat the following *a* times:
> Add 1 to the value of *b*.
> The result is given by the final value of *b*.

To add 3 to 7 by this schema, start with 7 and add 1 to it 3 times: 7, to 8, to 9, to 10. The last number, 10, is the answer. This is doing addition by counting. It's a sensible method. It will always work. The trouble is that it takes a fair amount of time and effort to do. A faster procedure is to learn particular schemas for specific pairs of numbers. Here is one such set:

> *Schema for adding two numbers.*
> If one number is 1 and the other number is:
> 1, the answer is 2.
> 2, the answer is 3.
> 3, the answer is 4.
>
> — — —
>
> If one number is 2 and the other number is:
> 2, the answer is 4.
> 3, the answer is 5.
> 4, the answer is 6.
>
> — — —
>
> If one number is 6 and the other number is:
> 6, the answer is 12.
> 7, the answer is 13.
> 8, the answer is 14.
>
> — — —

Here we have a set of particular schemas, each much easier to perform than the general schema we had before. Essentially, we have replaced the *variables* of the first schema with the particular values or *constants* of the second. The second set is done by what is called *table look-up*. The answer is faster than with the general schema and is derived with less use of computational resources. There is a cost, of course. Before, to add up any pair of numbers, we simply needed one single schema. Now, we must learn many schemas—45 different rules are needed for the pairs of numbers ranging from 1 to 9.

The arithmetic example vividly illustrates the difference between the power of general and particular schemas. A general schema can be applied to a variety of situations, even one not previously encountered. But the generality comes at the price of requiring computation, and this takes both resources and time. A particular schema gives great efficiency. It can give a particular result quickly, with little computation required. But the particularization comes at the price of requiring large numbers of particular schemas to cope with any variation in the set of applicable situations. Moreover, the particularization route will fail anytime a question is asked that does not fall into the range of the existing set of schemas. In such a case, we must fall back to the general schema.

To get back to juggling (or tennis, chess, or piano playing), one thing that the skilled practitioner acquires is a large set of particular schemas for dealing with specific situations. For each position of the hands, for each position and velocity of the ball, there must be a particular schema, yielding the proper response with a minimum of computation. Obviously, there must be thousands or millions of possible situations. Recall that we estimated that a master chess player might know 50,000 configurations. Perhaps that is why it takes years and years to acquire the skills of the professional.

This discussion of learning has revolved around several different issues. First, we introduced the notion of the memory schema as the organizational unit. Second, we indicated that in learning, one had to set up new memory schemas that were related to the old. Third, we showed that it was important to discover and correct bugs in the schemas. Fourth, we suggested that one role of practice might be the particularization of general schemas, making more efficient operations possible, but at the cost of an extensive learning period. Finally, it is wise to note that practice alone need not lead to improvement. It may require study, thought, or instruction to point out what needs to be learned (or unlearned). Developing particular schemas and debugging existing ones is a conceptual, cognitive task, which is why learning proceeds faster with guidance than without.

10
Unfinished Business

The different topics discussed in this book fit together into a general picture of the information processing structures of a person. Attention, perception, pattern recognition, memory—each term emphasizes a different aspect of processing, but all are related; none can be separated from the others. We have seen how the representation of information within memory reflects properties of the way that information is perceived and also of the way in which it is used. We have seen how the acquisition and interpretation of information requires the interaction of conceptually driven and data driven processing, and that the study of attention is, in part, the study of the limitations on these interacting mechanisms. We have studied the importance of the mental operations that people perform on the information presented to them, both in determining how information is perceived and also in determining the likelihood that the information will ever be retrieved again. And we have examined some practical implications of the principles covered in the preceding chapters.

In the treatment of topics in this book, many important areas have not been mentioned. In part, this is because it is impossible to cover everything in a single survey of the type undertaken here. However, some topics are too important to ignore. In general, these are topics that have not yet reached full treatment or understanding within the literature of experimental psychology, which is why they were not included within other chapters. They represent important new developments and are likely to be the source of important new work in coming years. It is not proper to end this book without mentioning these topics and providing a brief introduction to them.

INDIVIDUAL DIFFERENCES

In this book, all the discussions have implied that all people are the same, and that the principles discussed in the book apply to everyone equally. But people are not all the same. Some seem to do better at one set of tasks, some at others. Some people have an extremely good ability to remember people's names, others seem to have a complete lack of memory for names. Some people are good musicians, others are good at sports, some are good at both. Some people do well in school, others have great difficulty. Just what are the sources of these distinctions?

A major belief of most cognitive psychologists is that the basic mechanisms of memory, attention, and cognition are similar for all people. That is, everyone has the same form of attentional and memory structures. Everyone has a short-term memory of about the same size. Everyone has the same rehearsal processes available to them, and everyone has similar representational powers available to them. This does not mean that there might not be quantitative differences among people. Someone's short-term memory span might be larger than another's. Someone's rate of rehearsal might be higher, thereby giving that person an edge at performing some kinds of tasks. It is possible that some people have more attentional resources—not different kinds, but simply more than other people.

There are two major ways in which people might differ, however, and these are probably more important than small differences in such things as short-term memory capacity. One way concerns mental strategies, the other the role of prior knowledge and experience. Recall in Chapters 3 and 4 that we distinguished between data driven and conceptually driven processing. It is possible to use this distinction to characterize different processing styles of individual people. People who are primarily data driven will do whatever is in front of them at the moment. If there is food, they will eat it (whether hungry or not); if someone walks past the door while they are doing something else, they will be distracted. In general, data driven people ought to be more distractable than conceptually driven people. In turn, conceptually driven people ought, to be less easily interrupted when engaged in some task, and they ought not to notice events in the environment that they were not expecting. It is quite conceivable that if we could develop a good classification of data-driven and conceptually driven people, they would do differently on tests of attention. (See the Suggested Readings for some possible approaches.)

Because the learning of new information depends critically on what has been previously acquired, one major source of differences among individuals is simply the differences in their exposure to information.

One major place where these differences might be noted is in comparing the performance of people of one culture with that of another. Cole and Scribner (1974) surveyed the literature on differences in cognitive abilities across different cultures and then performed their own experiments. They documented the extreme difficulty in drawing conclusions about the differences among cultures, for the basic knowledge and style and worldview of each culture become the overwhelming variables in determining how well a person can perform on some psychological test. Anyone interested in individual differences, or in cultural differences, should read their book. Even the most innocuous appearing test often has cultural implications, and some people seem unable to perform well at some skill on a test, despite the fact that they may use the very same skill at a high level of performance in a natural surrounding.

HEMISPHERIC SPECIALIZATION

One major topic, closely related to the study of consciousness, is the area called *laterality* or *hemispheric specialization*. The upper part of the human brain is called the cerebral cortex. In reality, there are two cortices—one on the right side of the brain, the other on the left. They are called the right and left hemispheres. The two cortices are interconnected by a massive band of neurones called the *corpus collosum* that runs under the cortex crosswise, interrelating the corresponding parts of the two hemispheres. There is overwhelming evidence that each hemisphere performs specialized processing functions. In particular, for most individuals (especially right-handed individuals) the left hemisphere seems to be specialized to perform language oriented tasks and the right hemisphere seems to be better at nonlinguistic tasks.[1]

In recent years, there has been increasing excitement about the implications of such division of processing. Unfortunately, despite the excitement, there is still little that can be said, although all the fuss has made many people overexpectant. What does it mean to say that there are two separate processing centers in the head? Does it mean that we have two independent minds, one that does language, another that does

---

[1] The brain is connected to the sensory organs and the muscle controls through a crossover of sides. In general, the signals to and from the left half of the body go directly to the right half of the brain and, similarly, signals to and from the right half of the body go to the left half of the brain. There are minor exceptions. The auditory system, for example, actually goes directly to both halves of the brain, but still, the major pathways from the right ear go to the left hemisphere, and vice versa. With the eyes, the division is related to the perceptual field, not to the location of the retinas. When you look straight ahead, information from objects that you see to the right of the point where you are focusing will end up in the left hemisphere, and information from objects to the left of your focal point will end up in the right hemisphere.

nonlanguage processing? Some people seem to think so. Some people believe that esoteric methods of "expanding one's consciousness" or of biofeedback allow the nondominant hemisphere to take over. Consistent with this belief is the notion that the left hemisphere does the methodological, analytic, well-reasoned part of human thought (language oriented), and that the right hemisphere is synthetic, intuitive, and less constrained by rational scientific logic. The mental operations of a philosopher or a scientist, according to this theory, are controlled by the left hemisphere. If one lets the right hemisphere take over, one becomes creative, emotional, synthetic—an artist rather than a scientist, one whose life is experiential rather than analytical. It has been suggested that the two hemispheres might retain different representations of the same information. Recall the discussions on the representation of knowledge in Chapter 8. There we characterized the representation of information by saying that there were two extreme emphases we could place on a representation, one highly categorical or propositional, the other more analogical. Some people have suggested that the left hemisphere maintains a propositional representation, while the right hemisphere is more analogical.[2]

The literature on hemispheric specialization makes for interesting reading. It clearly is studying an important aspect of human processing, one that seems highly relevant to the concepts of attention and memory studied in this book. But despite the work and all the publicity, little is yet known about what really happens beyond the simple and undisputed fact that specialization of language processing does occur. Beyond that statement, we really know too little about thought, representation, and consciousness to do more than make wild guesses.

In reviewing the literature (the Suggested Readings for this chapter show places to start), remember that the strong, oversimplified separation of processing styles implied by some people working in these areas probably does not exist. The two hemispheres are strongly interconnected, because many of the sensory systems send signals to both hemispheres, and because the corpus collosum richly interconnects both hemispheres. Furthermore, sheer logic alone indicates that the distinction between two modes of thought or consciousness simply isn't that strong. Just as the chapter on representation of knowledge (Chapter 8) demonstrated that all representations must be both propositional and analogical, so is all thought both analytic and synthetic. To be carried away by the rhythms of a musical experience is to be synthetic, or experiential, or analogical. But as soon as one rhythm is noticed as a

---

[2] Note that with some people the sides are reversed, and the right hemisphere handles language. This tends to be true for left-handed individuals. For these people the same arguments apply, but with the sides interchanged.

repetition of another, or as a subtle transformation of one heard earlier, or perhaps as a counterpoint to another one at the same time, that act of noticing is analytic. We can fluctuate between different modes of thought with reasonable ease, a factor that adds to our ability both to understand and to create.

Whatever the eventual discoveries and outcomes of studies of hemispheric specialization, there is no doubt that they will have important implications for our understanding of the human processing system. Today, the studies still do not say much about processing structures relevant to the issues of this book, which is why this discussion was left for this final chapter.

CONSCIOUSNESS

Despite the many topics covered in our pursuit of memory and attention, one major issue has not received its proper discussion: consciousness. The word has continually appeared thoughout the book, but has not been defined. Consciousness is closely coupled with the inner voice with which we "speak" to ourselves and which appears to analyze our experiences and our actions. Consciousness is clearly closely linked to the concepts of attention and to short-term memory. We feel we consciously can direct our attention to one thing or another. We say that we are conscious of the immediate present. To recall the past, we need to retrieve it, to "bring it back" into conscious awareness.

At this point, however, little can be said about the properties or the nature of consciousness except that it clearly exists, and that it is an important central aspect of human performance. Some people would call it *the* most important aspect. In the chapter on attention we spoke of conscious processing. In the chapters on memory, we saw how conscious decision making appears to be involved in the storage and retrieval of information. Studies of nontraditional views of consciousness (Ornstein, 1972) indicate that the phenomenological state can be controlled and even altered. Many methods of meditation require explicit methods of controlling attention—saying one word (a mantra) over and over again, counting breaths, concentrating on a single fixed object. By controlling attention, one can still the inner voice and enter a different state of consciousness than traditionally experienced. Control of attentional states is one of the keys to entering new states of conscious awareness of the world (see the Suggested Readings for Chapter 4).

But what is consciousness? What are the psychological mechanisms and reasons? At the moment, there is nothing but speculation. Some believe that conscious processes play a central role in guiding us through our activities. Conscious processes act at the highest level of decision making, initiating high-level operations and choosing between courses of action whenever there are conflicts (Shallice, 1972). In learning, we are quite often conscious of the acts we perform in attempting to make sense of the material before us and in attempting to organize it in such a way that we can later retrieve it. Thus, rehearsal, explicit comparison with other concepts, and explicit search for relations that can be formed often mark our conscious awareness of the operations of learning.

George Mandler (1975a, 1975b) argued that consciousness plays an important adaptive role for the human organism. He views it as a planning process, a mental "scratchpad" on which one can plan the possible results of future actions, allowing for more intelligent, reasoned choice than would be possible otherwise. Thus, consciousness allows selected information from long-term memory to be considered in determining courses of action.

One important aspect of consciousness is the state of self awareness. By being aware of the courses of action that one is contemplating, there can be self-criticism and evaluation of the actions prior to their use. Similarly, while some activity is underway, or after it has been completed, this awareness allows for intelligent evaluation of the results and for suggested modifications for future actions. Consciousness and self-awareness may play an important critical role in the process of learning. To learn effectively, one must be able to do mental evaluation, to analyze the possible outcomes of several courses of action, and to modify existing schemas in ways relevant to the new analyses. One is struck by the important roles that conscious evaluation might play in learning.

Earlier in the book we stressed the differences between data driven, bottom-up processing and conceptually driven, top-down processing. Conscious planning and initiation of actions would appear to be one of the sources of conceptually driven processing. Consciousness is at the top of the layers of processing structures. We have not specifically discussed purposeful behavior; that is, we have analyzed the mechanisms that make possible attention, perception, memory, and learning, but we have not at all discussed why a person does these activities. Just why a person performs the activities of daily life is a complex problem that will not even be attempted here. But we can speculate a bit on how the higher-order goals of life are transformed into the detailed bits of human behavior that we enact in order to achieve the goals. Here, conscious processing would appear to be of great importance. It would appear that the highest level of conceptual guidance comes from conscious decision making, that this guidance invokes memory schemas that can govern the pattern of daily activities, and that these schemas may, in turn, initiate other memory schemas that handle more basic details. As we do our daily tasks, when there are new decisions to be made or discrepancies between expectations and actuality, then conscious processes can play the part of making the necessary decisions to keep the operations going.

REMEMBERING

Despite all the emphasis on memory in this book, there has been strikingly little work reported on how people remember things. The work that has been performed is both interesting and also potentially of great importance to our understanding of the memory system. Unfortunately, there is very little of it. As yet, there is no real discipline of research on how one retrieves information.

In this section we will examine some of the research that has been performed. Each of these efforts stands alone, apart from each other and from the research discussed within this book. This situation will not last long. The general trend of research in the area of human memory is clearly toward the study of the types of issues to be discussed here. Moreover, there are tentative connections between the issues discussed earlier in the book and the material in this section, but the final connections are still to be made.

The Tip-of-the-Tongue Problem

One particularly tantalizing phenomenon, especially rich in the insight it gives into the working of retrieval from memory, occurs when we get into a state of partial knowledge about a word. In this particular state, we search for a particular word in memory. Yet, even though we are certain that we know the item we seek, we cannot quite snatch it into consciousness; we say that the word is "on the tip cf the tongue."

The aspect of the tip-of-the-tongue state that most frustrates those who experience it is the extremely long duration that it may last. It is just this point, however, that makes the state valuable to the experimental psychologist: there is time to find out what is happening. Two psychologists at Harvard University, Brown and McNeill, have used the results of their studies of the tip-of-the-tongue state to speculate on the organization of human memory. In order to do their studies, Brown and McNeill first had to devise an experimental technique for inducing the tip-of-the-tongue state in their laboratory subjects. Then they had to develop a procedure for probing the subjects to see how much was really known about the words the subjects claimed to have found in their memories, yet were unable to extract. Brown and McNeill described their study in this way:

The "Tip-of-the-Tongue" Phenomenon*

ROGER BROWN and DAVID MC NEILL

William James wrote, in 1890: "Suppose we try to recall a forgotten name. The state of our consciousness is peculiar. There is a gap therein; but no mere gap. It is a gap that is intensely active. A sort of wraith of the name is in it, beckoning us in a given direction, making us at moments tingle with the sense of our closeness and then letting us sink back without the longed-for term. If wrong names are proposed to us, this singularly definite gap acts immediately so as to negate them. They do not fit into its mould. And the gap of one word does not feel like the gap of another, all empty of content as both might seem necessarily to be when described as gaps."

The "tip-of-the-tongue" (TOT) state involves a failure to recall a word of which one has knowledge. The evidence of knowledge is either an eventually successfully recall or else an act of recognition that occurs, without additional training, when recall has failed. The class of cases defined by the conjunction of knowledge and a failure of recall is a large one. The TOT state, which James described, seems to be a small subclass in which recall is felt to be imminent.

For several months we watched for TOT states in ourselves. Unable to recall the name of the street on which a relative lives, one of us thought of *Congress* and *Corinth* and *Concord* and then looked up the address and learned that it was *Cornish*. The words that had come to mind have certain properties in common with the word that had been sought (the "target word") ; all four begin with *Co*; all are two-syllable words; all put the primary stress on the first syllable. After this experience we began putting direct questions to ourselves when we fell into the TOT state, questions as to the number of syllables in the target word, its initial letter, etc.

Brown and McNeill devised an experimental technique for inducing the TOT state in their subjects. The procedure was simple: subjects were presented with the definition of an uncommon English word and were asked to supply the word. In a preliminary experiment on nine subjects, the procedure appeared to be successful. To quote Brown and McNeill:

In 57 instances a subject (S) was, in fact, "seized" by a TOT state. The signs of it were unmistakable; he would appear to be in a mild torment, something like the brink of a sneeze, and if he found the word his relief was considerable. While searching for the target S told us all the words that came to his mind. He volunteered the information that some of them resembled the

* R. Brown and D. McNeill. The "tip-of-the-tongue" phenomenon. Journal of Verbal Learning and Verbal Behavior. 1966, 5, 325–337. Copyright © 1966 by Academic Press, Inc. Reprinted by permission.

target in sound but not in meaning; others he was sure were similar in meaning, but not in sound. The E [experimenter] intruded on S's agony with two questions: (a) How many syllables has the target word? (b) What is its first letter? Answers to the first question were correct in 47 percent of all cases and answers to the second were correct in 51 percent of the cases.

The procedure was refined by eliciting more information from the subjects about the exact state of their knowledge of the target word while in the TOT state. In a test of 56 subjects, the experimental procedure was able to yield 360 instances of a TOT state. Of this total, 233 of the instances yielded usable data. Brown and McNeill analyzed their data for the types of partial information that their subjects were able to give: number of syllables, initial letter, syllabic stress, letters in various positions, suffixes, and other aspects.

The preliminary characterization of the data was that "when complete recall of a word is not presently possible but is felt to be imminent, one can often correctly recall the general type of the word; *generic* recall may succeed when particular recall fails." After the analysis of the data had been completed, Brown and McNeill were able to develop this survey of their experimental and theoretical conclusions:

CONCLUSIONS

When complete recall of a word has not occurred but is felt to be imminent there is likely to be accurate generic recall. Generic recall of the *abstract form* variety is evidenced by S's knowledge of the number of syllables in the target and of the location of the primary stress. Generic recall of the *partial* variety is evidenced by S's knowledge of letters in the target word. This knowledge shows a bowed serial-position effect since it is better for the ends of a word than for the middle and somewhat better for beginning positions than for final positions. The accuracy of generic recall is greater when S is near the target (complete recall is imminent) than when S is far from the target. A person experiencing generic recall is able to judge the relative similarity to the target of words that occur to him and these judgments are based on the features of words that figure in partial and abstract form recall.

— — —

THE REASON FOR GENERIC RECALL

In adult minds words are stored in both visual and auditory terms and between the two there are complicated rules of translation. Generic recall involves letters (or phonemes), affixes, syllables, and stress location. In this section we will discuss only letters (legible forms) and will attempt to explain a single effect—the serial position effect in the recall of letters. It is not clear how far the explanation can be extended.

In brief overview this is the argument. The design of the English language is such that one word is usually distinguished from all others in a more-than-minimal way, i.e., by more than a single letter in a single position. It is consequently *possible* to recognize words when one has not stored the complete letter sequence. The evidence is that we do not store the complete sequence if we do not have to. We begin by attending chiefly to initial and final letters and storing these. The order of attention and of storage favors the ends of words because the ends carry more information than the middles. An incomplete entry will serve for recognition, but if words are to be produced (or recalled) they must be stored in full. For most words, then, it is eventually necessary to attend to the middle letters. Since end letters have been attended to from the first they should always be more clearly entered or more elaborately connected than middle letters. When recall is required, of words that are not very familiar to S, as it was in our experiment, the end letters should often be accessible when the middle are not.

In building pronounceable sequences the English language, like all other languages, utilizes only a small fraction of its combinatorial possibilities. If a language used all possible sequences of phonemes (or letters) its words could be shorter, but they would be much more vulnerable to misconstruction. A change of any single letter would result in reception of a different word. As matters are actually arranged, most changes result in no word at all; for example: *textant, sixtant, sektant*. Our words are highly redundant and fairly indestructible.

The model of memory described by Brown and McNeill assumes that words are stored at specific locations in memory. At each location there are special "markers" that specify the semantic content and associations of the words. In their model, Brown and McNeill suggested that the information necessary to translate from the acoustical representation of each word to the semantic representation is also contained at each storage location. It takes less information about a word to interpret it than it does to generate it, primarily because the interpretation process requires only sufficient information about the word to distinguish it from all other possibilities. Any lack of information about the middle of a word does not necessarily harm the understanding of spoken words. by pronouncing the beginning and ending and mumbling the middle.

It is interesting that Brown and McNeill found no information about the visual properties of words in the TOT state. This might be an artifact of their testing procedure, but more likely it results from the nature of the memory system itself. In this sense, then, the results from the TOT studies are completely consistent with all the other studies we have examined. Somewhere, however, there must exist visual representations of words, for otherwise we would not be able to read and write them. Moreover, the visual representation must exist in long-term memory and must be used by whatever mechanism translates visual images to auditory images, presumably in the transference of words from visual information storage into short-term memory.

REMEMBERING OR RECONSTRUCTING

We now turn to a more complex subject: the storage for complex events, which introduces us to the techniques of inferring the properties of memory from the types of errors made by subjects. The investigations were performed in Cambridge, England, in the 1920s and 30s by Sir Frederic Bartlett. He used a variety of experimental methods, the most famous being the method of repeated reproduction. In this method, subjects were asked to study a story, an argumentative prose passage, or a drawing. After varying intervals of time, they were asked to reproduce the original material. By repeatedly testing his subjects, Bartlett hoped to find "something about the common types of change introduced by normal individuals into remembered material with increasing lapse of time."

Bartlett found that accuracy of report was the exception rather than the rule. His subjects appeared to reconstruct their material, rather than actually to remember it. As a result, the stories of pictures that they would report as "memories" were often quite distorted from the original version. When subjects were asked to recollect material after very long intervals of time (Bartlett calls this "long-distance remembering"), the constructive process was particularly evident. All that seemed to remain of the original material were "isolated but striking details." And even then, the details were remembered only if they fit into the subjects' preconceptions.

Bartlett proposed that we remember by organizing things within the framework of our experiences. Remembering is viewed more as a process of reconstruction than as a recollection. As a result, our organizational scheme relies heavily on the integration of present experience with that of the past. Sometimes we find it difficult to reconcile the two, and as a result, we often remember what we expected to perceive, rather than that which we actually did perceive.

Bartlett found that when his subjects tried to recall stories he had asked them to learn, their versions were shorter, the phraseology more modern, and the entire tale more coherent and consequential than the original. With time these errors increased, but the length of the story that was recalled did not necessarily change. Thus, there was much invention, or in Bartlett's terms "constructive remembering." Moreover, his subjects were often unaware that they were inventing rather than remembering, for often the very part that was created anew was the part that the subject was most pleased about and most certain.

These results fit quite beautifully into the structure we have devised to account for the power of mnemonics and organization. It is as if we cannot add anything too new or unique into our memory: things must be introduced gradually, slowly constructed onto the old framework. In many cases, this simplifies our task, for instead of learning all about some new material, we simply need to learn how it relates to something already known. The problem with this, as Bartlett showed so dramatically, is that after a while it is not possible to remember what actually did happen —the memory becomes blurred by past experiences.

Bartlett elaborated on these views in his theory of remembering. One of his most important contributions was a discussion of the organization imposed on stored material: what Bartlett called a *schema*. He described a schema as "an active organization of past reactions, or of past experiences." Various schemas go together into one active, organized setting, all interconnected by common factors. According to Bartlett, we do not remember by activating some fixed trace of memory image. Rather we reactivate a whole mass of images, we energize the relevant schemas, and we re-create anew the event we are attempting to revive. But in this method, we may err by creating too much, for we may recall what usually was or what ought to have been instead of what really was.

We have come across the notion of *schema* numerous times throughout this book. The problems of representation have been introduced, but not much has been said about how information might be interrelated. Growing interest in psychology and artificial intelligence in such organizational factors seems to have centered on a common notion: general information about concepts and situations is organized into structural units. Each structural unit guides the use of knowledge, the development of interrelationships, and the organization of new knowledge. Such structural units are called either *frames* or *schemas*. The word "frames" tends to be used in the literature on artificial intelligence (although it was used some time ago in psychology, as well—Woodworth, 1938, p. 798). The word "schema" tends to be used in psychology, and it also has a long history, but today it is mostly associated with the work of Bartlett (1932) and the Swiss psychologist Jean Piaget (e.g., 1936/1952).

REPRESENTATIVENESS AND AVAILABILITY

Quite often, our ability to make judgments about things results from our ability to retrieve relevant information from memory. Thus, memory retrieval plays an important role even in areas not directly related to memory. Amos Tversky and Daniel Kahneman, two psychologists at the Hebrew University in Jerusalem, studied what they call the effect of representativeness and availability of information on people's decisions. First let us look at their experiments, then at the practical implications.

Suppose we sample a word from an English text. Which is more likely, that the word starts with a *K* or that its third letter is a *K*? Most people do the task by thinking of words that start with *K* and then comparing that number with the words recalled whose third letter is *K*. This method is bound to be erroneous, because memory retrieval for words is efficient for a property at the start of a word, but quite inefficient for a property in the middle of a word.[3]

Memory retrieval has an effect even on simple judgments. To show this, Tversky and Kahneman asked a group of subjects to listen to lists of names and judge whether the lists contained more names of men than of women. Here is their description of the experiment:

Accessibility of Information*

AMOS TVERSKY and DANIEL KAHNEMAN

In this section we discuss several studies in which the subject is first exposed to a message (e.g., a list of names) and is later asked to judge the frequency of items of a given type that were included in the message. . . . The subject cannot recall and count all instances. Instead, we propose, he attempts to recall some instances and judges over all frequency by availability, i.e., by the ease with which instances come to mind. As a consequence, classes whose instances are readily recalled will be judged more numerous than classes of the same size whose instances are less available. This prediction is first tested in a study of the judged frequency of categories.

— — —

FAME, FREQUENCY, AND RECALL

The subjects were presented with a recorded list consisting of names of known personalities of both sexes. After listening to the list, some subjects judged whether it contained more names of men or of women, others attempted to recall the names in the list. Some of the names in the list were very famous (e.g., Richard Nixon, Elizabeth Taylor), others were less famous (e.g., William Fulbright, Lana Turner). Famous names are generally easier to recall. Hence, if frequency judgments are mediated by assessed availability,

* A. Tversky and D. Kahneman. Availability: A heuristic for judging frequency and probability. Cognitive Psychology. 1973, 5, 220–221. Copyright © 1973 by Academic Press, Inc. Reprinted by permission.

[3] Most people believe there to be more words that start with *K*. In fact, there are more likely to be twice as many words with a *K* in the third position than in the first position (Tversky and Kahneman, 1973).

then a class consisting of famous names should be judged more numerous than a comparable class consisting of less famous names.

Four lists of names were prepared, two lists of entertainers and two lists of other public figures. Each list included 39 names recorded at a rate of one name every 2 sec. Two of the lists (one of public figures and one of entertainers) included 19 names of famous women and 20 names of less famous men. The two other lists consisted of 19 names of famous men and 20 names of less famous women. Hence, fame and frequency were inversely related in all lists. The first names of all personalities always permitted an unambiguous identification of sex.

The subjects were instructed to listen attentively to a recorded message. Each of the four lists were presented to two groups. After listening to the recording, subjects in one group were asked to write down as many names as they could recall from the list. The subjects in the other group were asked to judge whether the list contained more names of men or of women.

Results

(a) Recall. On the average, subjects recalled 12.3 of the 19 famous names and 8.4 of the 20 less famous names. Of the 86 subjects in the four recall groups, 57 recalled more famous than nonfamous names, and only 13 recalled fewer famous than less famous names ($p < .001$, by sign test).

(b) Frequency. Among the 99 subjects who compared the frequency of men and women in the lists, 80 erroneously judged the class consisting of the more famous names to be more frequent ($p < .001$, by sign test).

These examples speak about the problems of access, not of prototypes. The accessibility of information appears to determine the judgment. Tversky and Kahneman also argued that prototypes affect judgments by the same mechanism: a prototype affects the accessibility of information. Just as accessibility affects how we make judgments about such mundane things as the number of words with *K* in them or the number of men or women on a list, so too will it affect our judgments about other things. A typical way to examine memory for information about a concept is to make up a prototypical scenario of an event, and then use that scenario as a source of information for the resulting decision. This procedure is only as accurate as the ability to retrieve information from memory. Alas, memory retrieval is not an accurate, unbiased process, and so many decisions are made incorrectly. Again, Tversky and Kahneman:

RETRIEVAL OF OCCURRENCES AND CONSTRUCTION OF SCENARIOS*

In all the empirical studies that were discussed in this paper, there existed an objective procedure for enumerating instances (e.g., words that begin with K or paths in a diagram), and hence each of the problems had an objectively correct answer. This is not the case in many real-life situations where probabilities are judged. Each occurrence of an economic recession, a successful medical operation, or a divorce, is essentially unique, and its probability cannot be evaluated by a simple tally of instances. Nevertheless, the availability heuristic may be applied to evaluate the likelihood of such events.

In judging the likelihood that a particular couple will be divorced, for example, one may scan one's memory for similar couples which this question brings to mind. Divorce will appear probable if divorces are prevalent among the instances that are retrieved in this manner. Alternatively, one may evaluate likelihood by attempting to construct stories, or scenarios, that lead to a divorce. The plausibility of such scenarios, or the ease with which they come to mind, can provide a basis for the judgment of likelihood. In the present section, we discuss the role of availability in such judgments, speculate about expected sources of bias, and sketch some directions that further inquiry might follow.

We illustrate availability biases by considering an imaginary clinical situation.[4] A clinician who has heard a patient complain that he is tired of life, and wonders whether that patient is likely to commit suicide may well recall similar patients he has known. Sometimes only one relevant instance comes to mind, perhaps because it is most memorable. Here, subjective probability may depend primarily on the similarity between that instance and the case under consideration. If the two are very similar, then one expects that what has happened in the past will recur. When several instances come to mind, they are probably weighted by the degree to which they are similar, in essential features, to the problem at hand.

How are relevant instances selected? In scanning his past experience does the clinician recall patients who resemble the present case, patients who attempted suicide, or patients who resemble the present case *and* attempted suicide? From an actuarial point of view, of course, the relevant class is that of patients who are similar, in some respects, to the present case, and the relevant statistic is the frequency of attemped suicide in this class:

---

* *Tversky and Kahneman.* op. cit. *1973. Pages 227–230.*
[4] This example was chosen because of its availability. We know of no reason to believe that intuitive predictions of stockbrokers, sportscasters, political analysts, or research psychologists are less susceptible to biases.

Memory search may follow other rules. Since attempted suicide is a dramatic and salient event, suicidal patients are likely to be more memorable and easier to recall than depressive patients who did not attempt suicide. As a consequence, the clinician may recall suicidal patients he has encountered and judge the likelihood of an attempted suicide by the degree of resemblance between these cases and the present patient. This approach leads to serious biases. The clinician who notes that nearly all suicidal patients he can think of were severely depressed may conclude that a patient is likely to commit suicide if he shows signs of severe depression. Alternatively, the clinician may conclude that suicide is unlikely if "this patient does not look like any suicide case I have met." Such reasoning ignores the fact that only a minority of depressed patients attempt suicide and the possibility that the present patient may be quite unlike any that the therapist has ever encountered.

Finally, a clinician might think only of patients who were both depressed and suicidal. He would then evaluate the likelihood of suicide by the ease with which such cases come to mind or by the degree to which the present patient is representative of this class. This reasoning, too, is subject to a serious flaw. The fact that there are many depressed patients who attempted suicide does not say much about the probability that a depressed patient will attempt suicide, yet this mode of evaluation is not uncommon.

— — —

Some events are perceived as so unique that past history does not seem relevant to the evaluation of their likelihood. In thinking of such events we often construct *scenarios,* i.e., stories that lead from the present situation to the target event. The plausibility of the scenarios that come to mind, or the difficulty of producing them, then serve as a clue to the likelihood of the event. If no reasonable scenario comes to mind, the event is deemed impossible or highly unlikely. If many scenarios come to mind, or if the one scenario that is constructed is particularly compelling, the event in question appears probable.

— — —

Perhaps the most obvious demonstration of availability in real life is the impact of the fortuitous availability of incidents or scenarios. Many readers must have experienced the temporary rise in the subjective probability of an accident after seeing a car overturned by the side of the road. Similarly, many must have noticed an increase in the subjective probability that an accident or malfunction will start a thermonuclear war after seeing a movie in which such an occurrence was vividly portrayed. Continued preoccupation with an outcome may increase its availability, and hence its perceived likelihood. People are preoccupied with highly desirable outcomes, such as winning the sweepstakes, or with highly undesirable outcomes, such as an airplane crash. Consequently availability provides a mechanism by which occurrences of extreme utility (or disutility) may appear more likely than they actually are.

Similar memory factors have important implications in many legal situations, where witnesses must testify about crimes. Despite the heavy reliance on eyewitnesses, there is overwhelming evidence that the eyewitness can often be quite unreliable. Moreover, just as in the experiments reported by Tversky and Kahneman, the person is unaware of making an error in memory or judgment. Thus, both decision-makers and witnesses make similar errors. Both may insist that their statements are accurate, despite the fact that they simply could not be (see Buckhout, 1974).

MEMORY FOR REAL EVENTS

> In the place you lived in three places ago, as you entered the front door, was the doorknob on the left or the right?

We discussed a very similar example in Chapter 8. Even so, it would be useful if you tried to answer this question now. As you do so, you will see several different stages of retrieval operating. First, there is the problem of getting to the correct location. Most people report that they must back up successively through the places in which they have lived until they arrive at the correct location. Next comes the task of locating the front door, usually a rapid process once the correct location has been determined. Now comes the problem: on which side is the doorknob? Most people can easily imagine either side, and therefore have considerable difficulty in determining the correct answer. Several tactics are useful at this point. You can attempt to remember the door from both sides. Or you can imagine walking up to the door with your arms full of packages, struggling to open the door. Or you can remember what was inside, behind the door, in an effort to decide which way it must have opened. One of these three attempts usually results in the retrieval of the correct answer. Note that the answer to the doorknob question requires that a lot of subsidiary information accompany the retrieval process. It simply is not possible to retrieve an isolated piece of information. Entire memory schemas seem to be necessary.

Other questions demonstrate the properties of human memory.

> Do you remember Isaac Newton, the scientist?
> What was Newton's telephone number?

Here, the question is absurd. But how do you know? Well, Newton died before there were telephones. True, but do you mean you first looked up the dates of Newton's life before trying to determine his telephone number? If so, consider the next sequence of questions.

> What is X's telephone number, where X is:
> John Smirnov

> Ernest Hemingway
> The President
> A local restaurant
> A friend

Starting from the top and working down there is increasing likelihood that you will know the answer. John Smirnov is a hypothetical person, so you cannot possibly know his number. But what of the rest? Most important, how do you know whether or not you know? What type of memory search operation is involved in determining whether or not some information is known? Evidently, some type of preprocessing of questions like these occurs to indicate whether detailed search is worthwhile.

Memory retrieval is often a process of problem solving. Thus, when a person attempts to get at some previously experienced event, the process of retrieval often follows interesting routes. Consider this illustration of the process of remembering something. You might try to answer the question yourself before reading the rest of the description.

Retrieval as Problem Solving*

PETER H. LINDSAY and DONALD A. NORMAN

Query: What were you doing on Monday afternoon in the third week of September two years ago?

Don't give up right away. Take some time to think about it and see if you can come up with the answer. Try writing down your thoughts as you attempt to recover this information. Better still, ask a friend to think out loud as he tries to answer the query.

The type of responses people typically produce when asked this kind of question go something like this:

1. *Come on. How should I know?* (Experimenter: Just try it, anyhow.)
2. *OK. Let's see: Two years ago. . . .*
3. *I would be in high school in Pittsburgh. . . .*
4. *That would be my senior year.*
5. *Third week in September—that's just after summer—that would be the fall term. . . .*
6. *Let me see. I think I had chemistry lab on Mondays.*
7. *I don't know. I was probably in the chemistry lab. . . .*

* P. H. Lindsay and D. A. Norman. Human Information Processing. *New York: Academic Press, 1972. Pages 379–380. Copyright © 1972 by Academic Press, Inc. Reprinted by permission.*

8. *Wait a minute—that would be the second week of school. I remember he started off with the atomic table—a big, fancy chart. I thought he was crazy, trying to make us memorize that thing.*
9. *You know, I think I can remember sitting. . . .*

Although this particular protocol is fabricated, it does catch the flavor of how the memory system works on this kind of retrieval problem. First, the question of whether or not to attempt the retrieval: The preliminary analysis suggests it is going to be difficult, if not impossible, to recover the requested information and the subject balks at starting at all (line 1). When he does begin the search, he does not attempt to recall the information directly. He breaks the overall question down into subquestions. He decides first to establish what he was doing two years ago (line 2). Once he has succeeded in answering this question (line 3), he uses the retrieved information to construct and answer a more specific question (line 4). After going as far as he can with the first clue, he returns to picking up more information in the initial query, "September, third week." He then continues with still more specific memories (lines 5 and 6). Most of what happened between lines 7 and 8 is missing from the protocol. He seems to have come to a dead end at line 7, but must have continued to search around for other retrieval strategies. Learning the periodic table seems to have been an important event in his life. The retrieval of this information seems to open up new access routes. By line 8, he once again appears to be on his way to piecing together a picture of what he was doing on a Monday afternoon two years ago.

Here memory appears as a looping, questioning activity. The search is active, constructive. When it cannot go directly from one point to another, the problem is broken up into a series of subproblems or subgoals. For each subproblem, the questions are: Can it be solved; will the solution move me closer to the main goal? When one subproblem gets solved, new ones are defined and the search continues. If successful, the system eventually produces a response, but the response is hardly a simple recall. It is a mixture of logical reconstruction of what must have been experienced with fragmentary recollections of what was in fact experienced.

This idea of memory as a problem-solving process is not a new notion. Similar ideas have been suggested by poets and philosophers for thousands of years. For psychologists, early and persuasive proponents were William James (1890) and Sir Frederic Bartlett (1932). What is new is that finally there are some analytic tools to deal with such processes in detail. The machinery is available to build and test models of memory that solve problems by breaking up questions into subgoals, that try to converge on solutions through continued reformulation and analysis of promising subquestions.

So ends our brief excursion into the studies of real remembrances. (Some sources of other studies are reported in the Suggested Readings.) On the whole, this area of research is one of the potentially most interesting and important of the studies of memory, but work has just barely begun.

SUGGESTED READINGS

Individual Differences

The study of individual differences has just barely been treated by those who study human information processing. Ruth Day has provided one fascinating description of the differences among people who are *language bound* and *stimulus bound* that appears to be very similar to what we called conceptually driven and data driven. Unfortunately, her work has not been published. (But the reader should check the *Psychological Abstracts* for reports that might appear after this book has been published.)

Hunt has established a research project aimed at discovering exactly what information processing correlations there are to individual differences in performance, especially attempting to determine the reasons behind differences in performances on intelligence tests. His papers mark perhaps the main research on this problem (see Hunt, 1974; Hunt, Frost, and Lunneborg, 1973; Hunt, Lunneborg, and Lewis, 1975).

Schachter and Rodin (1974) examined performance of obese people, comparing it to people of normal weight and to the performance found in animals made obese. They portrayed the obese individual (especially in their chapters 12, 13, and 14) as one whom we could describe as data driven. Obese individuals will only overeat if food is in front of them and if it is palatable. They are easily distracted. They are more responsive to external cues than are individuals of normal weight.

The strong influence that culture has on an individual's performance of cognitive tasks is examined by Cole and Scribner (1974) in an important study titled *Culture and Thought*. Even memory performance is affected by cultural style, and this book is important reading for anyone who wishes to study differences in the performances of people. Often, someone who performs badly on some test can actually do all the skills required in the test, but simply does not understand the appropriate application of the skills in the artificial, culturally stereotyped situation.

Hemispheric Specialization

The literature on hemispheric specialization is enormous. Almost any experimental journal publishes new studies. A good review of the issues is given by Gazzaniga (1970). Ornstein (1972) presented some of the arguments for different modes of thoughts, and his book of readings (1973) is also useful.

Consciousness

The literature on consciousness is very limited. Mandler (1975*a*, 1975*b*) provides an excellent introduction. Ornstein (1972), again, is relevant. Shallice (1972) also provides a good start, and Posner provides some experimental studies (Posner and Klein, 1973; Posner and Snyder, 1975). Smith (1975), in his book *Powers of Mind,* provides an appealing discussion of the non-scientific quest for new states of consciousness.

Memory

Studies of the use of memory in more natural environments are not very common. Norman (1973) provides a discussion of some of the issues. Norman, Gentner, and Stevens (1976) apply the notion of schemas to education. Linton has examined the memory for real events. She is studying how a single subject (herself) remembers the events of daily life by laboriously writing down about five experiences each day over a period of five years, and testing for the memory of those events. A preliminary report of this research is given in Linton (1975).

───────────────────────── **References** ─────────────────────────

The boldface numbers in brackets at the end of each citation refer to the chapter in which that reference is discussed.

Ad herennium, see *Rhetorica ad herennium.* **[7]**

Anderson, J. R., & Bower, G. H. *Human associative memory.* Washington, D.C.: Winston, 1973. (Distributed by Halsted Press, Wiley, New York.) **[8]**

Atkinson, R. C., & Raugh, M. R. An application of the mnemonic keyword method to the acquisition of a Russian vocabulary. *Journal of Experimental Psychology: Human Learning and Memory,* 1975, *104,* 126–133. **[7]**

Atkinson, R. C., & Shiffrin, R. M. Human memory: A proposed system and its control processes. In K. W. Spence & J. T. Spence (Eds.), *The psychology of learning and motivation,* Vol. 2. New York: Academic Press, 1968. **[6]**

Atkinson, R. C., & Shiffrin, R. M. The control processes of short-term memory. *Scientific American,* 1971, *224,* 82–90. **[6]**

Austin, H. *A computational view of the skill of juggling.* Unpublished report. Cambridge, Mass.: Artificial Intelligence Laboratory, Massachusetts Institute of Technology, December 1974. **[9]**

Bachrach, A. J. Diving behavior. In *Human performance and SCUBA diving.* Proceedings of the symposium on underwater physiology. Chicago: The Athletic Institute, 1970. **[4]**

Baddeley, A. D. The influence of acoustic and semantic similarity on long-term memory for word sequences. *Quarterly Journal of Experimental Psychology,* 1966, *18,* 302–309. **[5]**

Baddeley, A. D. Selective attention and performance in dangerous environments. *British Journal of Psychology,* 1972, *63,* 537–546. **[4]**

Baddeley, A. D., Grant, S., Wight, E., & Thomson, N. Imagery and visual working memory. In P. M. A. Rabbitt & S. Dornic (Eds.), *Attention and performance V.* London: Academic Press, 1975. **[8]**

Bartlett, F. C. *Remembering.* Cambridge, England: Cambridge University Press, 1932. **[10]**

Bellugi, U., Klima, E. S., & Siple, P. Remembering in signs. *Cognition: International Journal of Cognitive Psychology,* 1974–1975, 3–2, 93–125. **[5]**

Bjork, R. A. Theoretical implications of directed forgetting. In A. W. Melton (Ed.), *Coding processes in human memory.* Washington, D. C.: Winston, 1972. [**6**]

Bjork, R. A. Short-term storage: The ordered output of a central processor. In F. Restle, R. M. Shiffrin, N. J. Castellan, H. R. Lindeman, & D. B. Pisoni (Eds.), *Cognitive theory,* Vol. 1. Hillside, N. J.: Lawrence Erlbaum Associates, 1975. [**6**]

Bjork, R. A., & Jongeward, R. H., Jr. *Rehearsal and mere rehearsal.* Unpublished manuscript, 1975. [**6**]

Bjork, R. A., & McClure, P. *Encoding to update one's memory.* Paper presented at the meeting of the Midwestern Psychological Association, Chicago, May 1974. [**6**]

Bleuler, E. [*Dementia praecox of the group of schizophrenias.*] (J. Zinkin, trans.). New York: International Universities Press, 1950. (Originally published in 1911.) [**4**]

Bliss, J. C., Crane, H. D., Mansfield, P. K., & Townsend, J. T. Information available in brief tactile presentations. *Perception & Psychophysics,* 1966, *1,* 273–283. [**5**]

Bobrow, D. G. Dimensions of representation. In D. G. Bobrow & A. M. Collins (Eds.), *Representation and understanding: Studies in cognitive science.* New York: Academic Press, 1975. [**8**]

Bobrow, D. G., & Collins, A. M. (Eds.). *Representation and understanding: Studies in cognitive science.* New York: Academic Press, 1975. [**8**]

Bobrow, D. G., & Norman, D. A. Some principles of memory schemata. In D. G. Bobrow & A. M. Collins (Eds.), *Representation and understanding: Studies in cognitive science.* New York: Academic Press, 1975. [**8**]

Bousfield, W. A. The occurrence of clustering in the recall of randomly arranged associates. *Journal of General Psychology,* 1953, *49,* 229–240. [**6**]

Bousfield, W. A., & Cohen, B. H. The occurrence of clustering in the recall of randomly arranged words of different frequencies-of-usage. *Journal of General Psychology,* 1955, *52,* 83–95. [**5,6**]

Bousfield, W. A., & Sedgewick, C. H. An anlysis of sequences of restricted associative responses. *Journal of General Psychology,* 1944, *30,* 149–165. [**6**]

Bower, G. H. Analysis of a mnemonic device. *American Scientist*, 1970a, *58*, 496–510. [**7**]

Bower, G. H. Organizational factors in memory. *Cognitive Psychology*, 1970b, *1*, 18–46. [**7**]

Bower, G. H. Mental imagery and associative learning. In L. W. Gregg (Ed.), *Cognition in learning and memory*. New York: Wiley, 1972a. [**7,8**]

Bower, G. H. A selective review of organizational factors in memory. In E. Tulving & W. Donaldson (Eds.), *Organization of memory*. New York: Academic Press, 1972b. [**6**]

Bower, G. H., & Bolton, L. S. Why are rhymes easy to learn? *Journal of Experimental Psychology*, 1969, *82*, 453–461. [**7**]

Bower, G. H., & Clark, M. C. Narrative stories as mediators for serial learning. *Psychonomic Science*, 1969, *14*, 181–182. [**7**]

Bower, G. H., & Reitman, J. S. Mnemonic elaboration in multilist learning. *Journal of Verbal Learning and Verbal Behavior*, 1972, *11*, 478–485. [**7**]

Bradshaw, J. L. Three interrelated problems in reading: A review. *Memory and Cognition*, 1975, *3*, 123–134. [**3**]

Broadbent, D. E. Speaking and listening simultaneously. *Journal of Experimental Psychology*, 1952, *43*, 267–273. [**2**]

Broadbent, D. E. *Perception and communication*. London: Pergamon Press, 1958. [**2**]

Broadbent, D. E. *Decision and stress*. New York: Academic Press, 1971. [**4**]

Brooks, L. R. Spatial and verbal components of the act of recall. *Canadian Journal of Psychology*, 1968, *22*, 349–368. [**8**]

Brown, J. Some tests of the decay theory of immediate memory. *Quarterly Journal of Experimental Psychology*, 1958, *10*, 12–21. [**5**]

Brown, J. Information, redundancy, and decay of the memory trace. In *The mechanization of thought processes*. London: H. M. Stationery Office, 1959. [**5**]

Brown, R., & McNeill, D. The "tip of the tongue" phenomenon. *Journal of Verbal Learning and Verbal Behavior*, 1966, *5*, 325–337. [**10**]

Buckhout, R. Eyewitness testimony. *Scientific American*, 1974, *231*, No. 6, 23–31. [**10**]

Carlo. *The juggling book.* New York: Random House, 1974. [9]

Carmichael, L., Hogan, H. P., & Walter, A. A. An experimental study of the effect of language on the reproduction of visually perceived form. *Journal of Experimental Psychology,* 1932, *15,* 73–86. [5]

Castaneda, C. *Tales of power.* New York: Simon and Schuster, 1974. [4,10]

Chapman, L. J., & Chapman, J. P. *Disordered thought in schizophrenia.* Englewood Cliffs, N.J.: Prentice-Hall, 1973. [4]

Chase, W. G., & Simon, H. A. Perception in chess. *Cognitive Psychology,* 1973, *4,* 55–81. [9]

Cherry, E. C. Some experiments on the recognition of speech, with one and with two ears. *Journal of the Acoustical Society of America,* 1953, *25,* 975–979. [2]

Cherry, E. C., & Taylor, W. K. Some further experiments on the recognition of speech with one and two ears. *Journal of the Acoustical Society of America,* 1954, *26,* 554–559. [2]

Cicero, M. T. *De oratore.* (E. W. Sutton, trans., completed, with an introduction, by H. Rackham). Cambridge, Mass.: Harvard University Press, 1942. [7]

Cicero, M. T. *De inventione.* (H. M. Hubbell, trans.) Cambridge, Mass.: Harvard University Press, 1949. [7]

Cofer, C. N. (Ed.). *The structure of human memory.* San Francisco: Freeman, 1976. [6,8]

Cohen, G., & Martin, M. Hemisphere differences in an auditory Stroop test. *Perception & Psychophysics,* 1975, *17,* 79–83. [3]

Cole, M., & Scribner, S. *Culture and thought.* New York: Wiley, 1974. [9,10]

Collins, A. M., & Loftus, E. F. A spreading-activation theory of semantic processing. *Psychological Review,* 1975, *82,* 407–428. [8]

Collins, A. M., & Quillian, M. R. Retrieval time from semantic memory. *Journal of Verbal Learning and Verbal Behavior,* 1969, *8,* 240–247. [8]

Collins, A. M., & Quillian, M. R. Facilitating retrieval from semantic memory: The effect of repeating part of an inference. *Acta Psychologica,* 1970, *33,* 304–314. [8]

Collins, A. M., & Quillian, M. R. Categories and subcategories in semantic memory. Paper presented at the Psychonomic Society, St. Louis, 1971. [8]

Collins, A. M., & Quillian, M. R. How to make a language user. In E. Tulving and W. Donaldson (Eds.), Organization of memory. New York: Academic Press, 1972. [8]

Conrad, R. Errors of immediate memory. British Journal of Psychology, 1959, 50, 349–359. [5]

Conrad, R. An association between memory errors and errors due to acoustic masking of speech. Nature, 1962, 196, 1314–1315. [5]

Conrad, R. Acoustic confusions in immediate memory. British Journal of Psychology, 1964, 55, 75–83. [5]

Conrad, R. Order error in immediate recall of sequences. Journal of Verbal Learning and Verbal Behavior, 1965, 4, 161–169. [5]

Conrad, R. Short-term memory processes in the deaf. British Journal of Psychology, 1970, 61, 179–195. [5]

Conrad, R., & Hull, A. J. Information, acoustic confusion and memory span. British Journal of Psychology, 1964, 55, 429–432. [5]

Cooper, L. A. Mental rotation of random two-dimensional shapes. Cognitive Psychology, 1975, 7, 20–43. [8]

Corteen, R. S., & Wood, B. Autonomic responses to shock-associated words in an unattended channel. Journal of Experimental Psychology, 1972, 94, 308–313. [2]

Craik, F. I. M., & Lockhart, R. S. Levels of processing: A framework for memory research. Journal of Verbal Learning and Verbal Behavior, 1972, 11, 671–684. [6]

Craik, F. I. M., & Tulving, E. Depth of processing and the retention of words in episodic memory. Journal of Experimental Psychology: General, 1975, 104, 268–294. [6]

Craik, F. I. M., & Watkins, M. J. The role of rehearsal in short-term memory. Journal of Verbal Learning and Verbal Behavior, 1973, 12, 599–607. [6]

Crovitz, H. F. Galton's walk: Methods for the analysis of thinking, intelligence, and creativity. New York: Harper and Row, 1970. [7]

Darwin, C. J., Turvey, M. T., & Crowder, R. G. An auditory analogue of the Sperling partial report procedure: Evidence for brief auditory storage. *Cognitive Psychology,* 1972, *3,* 255–267. [5]

DeGroot, A. D. *Thought and choice in chess.* The Hague: Mouton, 1965. [9]

DeGroot, A. D. Perception and memory versus thinking. In B. Kleinmuntz (Ed.), *Problem solving.* New York: Wiley, 1966. [9]

Deutsch, D., & Deutsch, J. A. (Eds.), *Short-term memory.* New York: Academic Press, 1975. [5]

Deutsch, J. A., & Deutsch, D. Attention: Some theoretical considerations. *Psychological Review,* 1963, *70,* 80–90. [2]

Deutsch, J. A., Deutsch, D., Lindsay, P. H., & Treisman, A. M. Comments on "selective attention: Perception or response?" and reply. *Quarterly Journal of Experimental Psychology,* 1967, *19,* 362–367. [2]

Dick, A. O. Iconic memory and its relation to perceptual processing and other memory mechanisms. *Perception & Psychophysics,* 1974, *16,* 575–596. [5]

Duda, R. O., & Hart, P. E. *Pattern classification and scene analysis.* New York: Wiley, 1973. [3]

Dyer, F. N. The Stroop phenomenon and its use in the study of perceptual, cognitive, and response processes. *Memory and Cognition,* 1973, *1,* 106–120. [3]

Eagle, M., & Ortoff, E. The effect of level of attention upon "phonetic" recognition errors. *Journal of Verbal Learning and Verbal Behavior,* 1967, *6,* 226–231. [6]

Easterbrook, J. A. The effect of emotion on the utilization and the organization of behavior. *Psychological Review,* 1959, *66,* 183–201. [4]

Egstrom, G. H., & Bachrach, A. J. Diver panic. *Skin Diver,* November 1971, 36–39. [4]

Epstein, W. Mechanisms of directed forgetting. In G. H. Bower (Ed.), *The psychology of learning and motivation,* Vol. 6. New York: Academic Press, 1972. [6]

Erdmann, B., & Dodge, R. *Psychologische unterschungen uber das lesen auf experimenteller grundlage.* Halle: Niemeyer, 1898. [5]

Estes, W. K. Phonemic encoding and rehearsal in short-term memory for letter strings. *Journal of Verbal Learning and Verbal Behavior,* 1973, *12,* 360–372. [5]

Estes, W. K. Redundancy of noise elements and signals in visual detection of letters. *Perception & Psychophysics,* 1974, *16,* 53–60. [**5**]

Feigenbaum, E. A., & Feldman, J. C. *Computers and thought.* New York: McGraw-Hill, 1963. [**8**]

Freeman, T., Cameron, J. L., & McGhie, A. *Chronic schizophrenia.* London: Tavistock Publications, 1958. [**4**]

Freeman, T., Cameron, J. L., & McGhie, A. *Studies on psychosis.* London: Tavistock Publications, 1966. [**4**]

Gazzaniga, M. S. *The bisected brain.* New York: Appleton, 1970. [**10**]

Geiselman, R. E. Semantic positive forgetting: Another cocktail problem. *Journal of Verbal Learning and Verbal Behavior,* 1975, *14,* 73–81. [**6**]

Gillogly, J. J. The TECHNOLOGY chess program. *Artificial Intelligence,* 1972, *3,* 145–163. [**3**]

Glucksberg, S., & Cowen, G. N., Jr. Memory for nonattended auditory material. *Cognitive Psychology,* 1970, *1,* 149–156. [**2**]

Goodman, N. *Language of art.* New York: Bobbs-Merrill, 1968. [**8**]

Gray, C. R., & Gummerman, K. The enigmatic eidetic image: A critical examination of methods, data, and theories. *Psychological Bulletin,* 1975, *82,* 383–407. [**8**]

Gray, J. A., & Wedderburn, A. A. I. Grouping strategies with simultaneous stimuli. *Quarterly Journal of Experimental Psychology,* 1960, *12,* 180–184. [**2**]

Haber, R. N. Eidetic images. *Scientific American,* 1969, *220,* 36–44. [**8**]

Hebb, D. O. Distinctive features of learning in the higher animal. In J. F. Delafresnaye (Ed.), *Brain mechanisms and learning.* London: Oxford University Press, 1961. [**5**]

Hellyer, S. Supplementary report: Frequency of stimulus presentation and short-term decrement in recall. *Journal of Experimental Psychology,* 1962, *64,* 650. [**5**]

Hilgard, E. R. Hypnosis. *Annual Review of Psychology,* 1975, *26,* 19–44. [**5**]

Hillyard, S. A., Hink, R. F., Schwent, V. L., & Picton, T. W. Electrical signs of selective attention in the human brain. *Science,* 1973, *182,* 177–180. [**4**]

Huey, E. B. *The psychology and pedagogy of reading.* Cambridge, Mass.: M.I.T. Press, 1968. (Originally published in 1908.) [**3**]

Hughes, E. Musical memory in piano playing and piano study. *The Musical Quarterly,* 1915, *1,* 592–603. [**9**]

Hunt, E. Quote the Raven? Nevermore! In L. W. Gregg (Ed.), *Knowledge and cognition.* Potomac, Md.: Lawrence Erlbaum Associates, 1974. [**10**]

Hunt, E., Frost, N., & Lunneborg, C. L. Individual differences in cognition: A new approach to intelligence. In G. Bower (Ed.), *Advances in learning and motivation,* Vol. 7. New York: Academic Press, 1973. [**10**]

Hunt, E., & Love, T. How good can memory be? In A. W. Melton & E. Martin (Eds.), *Coding processes in human memory.* Washington, D.C.: Winston, 1972. [**7**]

Hunt, E., Lunneborg, C., & Lewis, J. What does it mean to be high verbal? *Cognitive Psychology,* 1975, *7,* 194–227. [**10**]

James, W. *The principles of psychology.* New York: Dover, 1950. (Originally published in 1890.) [**2,5,10**]

Johnston, W. A., & Heinz, S. P. It takes attention to pay attention. Paper presented at the meeting of the Psychonomic Society, Boston, 1974. [**4**]

Julesz, B. *Foundations of cyclopean perception.* Chicago: University of Chicago Press, 1971. [**8**]

Kahneman, D. *Attention and effort.* Englewood Cliffs, N.J.: Prentice-Hall, 1973. [**4**]

Kanal, L. Patterns in pattern recognition: 1968–1974. *IEEE Transactions on Information Theory,* 1974, *IT-20,* 697–722. [**3**]

Keele, S. W. *Attention and human performance.* Pacific Palisades, Calif.: Goodyear, 1973. [**4**]

Keppel, G., & Underwood, B. J. Proactive inhibition in short-term retention of single items. *Journal of Verbal Learning and Verbal Behavior,* 1962, *1,* 153–161. [**5**]

King, B. J. *Tennis to win* (with K. Chapin). New York: Harper and Row, 1970. [9]

Kintsch, W. *Learning, memory, and conceptual processes.* New York: Wiley, 1970. [6]

Kintsch, W. *The representation of meaning in memory.* Hillsdale, N.J.: Lawrence Erlbaum Associates, 1974. [8]

Kolers, P. A., & Perkins, D. N. Spatial and ordinal components of form perception and literacy. *Cognitive Psychology,* 1975, *7,* 228–267. [3]

Kornblum, S. (Ed.). *Attention and performance IV.* New York: Academic Press, 1973. [4]

Kosslyn, S. M. Scanning visual images: Some structural implications. *Perception & Psychophysics,* 1973, *14,* 90–94. [8]

Kosslyn, S. M. Information representation in visual images. *Cognitive Psychology,* 1975, *7,* 341–370. [8]

Krueger, L. E. Familiarity effects in visual information processing. *Psychological Bulletin,* 1975, *82,* 949–974. [3]

Kuipers, B. A frame for frames: Representing knowledge for recognition. In D. G. Bobrow & A. M. Collins (Eds.), *Representation and understanding: Studies in cognitive science.* New York: Academic Press, 1975. [8]

LaBerge, D. Acquisition of automatic processing in perceptual and associative learning. In P. M. A. Rabbitt & S. Dornic (Eds.), *Attention and performance V.* London: Academic Press, 1975. [4]

LaBerge, D., & Samuels, S. J. Toward a theory of automatic information processing in reading. *Cognitive Psychology,* 1974, *6,* 293–323. [4]

Lakoff, G. Hedges: A study in meaning criteria and the logic of fuzzy concepts. In P. M. Peranteau, J. N. Levi, & G. C. Phares (Eds.), *Papers from the eighth regional meeting, Chicago Linguistics Society.* Chicago: University of Chicago, Linguistics Department, 1972. [8]

Lawson, E. A. Decisions concerning the rejected channel. *Quarterly Journal of Experimental Psychology,* 1966, *18,* 260–265. [4]

Lea, G. Chronometric analysis of the method of loci. *Journal of Experimental Psychology: Human Perception and Performance,* 1975, *104,* 94–104. [8]

Leach, J. *Table tennis made easy.* Hollywood, Calif.: Wilshire, 1971. **[9]**

Leask, J., Haber, R. N., & Haber, R. B. Eidetic imagery in children: II. Longitudinal and experimental results. *Psychonomic Monograph Supplements*, 1969, *3*, No. 35. **[8]**

Lewis, J. L. Semantic processing of unattended messages using dichotic listening. *Journal of Experimental Psychology*, 1970, *85*, 225–228. **[2]**

Lindsay, P. H., & Norman, D. A. *Human information processing.* New York: Academic Press, 1972. **[8,10]**

Linton, M. Memory for real-world events. In D. A. Norman, D. E. Rumelhart, & the LNR Research Group, *Explorations in cognition.* San Francisco: Freeman, 1975. **[10]**

Loess, H. Proactive inhibition in short-term memory. *Journal of Verbal Learning and Verbal Behavior*, 1964, *3*, 362–368. **[5]**

Loisette, A. *Assimilative memory or how to attend and never forget.* New York: Funk and Wagnalls, 1896. **[7]**

Lorayne, H., & Lucas, J. *The memory book.* New York: Stein and Day, 1974. (Also published in paperback by Ballantine Books, 1975.) **[7]**

Luria, A. R. [*The mind of a mnemonist.*] (L. Solotaroff, trans.). New York: Basic Books, 1968. **[7,8]**

Mandler, G. Response factors in human learning. *Psychological Review*, 1954, *61*, 235–244. **[4]**

Mandler, G. Organization and memory. In K. W. Spence & J. T. Spence (Eds.), *Psychology of learning and motivation*, Vol. 1. New York: Academic Press, 1967a. **[6]**

Mandler, G. Verbal learning. In *New directions in psychology III.* New York: Holt, 1967b. **[6]**

Mandler, G. Consciousness: Respectable, useful, and probably necessary. In R. L. Solso (Ed.), *Information processing and cognition: The Loyola symposium.* Hillsdale, N.J.: Lawrence Erlbaum Associates, 1975a. **[10]**

Mandler, G. *Mind and emotion.* New York: Wiley, 1975b. **[4,10]**

Massaro, D. W. Preperceptual images, processing time, and perceptual units in auditory perception. *Psychological Review*, 1972, *79*, 124–145. **[5]**

Massaro, D. W. *Experimental psychology and information processing.* Chicago: Rand McNally, 1975. [5]

Massaro, D. W. Preperceptual images, processing time, and perceptual units in speech perception. In D. W. Massaro (Ed.), *Understanding language: An information processing analysis of speech perception, reading, and psycholinguistics.* New York: Academic Press, 1975. [5]

McGhie, A. *Pathology of attention.* Baltimore: Penguin Books, 1969. [4]

McGhie, A., & Chapman, J. Disorders of attention and perception in early schizophrenia. *British Journal of Medical Psychology,* 1961, *34,* 103–116. [4]

McKay, D. G. Aspects of the theory and comprehension, memory and attention. *Quarterly Journal of Experimental Psychology,* 1973, *25,* 22–40. [2]

Melton, A. W. Implications of short-term memory for a general theory of memory. *Journal of Verbal Learning and Verbal Behavior,* 1963, *2,* 1–21. [5]

Miller, G. A. The magical number seven, plus or minus two: Some limits on our capacity for processing information. *Psychological Review,* 1956, *63,* 81–97. [5,7]

Miller, G. A. Decision units in the perception of speech. *IRE Transactions on Information Theory,* 1962, *IT-8,* 81–83. [3]

Miller, G. A., Galanter, E., & Pribram, K. *Plans and the structure of behavior.* New York: Holt, 1960. [7]

Miller, G. A., Heise, G. A., & Lichten, W. The intelligibility of speech as a function of the context of the test materials. *Journal of Experimental Psychology,* 1951, *41,* 329–335. [3]

Minsky, M. (Ed). *Semantic information processing.* Cambridge, Mass.: M.I.T. Press, 1968. [8]

Minsky, M. A framework for representing knowledge. In P. H. Winston (Ed.), *The psychology of computer vision.* New York: McGraw-Hill, 1975. [8]

Minsky, M., & Papert, S. *Artificial intelligence progress report* (Tech. Rep. 252). Cambridge, Mass.: M.I.T., Artificial Intelligence Laboratory, January 1972. [9]

Mitchell, J. M. Mnemonics. *Encyclopaedia Britannica*, 1910, *15*, 626–628. [**7**]

Moray, N. Attention in dichotic listening: Affective cues and the influence of instructions. *Quarterly Journal of Experimental Psychology*, 1959, *11*, 56–60. [**2**]

Moray, N. Where is capacity limited? A survey and a model. In A. Sanders (Ed.), *Attention and performance*. Amsterdam: North-Holland, 1967. [**6**]

Moray, N. *Attention: Selective processes in vision and hearing*. New York: Academic Press, 1970. [**2,4**]

Morton, J. A functional model for memory. In D. A. Norman (Ed.), *Models of human memory*. New York: Academic Press, 1970. [**6**]

Mowbray, G. H. Choice reaction times for skilled responses. *Quarterly Journal of Experimental Psychology*, 1960, *12*, 193–202. [**3**]

Moyer, R. S. Comparing objects in memory: Evidence suggesting an internal psychophysics. *Perception & Psychophysics*, 1973, *13*, 180–184. [**8**]

Naatanen, R. Selective attention and evoked potentials in humans—a critical review. *Biological Psychology*, 1975, *2*, 237–307. [**4**]

Neely, R. B. *On the use of syntax and semantics in a speech understanding system*. Pittsburgh: Carnegie-Mellon University, Computer Science Department, 1973. [**3**]

Newell, A., Barnett, J., Forgie, J., Green, C., Klatt, D., Licklider, J .C. R., Munson, J., Reddy, R., & Woods, W. *Speech understanding systems 1973*. Amsterdam: North-Holland, 1973. [**3**]

Newell, A., & Simon, H. A. *Human problem solving*. Englewood Cliffs, N.J.: Prentice-Hall, 1972. [**9**]

Nickerson, R. S. Short-term memory for complex meaningful visual configurations: A demonstration of capacity. *Canadian Journal of Psychology*, 1965, *19*, 155–160. [**8**]

Norman, D. A. Toward a theory of memory and attention. *Psychological Review*, 1968, *75*, 522–536. [**2**]

Norman, D. A. Memory while shadowing. *Quarterly Journal of Experimental Psychology*, 1969, *21*, 85–93. [**2**]

Norman, D. A. Memory, knowledge, and the answering of questions. In R. L. Solso (Ed.), *Contemporary issues in cognitive psychology: The Loyola symposium.* Washington, D. C.: Winston, 1973. [**10**]

Norman, D. A., & Bobrow, D. G. On data-limited and resource-limited processes. *Cognitive Psychology,* 1975, 7, 44–64. [**4**]

Norman, D. A., & Bobrow, D. G. On the role of active memory processes in perception and cognition. In C. N. Cofer (Ed.), *The structure of human memory.* San Francisco: Freeman, 1976. [**3**]

Norman, D. A., Gentner, D. R., & Stevens, A. L. Comments on learning: *Schemata and memory representation.* In D. Klahr (Ed.), *Cognitive approaches to education.* Hillsdale, N. J.: Lawrence Erlbaum Associates, 1976. [**8,10**]

Norman, D. A., Rumelhart, D. E., and the LNR Research Group. *Explorations in cognition.* San Francisco: Freeman, 1975. [**8**]

Ornstein, R. E. *The psychology of consciousness.* San Francisco: Freeman, 1972. (Also published by Viking, 1972.) [**4,10**]

Ornstein, R. E. *The nature of human consciousness.* San Francisco: Freeman, 1973. (Also published by Viking, 1973.) [**10**]

Paivio, A. *Imagery and verbal processes.* New York: Holt, 1971. [**7,8**]

Paivio, A. Perceptual comparisons through the mind's eye. *Memory and Cognition,* 1975, 3, 635–647. [**8**]

Palmer, S. E. Visual perception and world knowledge. In D. A. Norman, D. E. Rumelhart, & the LNR Research Group, *Explorations in cognition.* San Francisco: Freeman, 1975. [**3**]

Papert, S. Teaching children thinking. *Programmed Learning and Educational Technology,* 1972, 9. [**9**]

Peterson, L. R., & Peterson, M. J. Short-term retention of individual verbal items. *Journal of Experimental Psychology,* 1959, 58, 193–198. [**5**]

Piaget, J. [*The origins of intelligence in children.*] (M .Cook, trans.). New York: Norton, 1952. (Originally published in 1936.) [**10**]

Picton, T. W., & Hillyard, S. A. Human auditory evoked potentials. II: Effects of attention. *Electroencephalography and Clinical Neurophysiology,* 1974, 36, 191–199. [**4**]

Picton, T. W., Hillyard, S. A., Krausz, H. I., & Galambos, R. Human auditory evoked potentials. I: Evaluation of components. *Electroencephalography and Clinical Neurophysiology,* 1974, *36,* 179–190. [4]

Posner, M. I. Abstraction and the process of recognition. In G. H. Bower & J. T. Spence (Eds.), *Psychology of learning and motivation,* Vol. 3. New York: Academic Press, 1969. [4]

Posner, M. I. *Cognition: An introduction.* Glenview, Ill.: Scott, Foresman, 1973. [4]

Posner, M. I., & Boies, S. J. Components of attention. *Psychological Review,* 1971, *78,* 391–408. [4]

Posner, M. I., & Klein, R. M. On the functions of consciousness. In S. Kornblum (Ed.), *Attention and performance IV.* New York: Academic Press, 1973. [10]

Posner, M. I., & Snyder, C. R. R. Attention and cognitive control. In R. Solso (Ed.), *Information processing and cognition: The Loyola symposium.* Hillsdale, N. J.: Lawrence Erlbaum Associates, 1975. [10]

Postman, L. Verbal learning and memory. *Annual Review of Psychology,* 1975, *26,* 291–335. [6]

Pribram, K. H., & McGuinness, D. Arousal, activation, and effort in the control of attention. *Psychological Review,* 1975, *82,* 116–149. [4]

Pylyshyn, Z. W. What the mind's eye tells the mind's brain: A critique of mental imagery. *Psychological Bulletin,* 1973, *80,* 1–24. [8]

Quillian, M. R. *Semantic memory.* Unpublished doctoral dissertation, Carnegie Institute of Technology (now the Carnegie-Mellon University), 1966. (Published in part as Quillian, 1968.) [8]

Quillian, M. R. *Semantic memory.* In M. Minsky (Ed.), *Semantic information processing.* Cambridge, Mass.: MIT Press, 1968. [8]

Quintilianus, M. F. *The institutio oratoria.* (H. E. Butler, trans.) New York: Putnam, 1921. [7]

Rabbitt, P. M. A., & Dornic, S. (Eds.). *Attention and performance V.* London: Academic Press, 1975. [4]

Rabbitt, P. M. A., & Dornic, S. (Eds.). *Attention and performance VI.* London: Academic Press, in press. [4]

Raugh, M. R., & Atkinson, R. C. A mnemonic method for learning of a second language vocabulary. *Journal of Educational Psychology,* 1975, *67,* 1–16. [**7**]

Reddy, R. (Ed.). *Speech recognition: Invited papers presented at the IEEE symposium.* New York: Academic Press, 1975. [**3**]

Reddy, R., & Newell, A. Knowledge and its representation in a speech understanding system. In L. W. Gregg (Ed.), *Knowledge and cognition.* Potomac, Md.: Lawrence Erlbaum Associates, 1974. [**3**]

Reed, G. *The psychology of anomalous experience: A cognitive approach.* London: Hutchinson University Library, 1972. [**4**]

Reed, S. K. *Psychological processes in pattern recognition.* New York: Academic Press, 1973. [**3**]

Reicher, G. M. Perceptual recognition as a function of meaningfulness of stimulus material. *Journal of Experimental Psychology,* 1969, *81,* 275–281. [**3**]

Reitman, J. S. Mechanisms of forgetting in short-term memory. *Cognitive Psychology,* 1971, *2,* 185–195. [**5**]

Reitman, J. S. Without surreptitious rehearsal, information in short-term memory decays. *Journal of Verbal Learning and Verbal Behavior,* 1974, *13,* 365–377. [**5**]

Reitman, W. R. *Cognition and thought: An information-processing approach.* New York: Wiley, 1965. [**8**]

Reitman, W. R., Malin, J. T., Bjork, R. A., & Higman, B. Strategy control and directed forgetting. *Journal of Verbal Learning and Verbal Behavior,* 1973, *12,* 140–149. [**6**]

Restle, F. Sources of difficulty in learning paired associates. In R. C. Atkinson (Ed.), *Studies in mathematical psychology.* Stanford, Calif.: Stanford University Press, 1964. [**6**]

Restle, F., Shiffrin, R. M., Castellan, N. J., Lindeman, H. R., & Pisoni, D. B. (Eds.). *Cognitive theory,* Vol. 1. Hillside, N.J.: Lawrence Erlbaum Associates, 1975. [**6**]

Rhetorica ad herennium. (Author unknown.) (H. Caplan, trans.) Cambridge, Mass.: Harvard University Press, 1954. [**7**]

Richardson, A. *Mental imagery.* New York: Springer, 1969. [**8**]

Rips, L. J., Shoben, E. J., & Smith, E. E. Semantic distance and the verification of semantic relations. *Journal of Verbal Learning and Verbal Behavior,* 1973, *12,* 1–20. [8]

Rosch, E. H. On the internal structure of perceptual and semantic categories. In T. Moore (Ed.), *Cognitive development and the acquisition of language.* New York: Academic Press, 1973a. [8]

Rosch, E. H. Natural categories. *Cognitive Psychology,* 1973b, *4,* 328–350. [8]

Rosch, E. H. Cognitive representations of semantic categories. *Journal of Experimental Psychology: General,* 1975, *104,* 192–233. [8]

Rosch, E. H. Basic objects in natural categories. *Cognitive Psychology,* in press. [8]

Rumelhart, D. E. Notes on a schema for stories. In D. G. Bobrow & A. M. Collins (Eds.), *Representation and understanding: Studies in cognitive science.* New York: Academic Press, 1975. [8]

Rumelhart, D. E. *An introduction to human information processing.* New York: Wiley, in press. [**3,5**]

Rumelhart, D. E., Lindsay, P. H., & Norman, D. A. A process model for long-term memory. In E. Tulving & W. Donaldson (Eds.), *Organization of memory.* New York: Academic Press, 1972. [8]

Rumelhart, D. E., & Siple, P. The process of recognizing tachistoscopically presented words. *Psychological Review,* 1974, *81,* 99–118. [3]

Rundus, D. Analysis of rehearsal processes in free recall. *Journal of Experimental Psychology,* 1971, *89,* 63–77. [6]

Rundus, D., & Atkinson, R. C. Rehearsal procedures in free recall: A procedure for direct observation. *Journal of Verbal Learning and Verbal Behavior,* 1970, *9,* 99–105. [6]

Sanders, A. F. (Ed.). *Attention and performance.* Amsterdam: North-Holland, 1967. (A special edition of *Acta Psychologica,* Vol. 27.) [4]

Sanders, A. F. (Ed.). *Attention and performance III.* Amsterdam: North-Holland, 1970. (A special edition of *Acta Psychologica,* Vol. 33.) [4]

Schachter, S., & Rodin, J. *Obese humans and rats.* Hillside, N. J.: Lawrence Erlbaum Associates, 1974. [**10**]

Schank, R. C. The structure of episodes in memory. In D. G. Bobrow & A. M. Collins (Eds.), *Representation and understanding: Studies in cognitive science*. New York: Academic Press, 1975. [**8**]

Schank, R. C., & Colby, K. M. *Computer models of thought and language*. San Francisco: Freeman, 1973. [**8**]

Schilder, P. *Brain and personality*. New York: New York University Press, 1951. [**4**]

Selfridge, O. G., & Neisser, U. Pattern recognition by machine. *Scientific American*, 1960, *203*, 60–68. [**6**]

Shallice, T. Dual functions of consciousness. *Psychological Review*, 1972, *79*, 383–393. [**10**]

Shepard, R. N. Recognition memory for words, sentences, and pictures. *Journal of Verbal Learning and Verbal Behavior*, 1967, *6*, 156–163. [**8**]

Shepard, R. N., & Metzler, J. Mental rotation of three-dimensional objects. *Science*, 1971, *171*, 701–703. [**8**]

Shiffrin, R. M. Information persistence in short-term memory. *Journal of Experimental Psychology*, 1973, *100*, 39–49. [**5**]

Shiffrin, R. M., & Geisler, W. S. Visual recognition in a theory of information processing. In R. L. Solso (Ed.), *Contemporary issues in cognitive psychology: The Loyola symposium*. Washington, D. C.: Winston, 1973. [**5**]

Shulman, H. G. Encoding and retention of semantic and phonemic information in short-term memory. *Journal of Verbal Learning and Verbal Behavior*, 1970, *9*, 499–508. [**5**]

Shulman, H. G. Semantic confusion errors in short-term memory. *Journal of Verbal Learning and Verbal Behavior*, 1972, *11*, 221–227. [**5**]

Smith, A. *Powers of mind*. New York: Random House, 1975. (Adam Smith is a pen-name. The book might be filed in some libraries under the author's real name: G. J. W. Goodman. [**4**,**10**]

Smith, E. E., Shoben, E. J., & Rips, L. J. Structure and processes in semantic memory: A featural model for semantic decisions. *Psychological Review*, 1974, *81*, 214–241. [**8**]

Smith, E. E., & Spoehr, K. T. The perception of printed English: A theoretical perspective. In B. H. Kantowitz (Ed.), *Human information processing: Tutorials in performance and cognition*, Hillsdale, N. J.: Lawrence Erlbaum Associates, 1974. [**3**]

Smith, F. *Understanding reading.* New York: Holt, 1971. [**3**]

Sperling, G. A. The information available in belief visual presentation. *Psychological Monographs,* 1960, *74,* No. 498. [**5**]

Sperling, G. A. Short-term memory, long-term memory, and scanning in the processing of visual information. In A. Young & D. B. Lindsley (Eds.), *Early experience and visual information processing in perceptual and reading disorders.* Washington: National Academy of Sciences, 1970. [**6**]

Standing, L. Learning 10,000 pictures. *Quarterly Journal of Experimental Psychology,* 1973, *25,* 207–222. [**8**]

Sternberg, S. Memory scanning: New findings and current controversies. *Quarterly Journal of Experimental Psychology,* 1975, *27,* 1–32. Also in D. Deutsch & J. A. Deutsch (Eds.), *Short-term memory.* New York: Academic Press, 1975. [**5**]

Stromeyer, C. F., III. Eidetikers. *Psychology Today,* November 1970, 76–80. [**8**]

Stromeyer, C. F., III, & Psotka, J. The detailed texture of eidetic images. *Nature,* 1970, *225,* 346–349. [**8**]

Stroop, J. R. Studies of interference in serial verbal reactions. *Journal of Experimental Psychology,* 1935, *18,* 643–662. [**3**]

Sutherland, N. S. Outlines of a theory of visual pattern recognition in animals and man. *Proceedings of the Royal Society,* Series B, 1968, *171,* 297–317. [**6**]

Thompson, D. M., & Tulving, E. Associative encoding and retrieval: Weak and strong cues. *Journal of Experimental Psychology,* 1970, *86,* 225–262. [**6**]

Titchener, E. B. *Lectures on the elementary psychology of feeling and attention.* New York: Macmillan, 1908. [**2**]

Treisman, A. M. Monitoring and storage of irrelevant messages in selective attention. *Journal of Verbal Learning and Verbal Behavior,* 1964a, *3,* 449–459. [**6**]

Treisman, A. M. Verbal cues, language and meaning in selective attention. *American Journal of Psychology,* 1964b, *77,* 206–219. [**2**]

Treisman, A. M. Strategies and models of selective attention. *Psychological Review,* 1969, *76,* 282–299. [**4**]

Treisman, A. M., & Geffen, G. Selective attention: Perception or response? *Quarterly Journal of Experimental Psychology,* 1967, *19,* 1–17. (Also see Deutsch, et al., 1967.) [**2,4**]

Treisman, A. M., Russell, R., & Green, J. Brief visual storage of shape and movement. In P. M. A. Rabbitt & S. Dornic (Eds.), *Attention and performance V.* New York: Academic Press, 1975. [**5**]

Tulving, E. Subjective organization in free recall of "unrelated" words. *Psychological Review,* 1962, *69,* 344–354. [**6**]

Tulving, E. Intratrial and intertrial retention: Notes towards a theory of free recall verbal learning. *Psychological Review,* 1964, *71,* 219–237. [**6**]

Tulving, E. Episodic and semantic memory. In E. Tulving & W. Donaldson (Eds.), *Organization of memory.* New York: Academic Press, 1972. [**8**]

Tulving, E., & Donaldson, W. (Eds.). *Organization of memory.* New York: Academic Press, 1972. [**8**]

Tulving, E., & Madigan, S. A. Memory and verbal learning. *Annual Review of Psychology,* 1970, *21,* 437–484. [**6**]

Tversky, A., & Kahneman, D. Availability: A heuristic for judging frequency and probability. *Cognitive Psychology,* 1973, *5,* 207–232. [**10**]

Von Wright, J. M., Anderson, K., & Stenman, U. Generalization of conditioned GSRs in dichotic listening. In P. M. A. Rabbitt & S. Dornic (Eds.), *Attention and performance V.* London: Academic Press, 1975. [**2**]

Walley, R. E., & Weiden, T. D. Lateral inhibition and cognitive masking: A neuropsychological theory of attention. *Psychological Review,* 1973, *80,* 284–302. [**4**]

Watkins, M. J., Watkins, O. C., Craik, F. I. M., & Mazuryk, G. Effect of nonverbal distraction on short-term storage. *Journal of Experimental Psychology,* 1973, *101,* 296–300. [**5**]

Waugh, N. C. Free versus serial recall. *Journal of Experimental Psychology,* 1961, *62,* 496–502. [**5**]

Waugh, N. C., & Norman, D. A. Primary memory. *Psychological Review,* 1965, *72,* 89–104. [**5**]

Weinland, J. D. *How to improve your memory.* New York: Barnes and Noble, 1957. [**7**]

Welford, A. T. *Ageing and human skill.* Oxford, England: Oxford University Press, 1958. [4]

Wheeler, D. D. Processes in word recognition. *Cognitive Psychology,* 1970, *1,* 59–85. [3]

Wickelgren, W. A. Distinctive features and errors in short-term memory for English vowels. *Journal of the Acoustical Society of America,* 1965a, *38,* 583–588. [5]

Wickelgren, W. A. Acoustic similarity and intrusion errors in short-term memory. *Journal of Experimental Psychology,* 1965b, 102–108. [5]

Wickelgren, W. A. Distinctive features and errors in short-term memory for English consonants. *Journal of the Acoustical Society of America,* 1966a, *39,* 388–398. [5]

Wickelgren, W. A. Phonemic similarity and interference in short-term memory for single letters. *Journal of Experimental Psychology,* 1966b, *71,* 396–404. [5]

Wickelgren, W. A. Associative intrusions in short-term recall. *Journal of Experimental Psychology,* 1966c, *72,* 853–858. [5]

Winston, P. H. Learning structural descriptions from examples. In P. H. Winston (Ed.), *The psychology of computer vision.* New York: McGraw-Hill, 1975a. [8]

Winston, P. H. (Ed.). *The psychology of computer vision.* New York: McGraw-Hill, 1975b. [8]

Winograd, T. Frame representations and the declarative-procedural controversy. In D. G. Bobrow & A. M. Collins (Eds.), *Representation and understanding: Studies in cognitive science.* New York: Academic Press, 1975. [8]

Woodrow, H. The effect of type of training upon transference. *Journal of Educational Psychology,* 1927, *18,* 159–172. [7]

Woodward, A. E., Jr., Bjork, R. A., & Jongeward, R. H., Jr. Recall and recognition as a function of primary rehearsal. *Journal of Verbal Learning and Verbal Behavior,* 1973, *12,* 608–617. [6]

Woodworth, R. S. *Experimental psychology.* New York: Holt, 1938. [10]

Yates, F. A. *The art of memory.* Chicago: University of Chicago Press, 1966. [1,7]

Yerkes, R. M., & Dodson, J. D. The relation of strength of stimulus to rapidity of habit-formation. *Journal of Comparative Neurology of Psychology,* 1908, *18,* 459–482. [4]

Young, M. N. *Bibliography of memory.* Philadelphia: Chilton, 1961. [7]

Young, M. N., & Gibson, W. B. *How to develop an exceptional memory.* Hollywood, Calif.: Wilshire, 1962. [7]

Index

WIDENER UNIVERSITY
WOLFGRAM
LIBRARY
CHESTER, PA